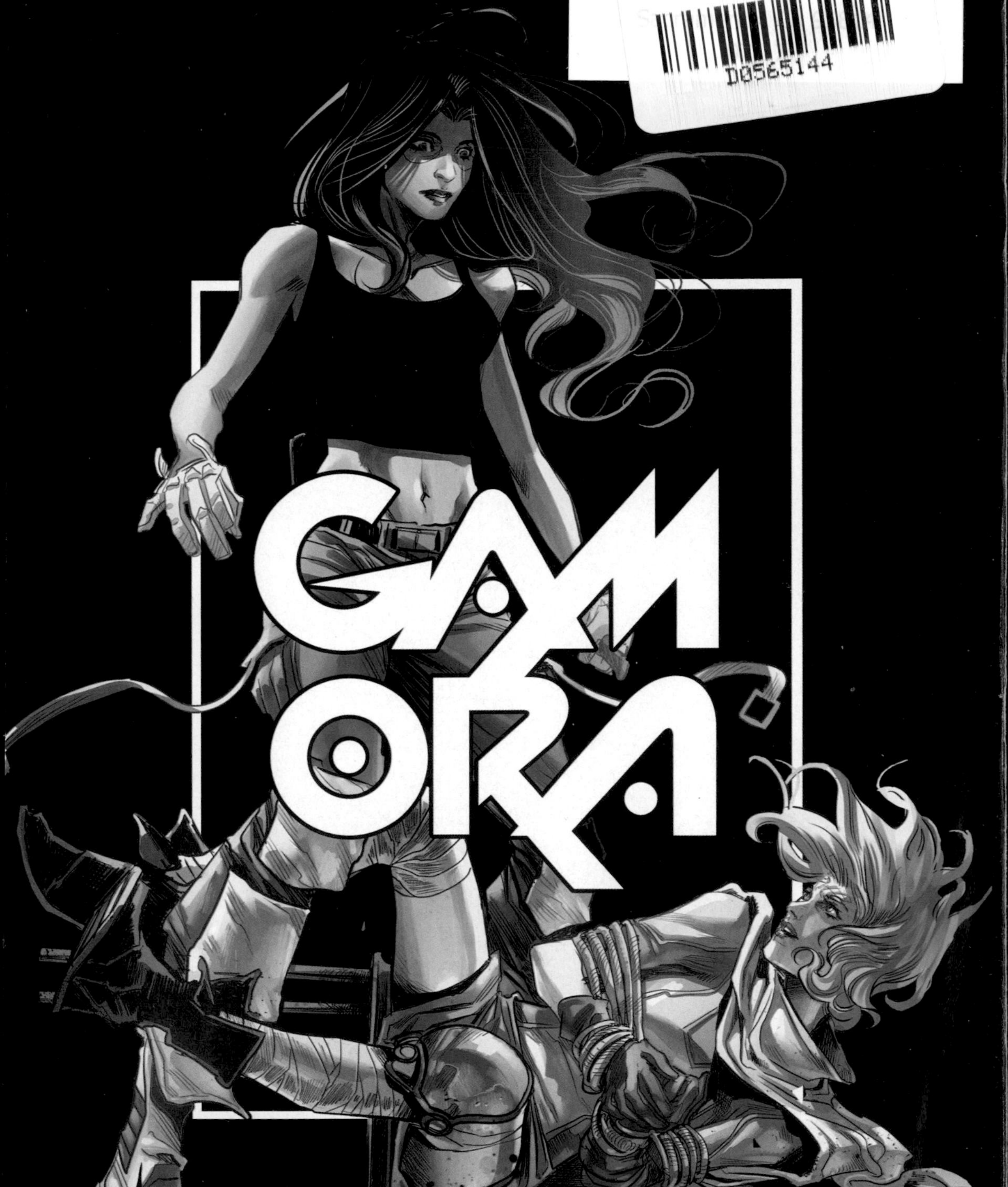
GAM
ORA

BEFORE SHE WAS A GUARDIAN OF THE GALAXY, GAMORA WAS AN ASSASSIN-IN-TRAINING AND WARD TO THE MAD TITAN, THANOS. ORPHANED BY THE GENOCIDE OF HER PEOPLE, GAMORA WAS RAISED BY THANOS TO KILL WITHOUT MERCY AND WITHOUT CONSCIENCE. THIS IS HOW SHE BECAME KNOWN AS THE DEADLIEST WOMAN IN THE GALAXY.

GAMORA

MEMENTO MORI

NICOLE PERLMAN
WRITER

MARCO CHECCHETTO
ARTIST

ANDRES MOSSA
COLOR ARTIST

ESAD RIBIC
COVER ART

VC's TRAVIS LANHAM
LETTERER

CHRISTINA HARRINGTON, KATIE KUBERT & BILL ROSEMANN
EDITORS

NICK LOWE
EXECUTIVE EDITOR

JENNIFER GRÜNWALD
COLLECTION EDITOR

CAITLIN O'CONNELL
ASSISTANT EDITOR

KATERI WOODY
ASSOCIATE MANAGING EDITOR

MARK D. BEAZLEY
EDITOR, SPECIAL PROJECTS

JEFF YOUNGQUIST
VP PRODUCTION & SPECIAL PROJECTS

DAVID GABRIEL
SVP PRINT, SALES & MARKETING

JAY BOWEN
BOOK DESIGNER

AXEL ALONSO
EDITOR IN CHIEF

JOE QUESADA
CHIEF CREATIVE OFFICER

DAN BUCKLEY
PRESIDENT

ALAN FINE
EXECUTIVE PRODUCER

GAMORA: MEMENTO MORI. Contains material originally published in magazine form as GAMORA #1-5. First printing 2017. ISBN# 978-0-7851-9782-9. Published by MARVEL WORLDWIDE, INC., a subsidiary of MARVEL ENTERTAINMENT, LLC. OFFICE OF PUBLICATION: 135 West 50th Street, New York, NY 10020. Copyright © 2017 MARVEL No similarity between any of the names, characters, persons, and/or institutions in this magazine with those of any living or dead person or institution is intended, and any such similarity which may exist is purely coincidental. Printed in Canada. DAN BUCKLEY, President, Marvel Entertainment; JOE QUESADA, Chief Creative Officer; TOM BREVOORT, SVP of Publishing; DAVID BOGART, SVP of Business Affairs & Operations, Publishing & Partnership; C.B. CEBULSKI, VP of Brand Management & Development, Asia; DAVID GABRIEL, SVP of Sales & Marketing, Publishing; JEFF YOUNGQUIST, VP of Production & Special Projects; DAN CARR, Executive Director of Publishing Technology; ALEX MORALES, Director of Publishing Operations; SUSAN CRESPI, Production Manager; STAN LEE, Chairman Emeritus. For information regarding advertising in Marvel Comics or on Marvel.com, please contact Vit DeBellis, Integrated Sales Manager, at vdebellis@marvel.com. For Marvel subscription inquiries, please call 888-511-5480. Manufactured between 5/12/2017 and 6/13/2017 by SOLISCO PRINTERS, SCOTT, QC, CANADA.

10 9 8 7 6 5 4 3 2 1

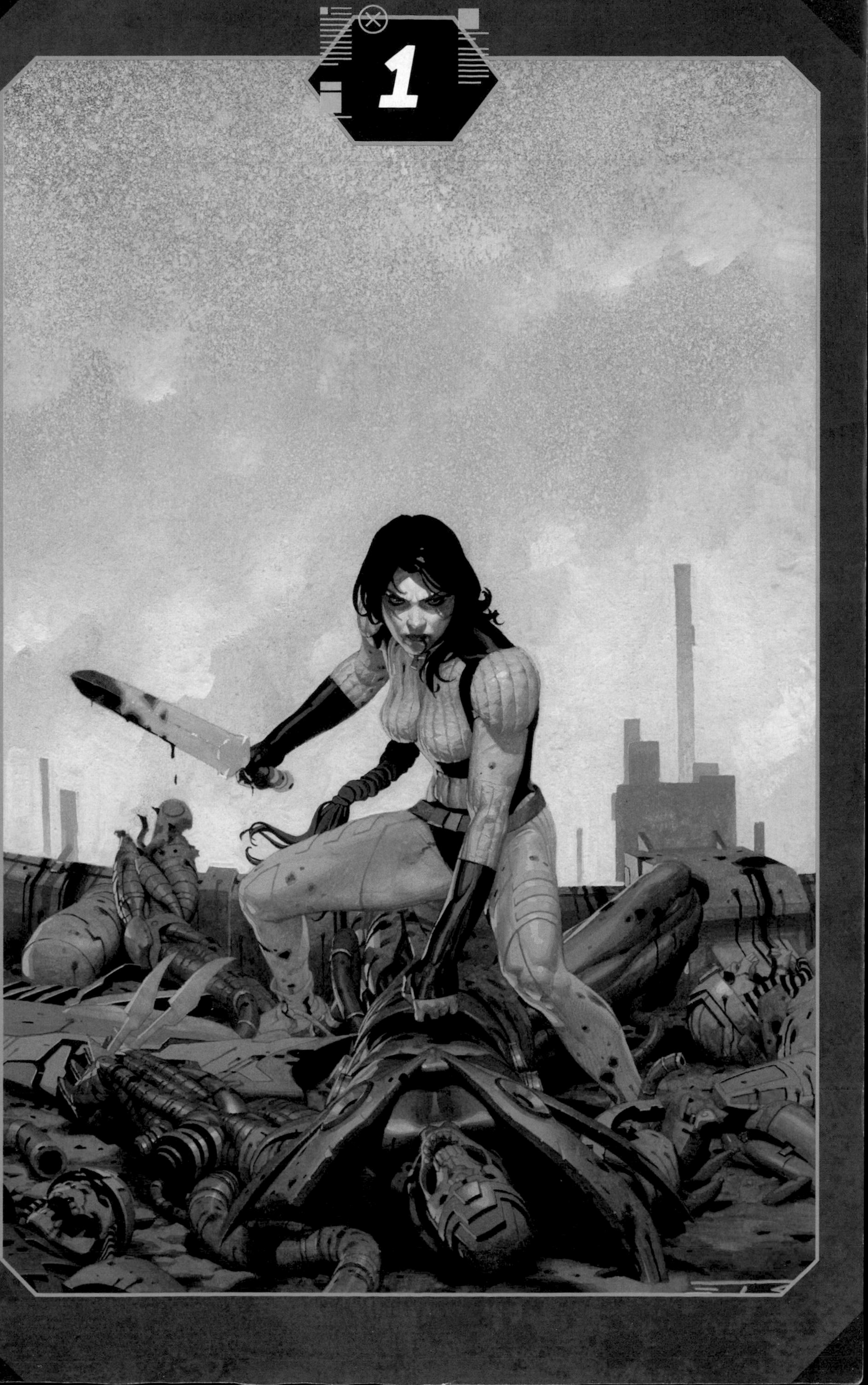
1

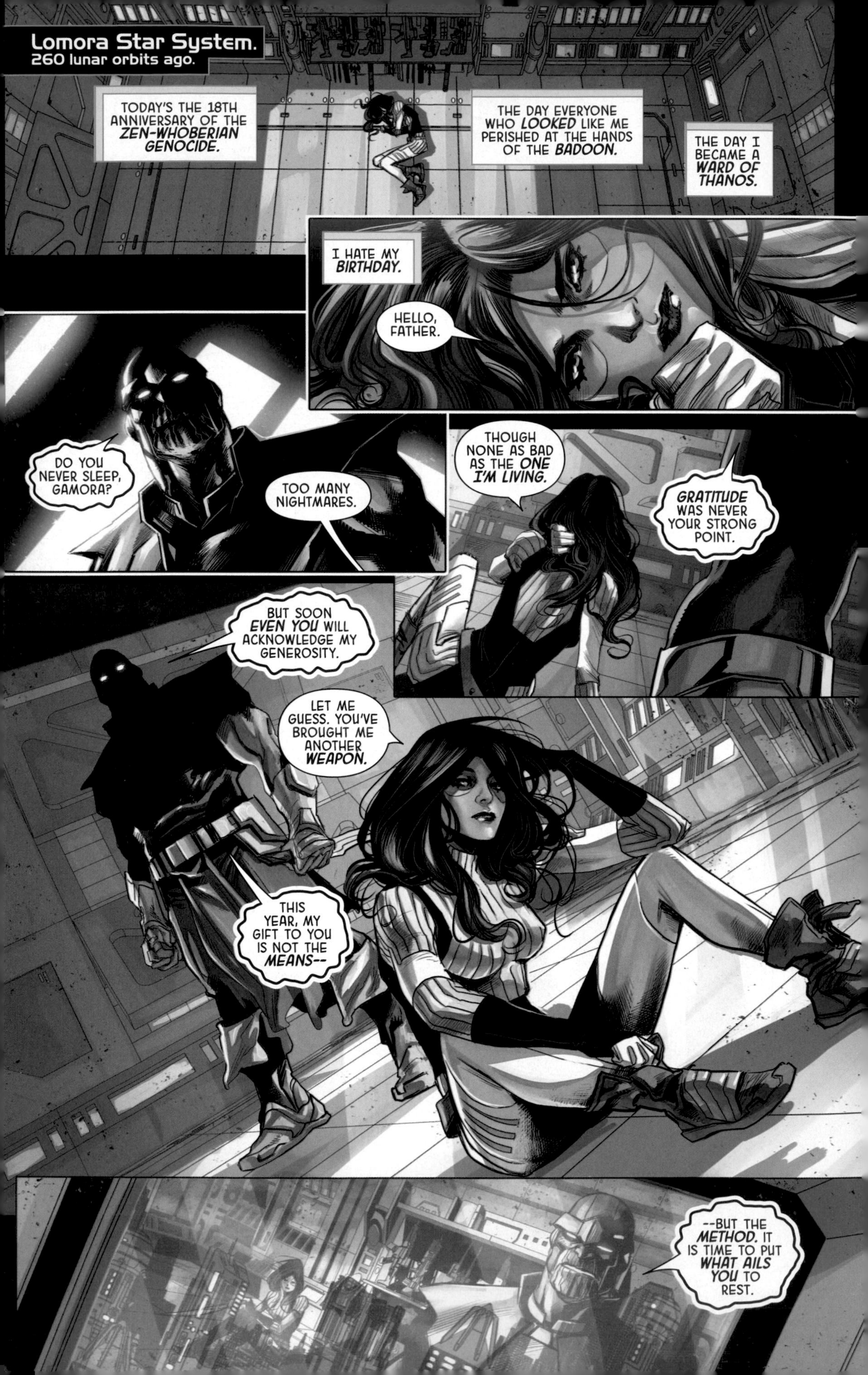
Lomora Star System.
260 lunar orbits ago.
TODAY'S THE 18TH ANNIVERSARY OF THE ZEN-WHOBERIAN GENOCIDE.
THE DAY EVERYONE WHO LOOKED LIKE ME PERISHED AT THE HANDS OF THE BADOON.
THE DAY I BECAME A WARD OF THANOS.
I HATE MY BIRTHDAY.
HELLO, FATHER.
DO YOU NEVER SLEEP, GAMORA?
TOO MANY NIGHTMARES.
THOUGH NONE AS BAD AS THE ONE I'M LIVING.
GRATITUDE WAS NEVER YOUR STRONG POINT.
BUT SOON EVEN YOU WILL ACKNOWLEDGE MY GENEROSITY.
LET ME GUESS. YOU'VE BROUGHT ME ANOTHER WEAPON.
THIS YEAR, MY GIFT TO YOU IS NOT THE MEANS--
--BUT THE METHOD. IT IS TIME TO PUT WHAT AILS YOU TO REST.

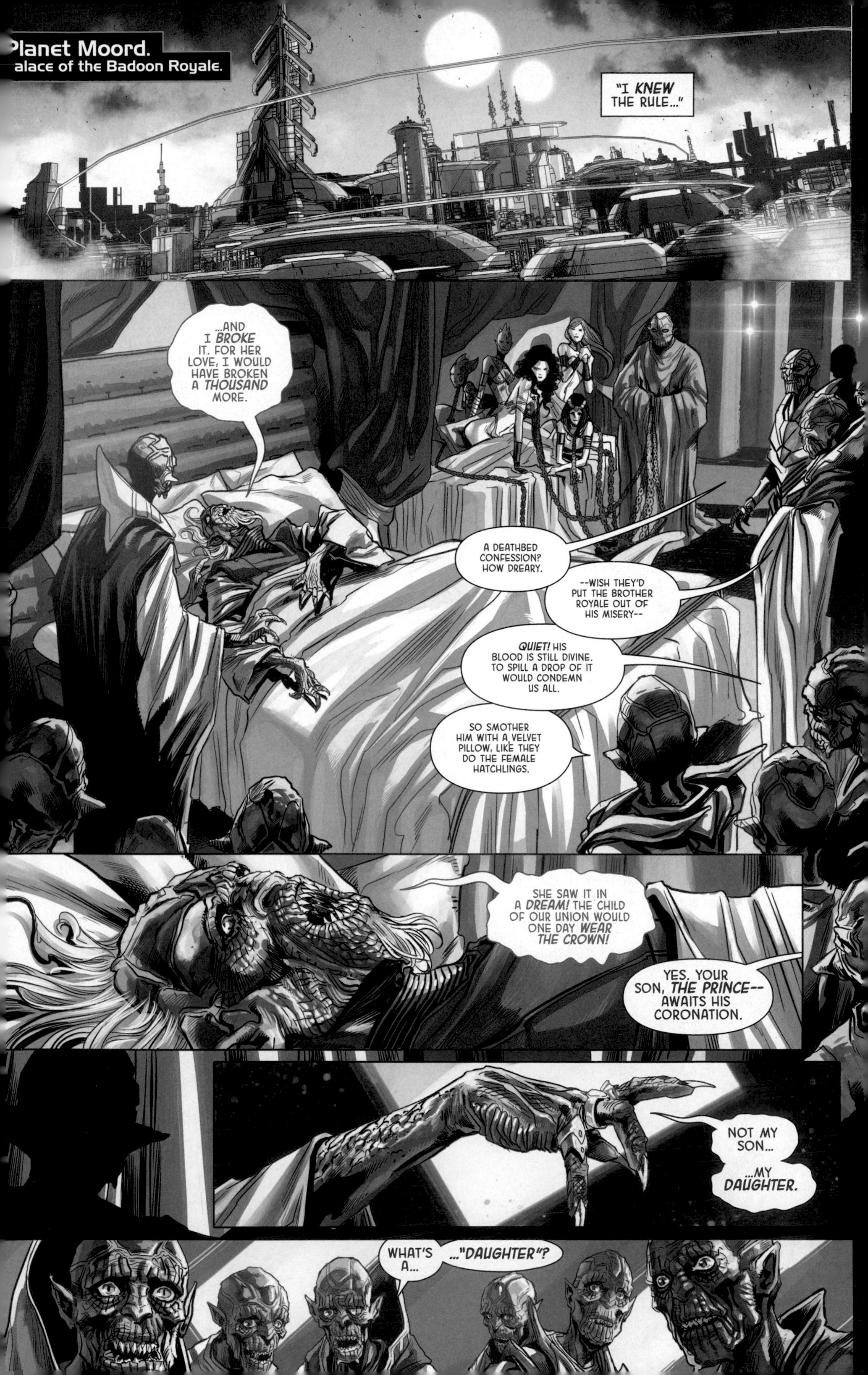
Planet Moord.
alace of the Badoon Royale.
"I KNEW THE RULE..."
...AND I BROKE IT. FOR HER LOVE, I WOULD HAVE BROKEN A THOUSAND MORE.
A DEATHBED CONFESSION? HOW DREARY.
--WISH THEY'D PUT THE BROTHER ROYALE OUT OF HIS MISERY--
QUIET! HIS BLOOD IS STILL DIVINE. TO SPILL A DROP OF IT WOULD CONDEMN US ALL.
SO SMOTHER HIM WITH A VELVET PILLOW, LIKE THEY DO THE FEMALE HATCHLINGS.
SHE SAW IT IN A DREAM! THE CHILD OF OUR UNION WOULD ONE DAY WEAR THE CROWN!
YES. YOUR SON, THE PRINCE--AWAITS HIS CORONATION.
NOT MY SON...
...MY DAUGHTER.
WHAT'S A...
..."DAUGHTER"?

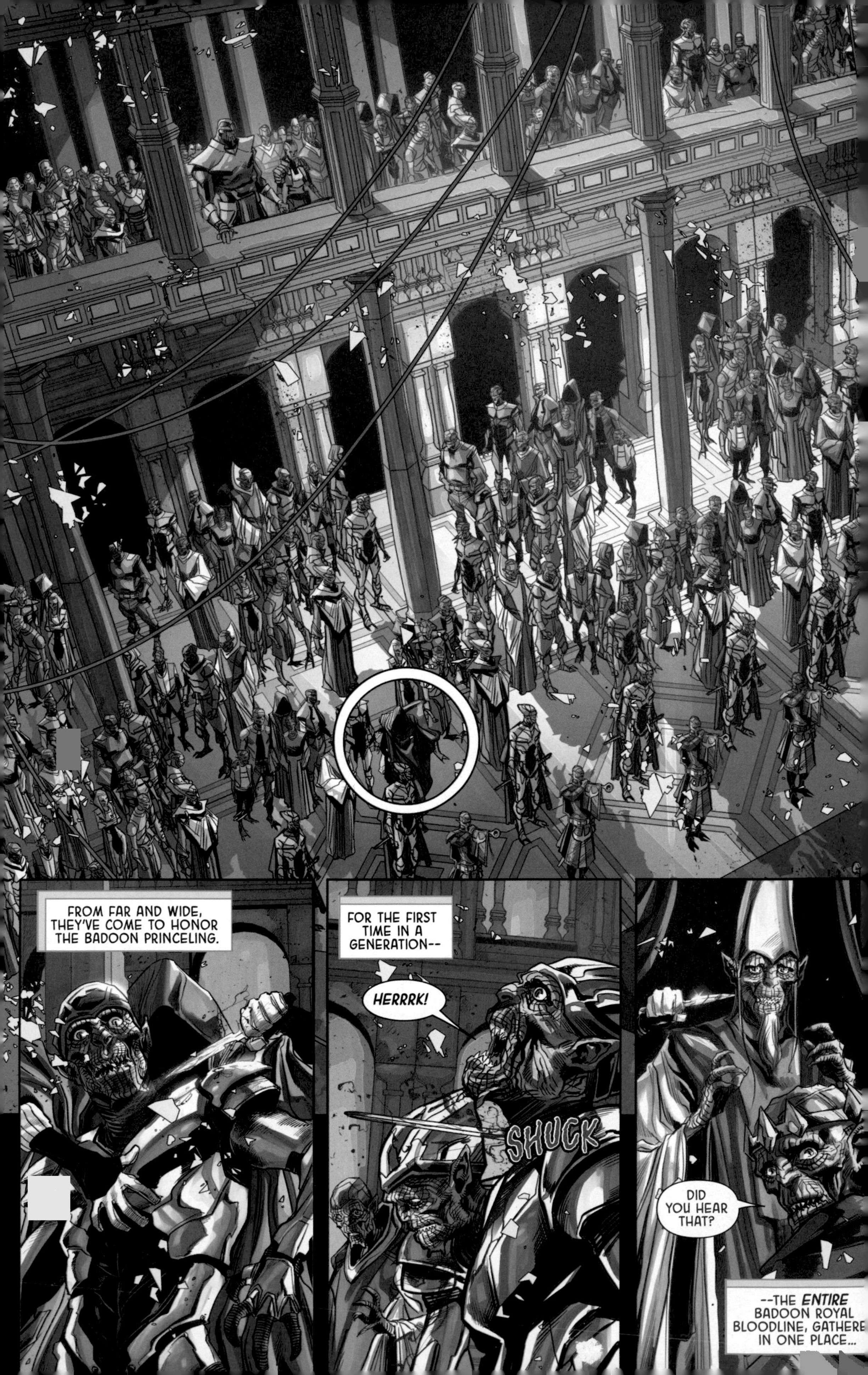
FROM FAR AND WIDE, THEY'VE COME TO HONOR THE BADOON PRINCELING.
FOR THE FIRST TIME IN A GENERATION--
HERRRK!
SHUCK
DID YOU HEAR THAT?
--THE ENTIRE BADOON ROYAL BLOODLINE, GATHERE IN ONE PLACE...

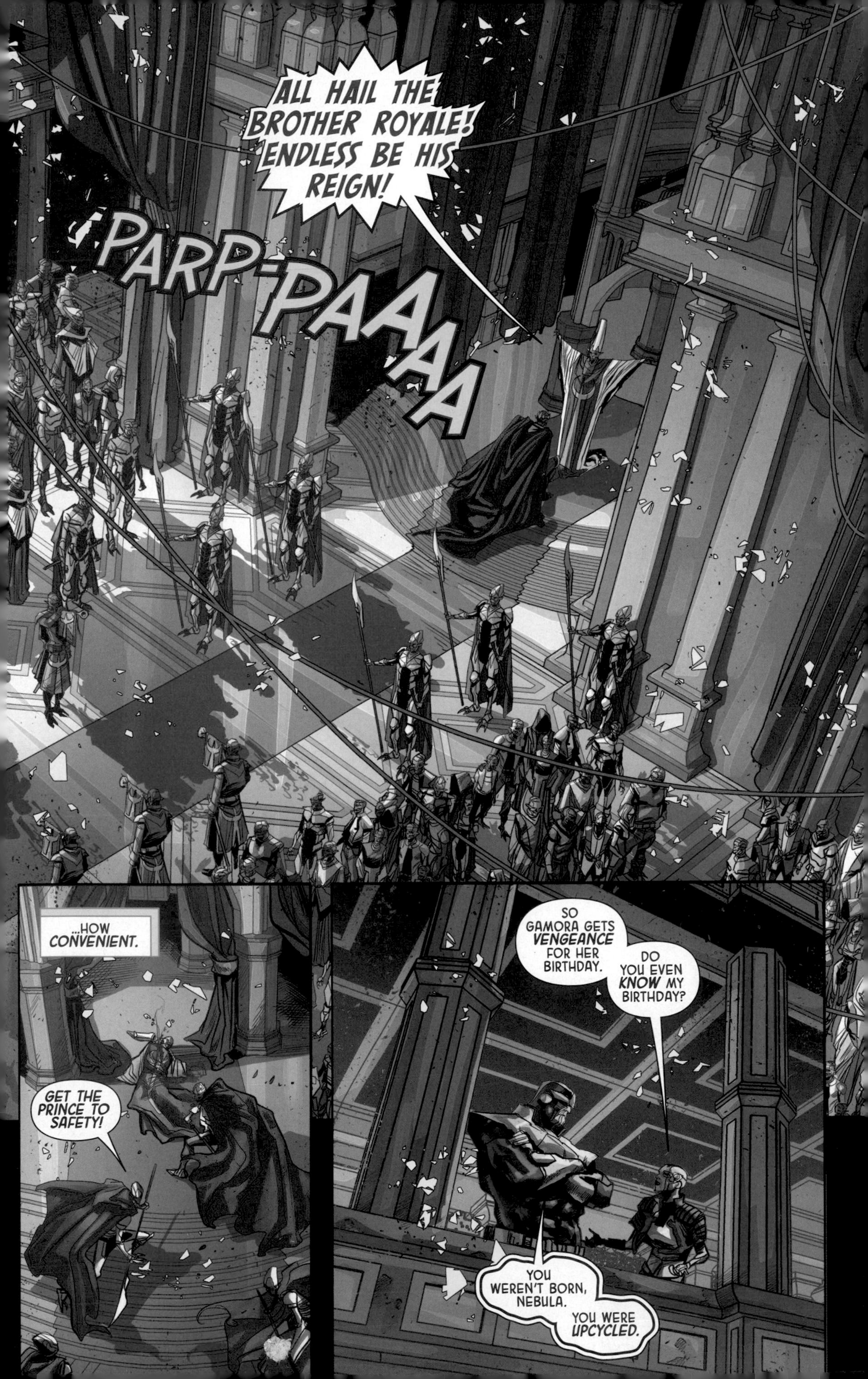
ALL HAIL THE BROTHER ROYALE! ENDLESS BE HIS REIGN!
PARP-PAAAAA
...HOW CONVENIENT.
GET THE PRINCE TO SAFETY!
SO GAMORA GETS VENGEANCE FOR HER BIRTHDAY.
DO YOU EVEN KNOW MY BIRTHDAY?
YOU WEREN'T BORN, NEBULA.
YOU WERE UPCYCLED.

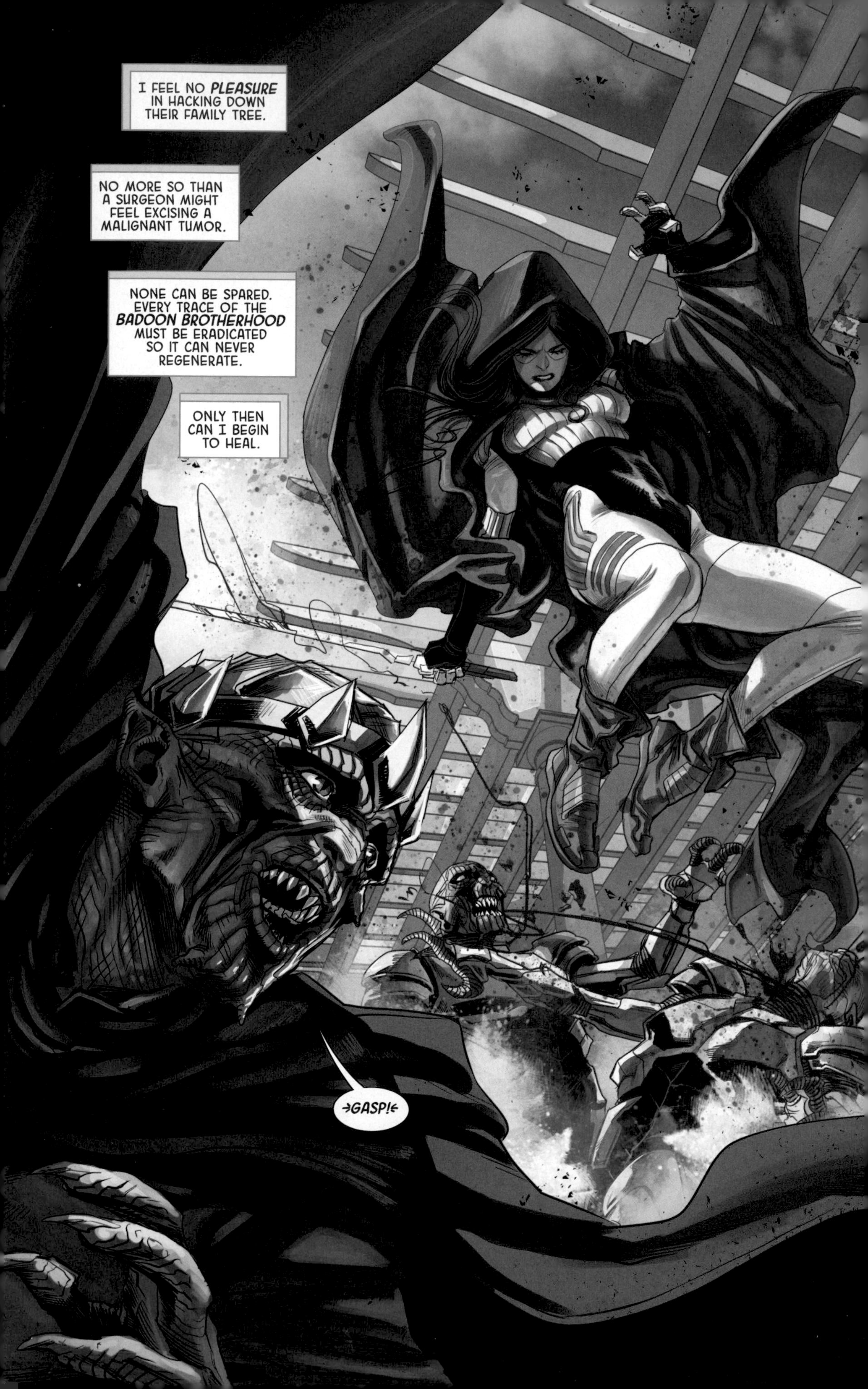
I FEEL NO PLEASURE IN HACKING DOWN THEIR FAMILY TREE.
NO MORE SO THAN A SURGEON MIGHT FEEL EXCISING A MALIGNANT TUMOR.
NONE CAN BE SPARED. EVERY TRACE OF THE BADOON BROTHERHOOD MUST BE ERADICATED SO IT CAN NEVER REGENERATE.
ONLY THEN CAN I BEGIN TO HEAL.
GASP!

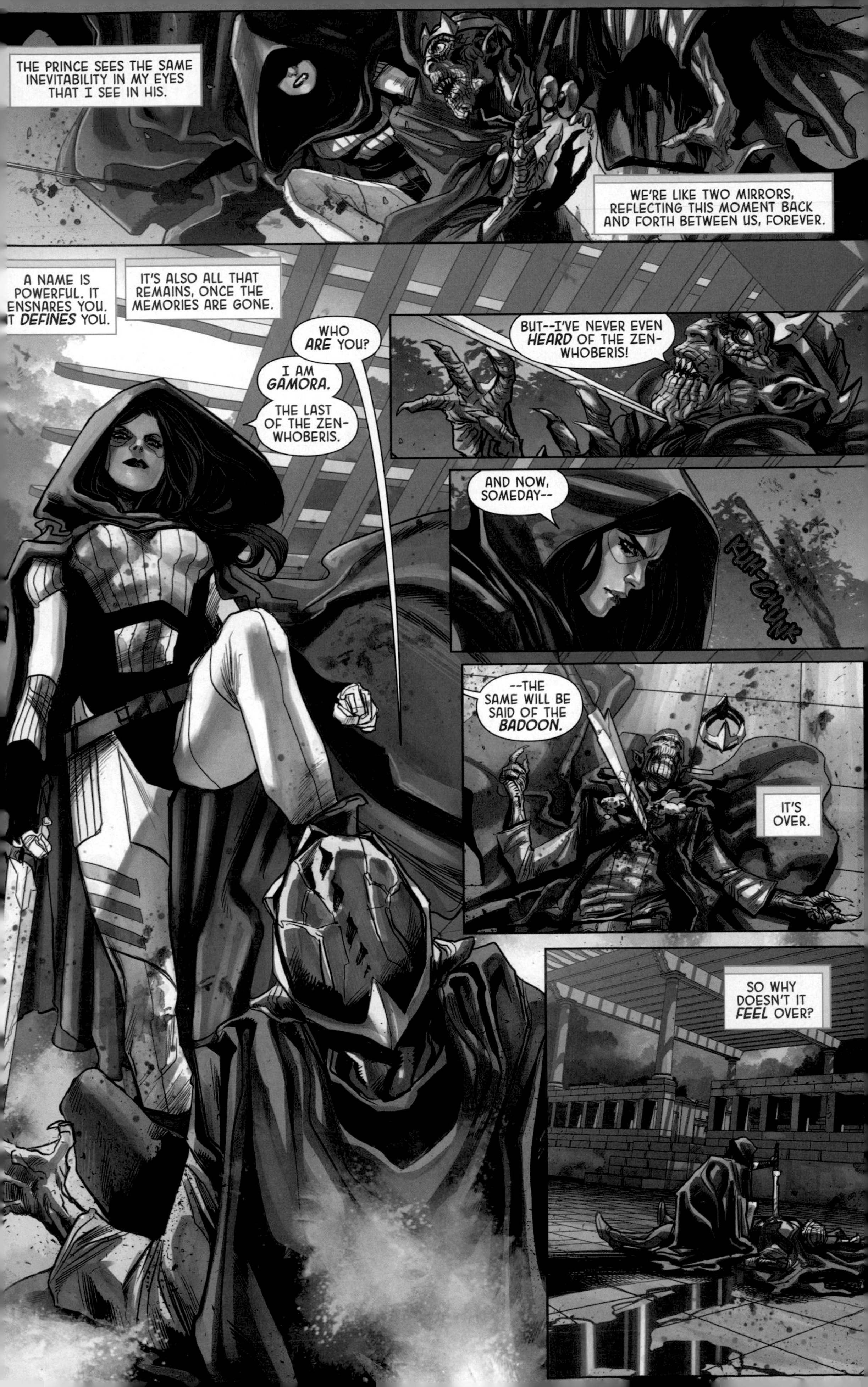
THE PRINCE SEES THE SAME INEVITABILITY IN MY EYES THAT I SEE IN HIS.
WE'RE LIKE TWO MIRRORS, REFLECTING THIS MOMENT BACK AND FORTH BETWEEN US, FOREVER.
A NAME IS POWERFUL. IT ENSNARES YOU. IT DEFINES YOU.
IT'S ALSO ALL THAT REMAINS, ONCE THE MEMORIES ARE GONE.
WHO ARE YOU?
I AM GAMORA.
THE LAST OF THE ZEN-WHOBERIS.
BUT--I'VE NEVER EVEN HEARD OF THE ZEN-WHOBERIS!
AND NOW, SOMEDAY--
KUH-CHUNK
--THE SAME WILL BE SAID OF THE BADOON.
IT'S OVER.
SO WHY DOESN'T IT FEEL OVER?

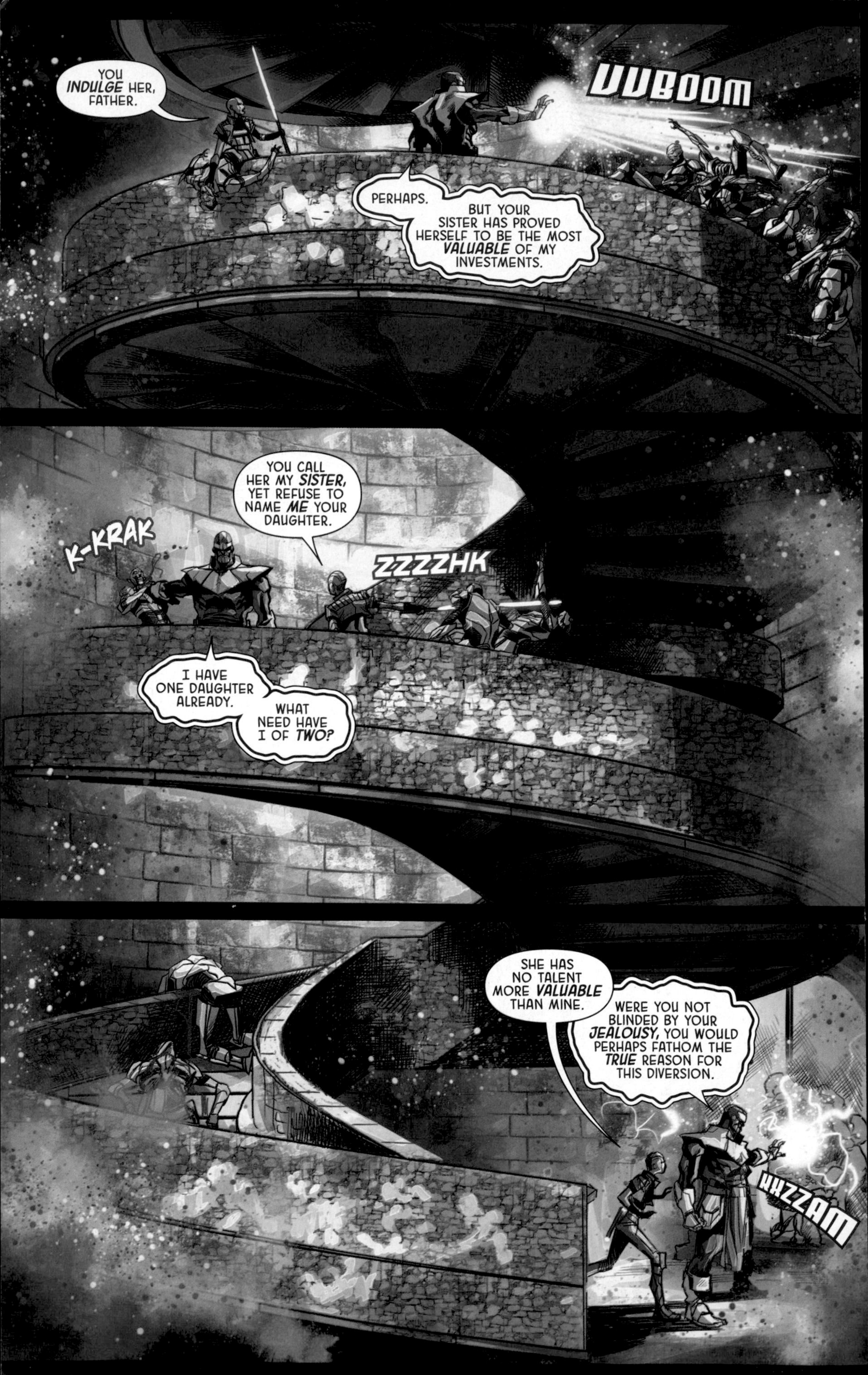
YOU INDULGE HER, FATHER.
VVBOOM
PERHAPS.
BUT YOUR SISTER HAS PROVED HERSELF TO BE THE MOST VALUABLE OF MY INVESTMENTS.
YOU CALL HER MY SISTER, YET REFUSE TO NAME ME YOUR DAUGHTER.
K-KRAK
ZZZZHK
I HAVE ONE DAUGHTER ALREADY.
WHAT NEED HAVE I OF TWO?
SHE HAS NO TALENT MORE VALUABLE THAN MINE.
WERE YOU NOT BLINDED BY YOUR JEALOUSY, YOU WOULD PERHAPS FATHOM THE TRUE REASON FOR THIS DIVERSION.
KKZZAM

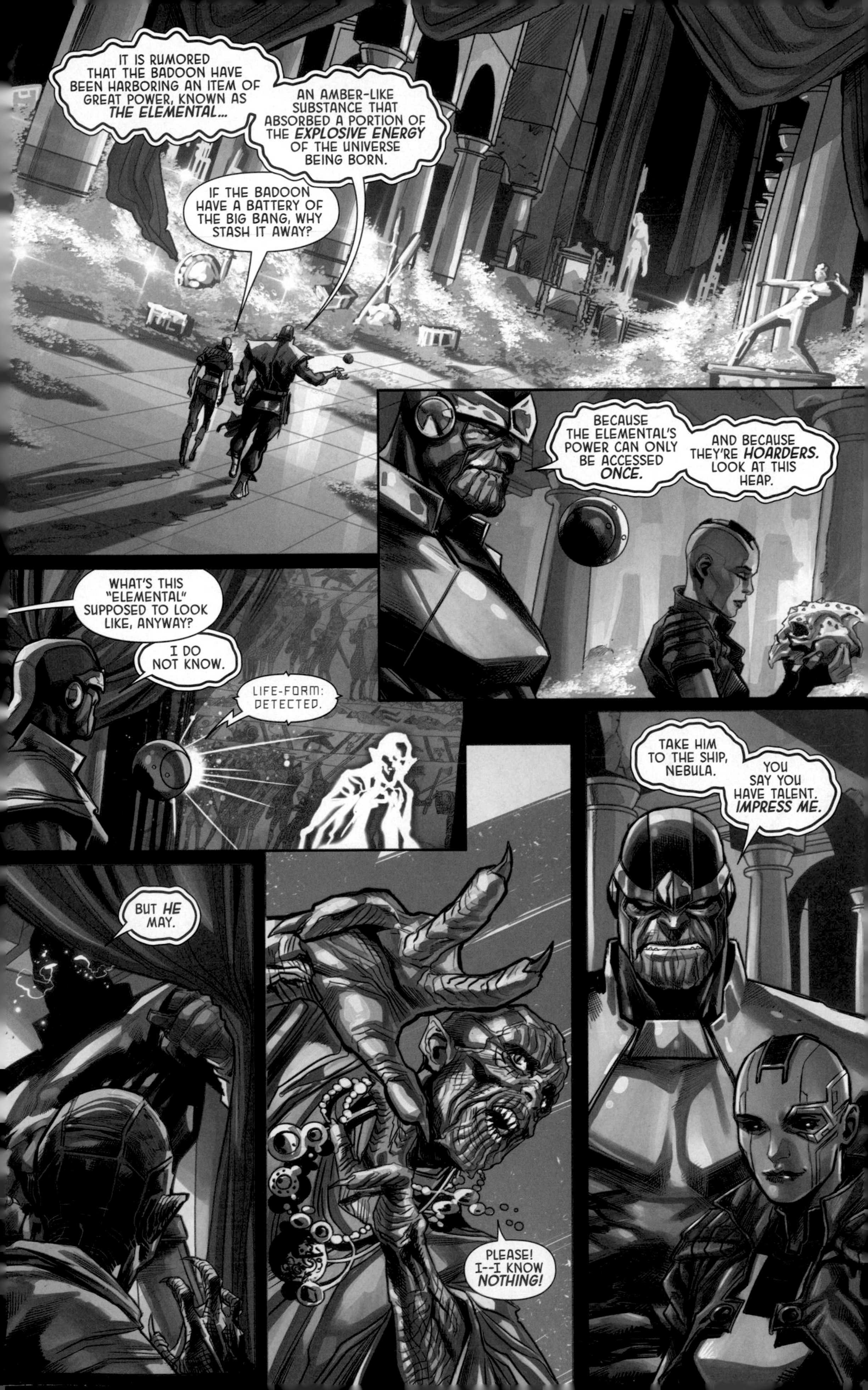
IT IS RUMORED THAT THE BADOON HAVE BEEN HARBORING AN ITEM OF GREAT POWER, KNOWN AS THE ELEMENTAL...
AN AMBER-LIKE SUBSTANCE THAT ABSORBED A PORTION OF THE EXPLOSIVE ENERGY OF THE UNIVERSE BEING BORN.
IF THE BADOON HAVE A BATTERY OF THE BIG BANG, WHY STASH IT AWAY?
BECAUSE THE ELEMENTAL'S POWER CAN ONLY BE ACCESSED ONCE.
AND BECAUSE THEY'RE HOARDERS. LOOK AT THIS HEAP.
WHAT'S THIS "ELEMENTAL" SUPPOSED TO LOOK LIKE, ANYWAY?
I DO NOT KNOW.
LIFE-FORM: DETECTED.
BUT HE MAY.
PLEASE! I--I KNOW NOTHING!
TAKE HIM TO THE SHIP, NEBULA.
YOU SAY YOU HAVE TALENT. IMPRESS ME.

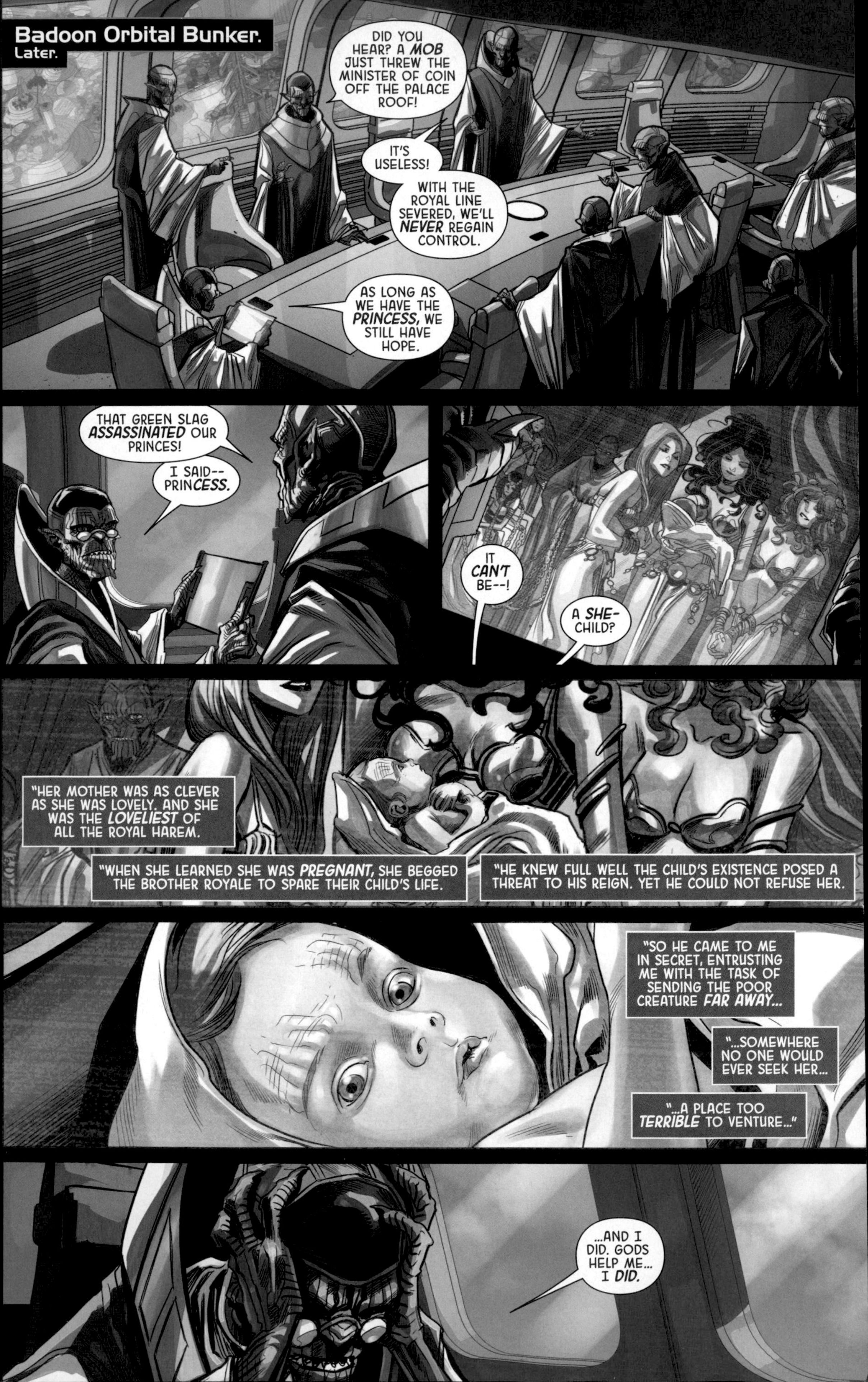
Badoon Orbital Bunker.
Later.
DID YOU HEAR? A MOB JUST THREW THE MINISTER OF COIN OFF THE PALACE ROOF!
IT'S USELESS!
WITH THE ROYAL LINE SEVERED, WE'LL NEVER REGAIN CONTROL.
AS LONG AS WE HAVE THE PRINCESS, WE STILL HAVE HOPE.
THAT GREEN SLAG ASSASSINATED OUR PRINCES!
I SAID-- PRINCESS.
IT CAN'T BE--!
A SHE-CHILD?
"HER MOTHER WAS AS CLEVER AS SHE WAS LOVELY. AND SHE WAS THE LOVELIEST OF ALL THE ROYAL HAREM.
"WHEN SHE LEARNED SHE WAS PREGNANT, SHE BEGGED THE BROTHER ROYALE TO SPARE THEIR CHILD'S LIFE.
"HE KNEW FULL WELL THE CHILD'S EXISTENCE POSED A THREAT TO HIS REIGN. YET HE COULD NOT REFUSE HER.
"SO HE CAME TO ME IN SECRET, ENTRUSTING ME WITH THE TASK OF SENDING THE POOR CREATURE FAR AWAY...
"...SOMEWHERE NO ONE WOULD EVER SEEK HER...
"...A PLACE TOO TERRIBLE TO VENTURE..."
...AND I DID. GODS HELP ME... I DID.

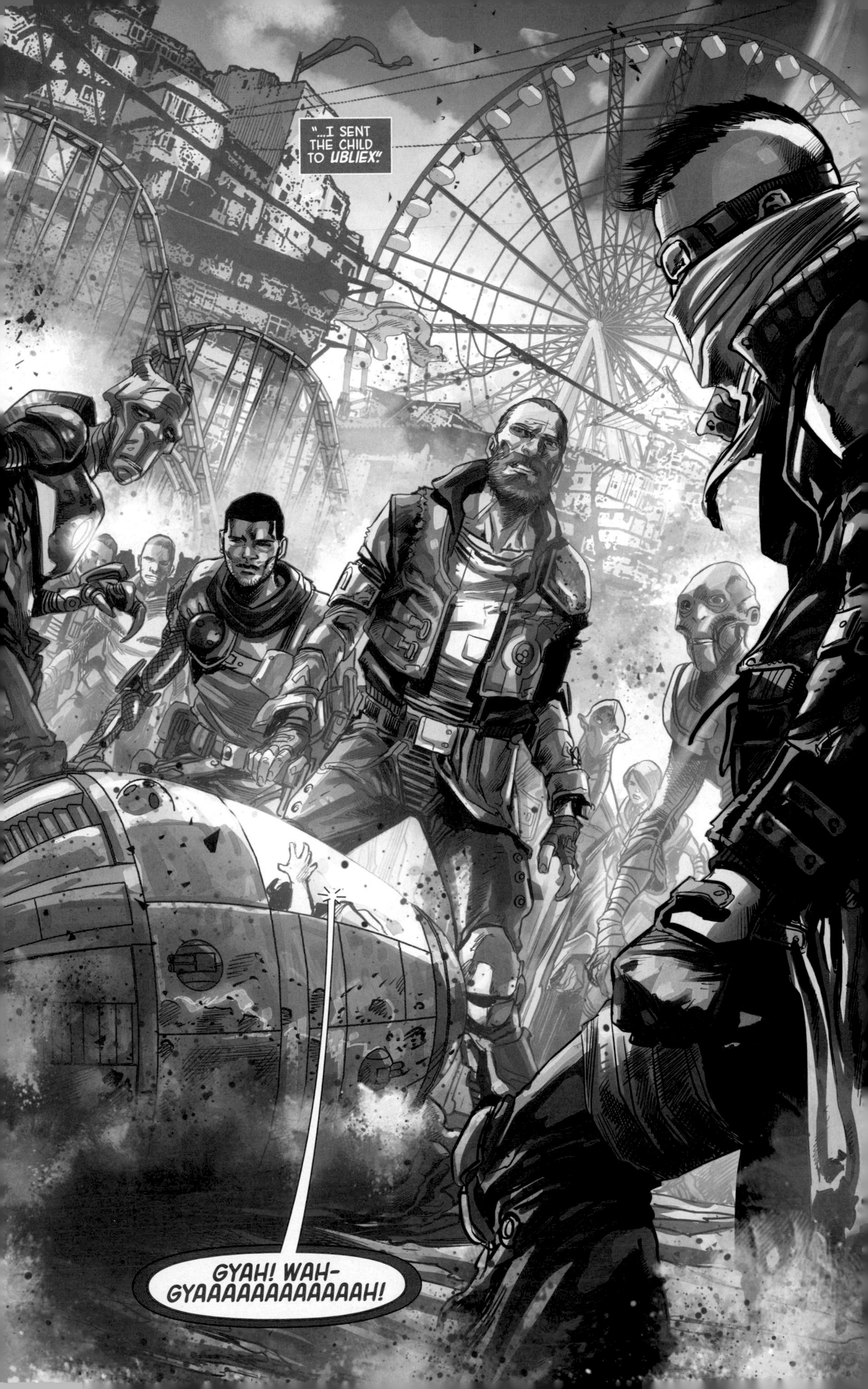
"...I SENT THE CHILD TO UBLIEX."
GYAH! WAH-GYAAAAAAAAAAAAH!

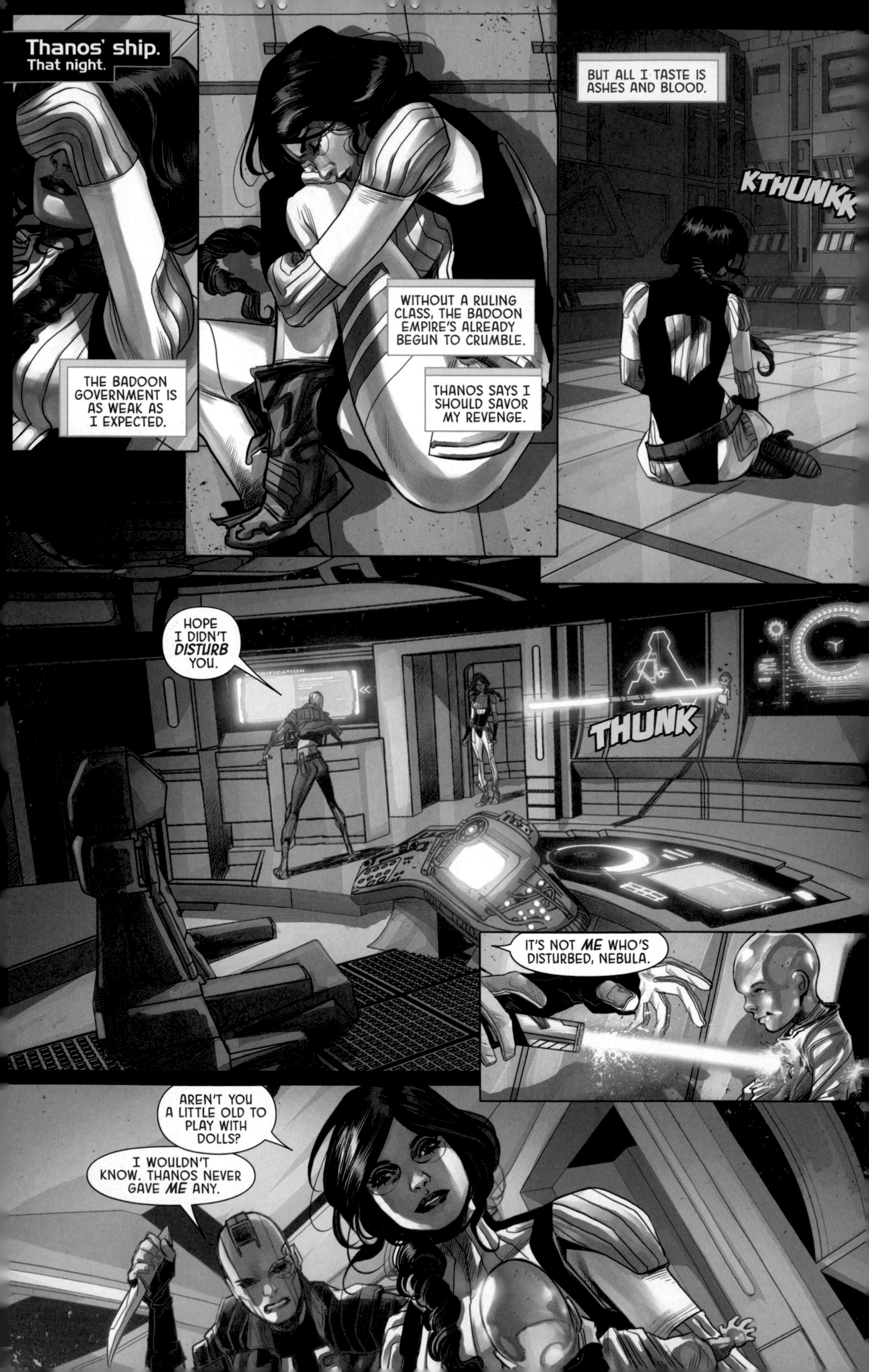
Thanos' ship.
That night.
THE BADOON GOVERNMENT IS AS WEAK AS I EXPECTED.
WITHOUT A RULING CLASS, THE BADOON EMPIRE'S ALREADY BEGUN TO CRUMBLE.
THANOS SAYS I SHOULD SAVOR MY REVENGE.
BUT ALL I TASTE IS ASHES AND BLOOD.
KTHUNKK
HOPE I DIDN'T DISTURB YOU.
THUNK
IT'S NOT ME WHO'S DISTURBED, NEBULA.
AREN'T YOU A LITTLE OLD TO PLAY WITH DOLLS?
I WOULDN'T KNOW. THANOS NEVER GAVE ME ANY.

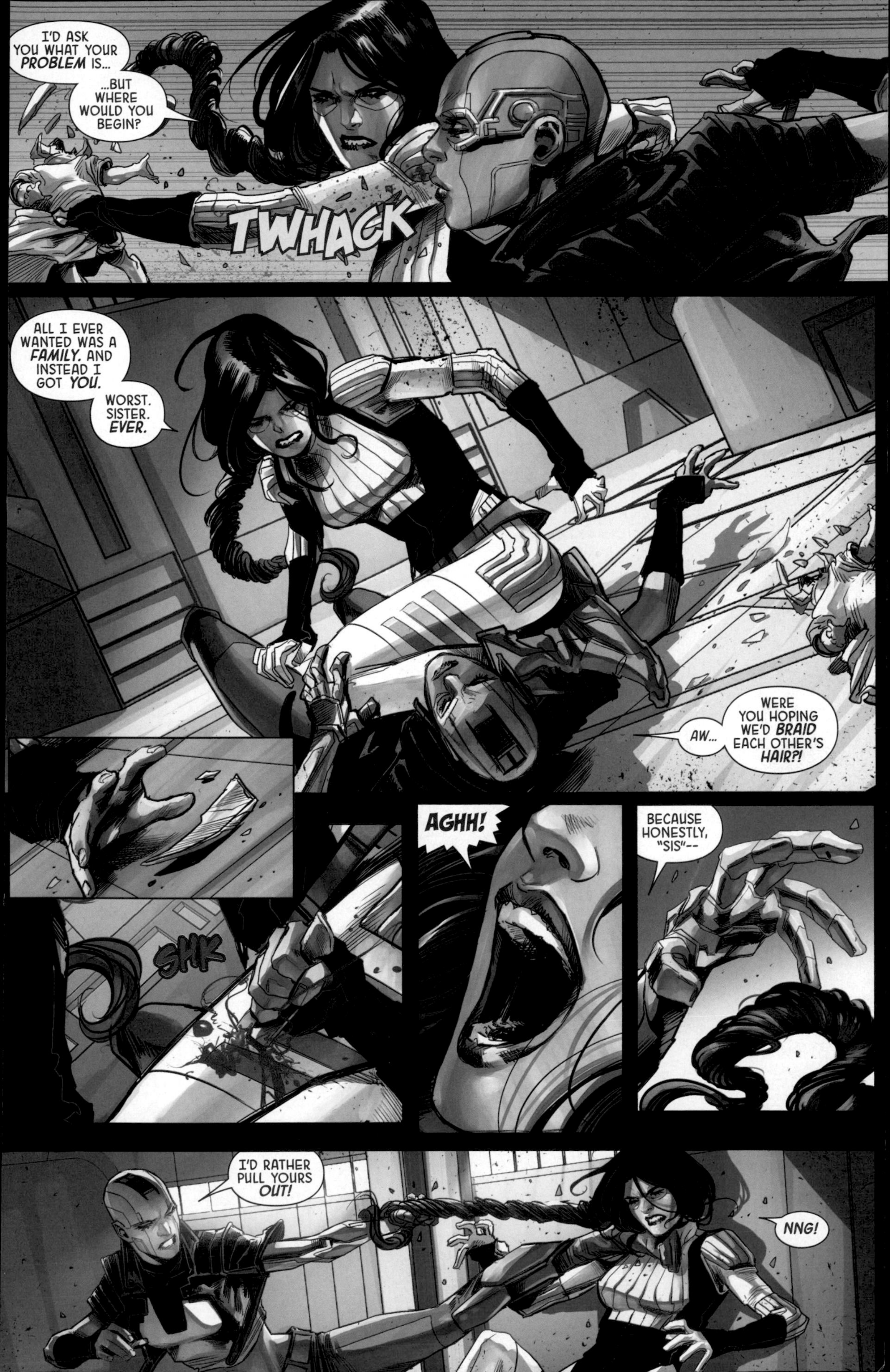

I'D ASK YOU WHAT YOUR PROBLEM IS...
...BUT WHERE WOULD YOU BEGIN?
TWHACK
ALL I EVER WANTED WAS A FAMILY. AND INSTEAD I GOT YOU.
WORST. SISTER. EVER.
AW...
WERE YOU HOPING WE'D BRAID EACH OTHER'S HAIR?!
SHK
AGHH!
BECAUSE HONESTLY, "SIS"--
I'D RATHER PULL YOURS OUT!
NNG!

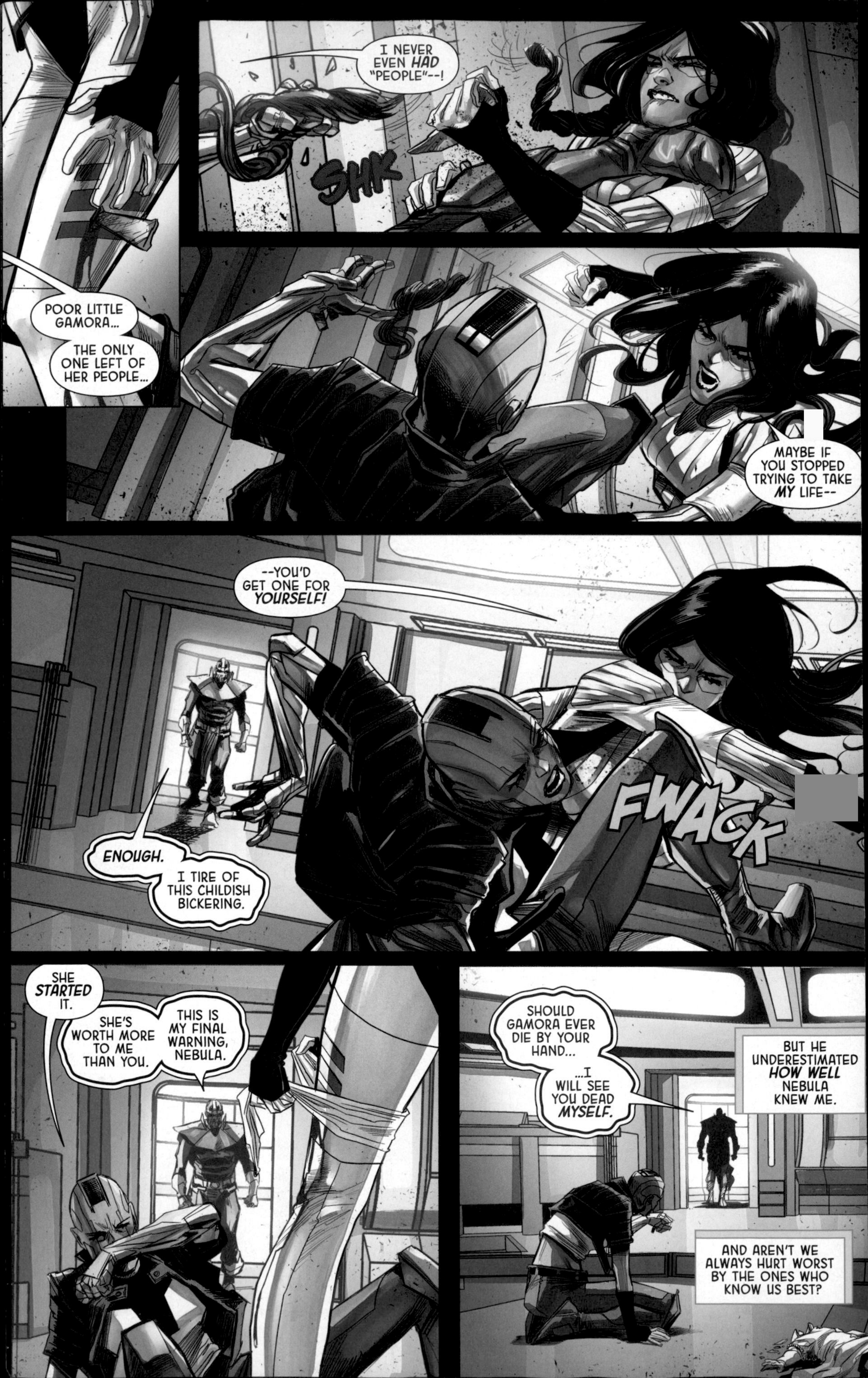
I NEVER EVEN *HAD* "PEOPLE"--!
SHK
POOR LITTLE GAMORA...
THE ONLY ONE LEFT OF HER PEOPLE...
MAYBE IF YOU STOPPED TRYING TO TAKE *MY* LIFE--
--YOU'D GET ONE FOR *YOURSELF!*
FWACK
ENOUGH.
I TIRE OF THIS CHILDISH BICKERING.
SHE *STARTED* IT.
SHE'S WORTH MORE TO ME THAN YOU.
THIS IS MY FINAL WARNING, NEBULA.
SHOULD GAMORA EVER DIE BY YOUR HAND...
...I WILL SEE YOU DEAD *MYSELF.*
BUT HE UNDERESTIMATED *HOW WELL* NEBULA KNEW ME.
AND AREN'T WE ALWAYS HURT WORST BY THE ONES WHO KNOW US BEST?

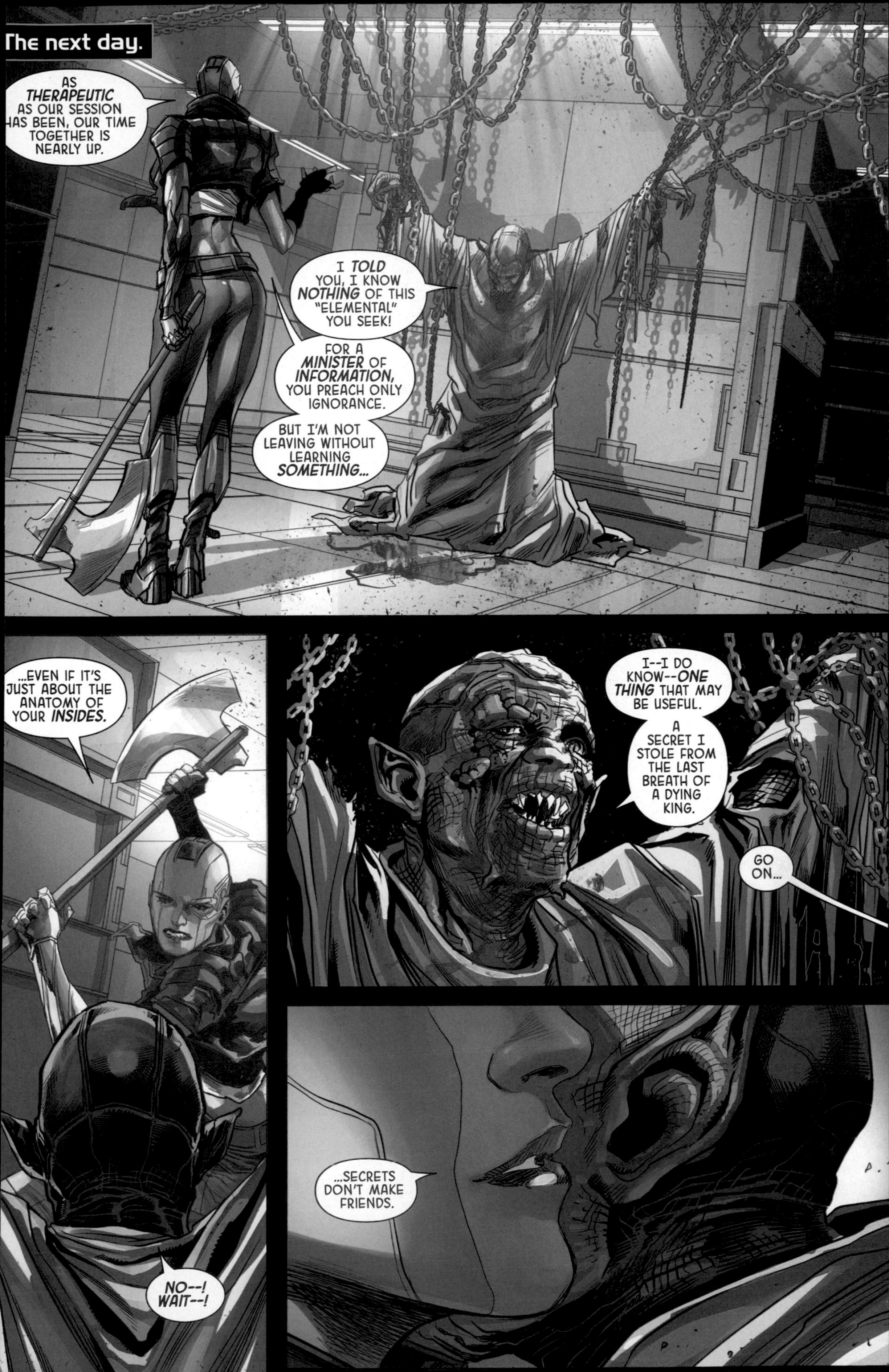
The next day.
AS THERAPEUTIC AS OUR SESSION HAS BEEN, OUR TIME TOGETHER IS NEARLY UP.
I TOLD YOU, I KNOW NOTHING OF THIS "ELEMENTAL" YOU SEEK!
FOR A MINISTER OF INFORMATION, YOU PREACH ONLY IGNORANCE.
BUT I'M NOT LEAVING WITHOUT LEARNING SOMETHING...
...EVEN IF IT'S JUST ABOUT THE ANATOMY OF YOUR INSIDES.
NO--! WAIT--!
I--I DO KNOW--ONE THING THAT MAY BE USEFUL.
A SECRET I STOLE FROM THE LAST BREATH OF A DYING KING.
GO ON...
...SECRETS DON'T MAKE FRIENDS.

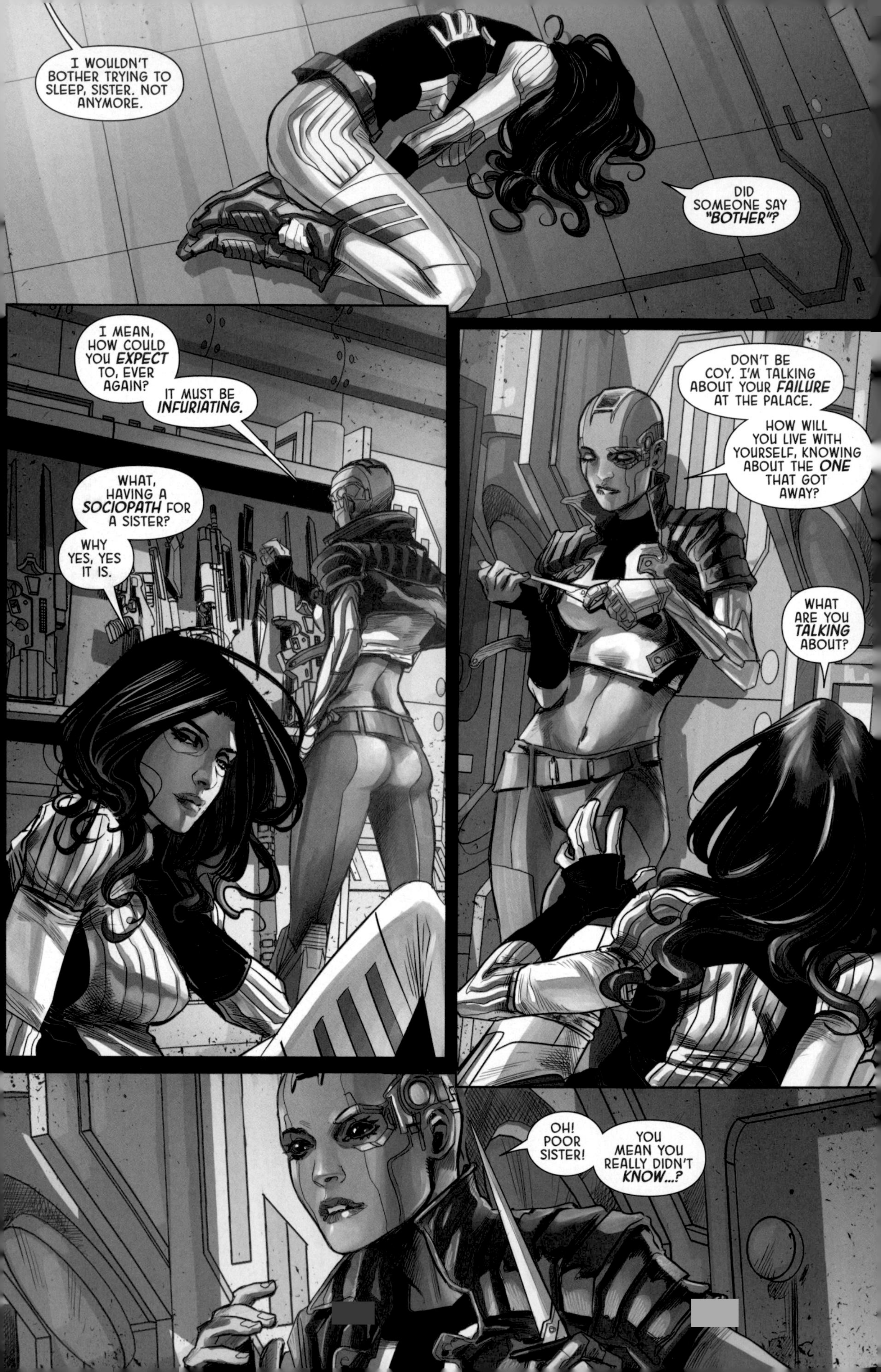
I WOULDN'T BOTHER TRYING TO SLEEP, SISTER. NOT ANYMORE.
DID SOMEONE SAY "BOTHER"?
I MEAN, HOW COULD YOU EXPECT TO, EVER AGAIN?
IT MUST BE INFURIATING.
WHAT, HAVING A SOCIOPATH FOR A SISTER?
WHY YES, YES IT IS.
DON'T BE COY. I'M TALKING ABOUT YOUR FAILURE AT THE PALACE.
HOW WILL YOU LIVE WITH YOURSELF, KNOWING ABOUT THE ONE THAT GOT AWAY?
WHAT ARE YOU TALKING ABOUT?
OH! POOR SISTER!
YOU MEAN YOU REALLY DIDN'T KNOW...?

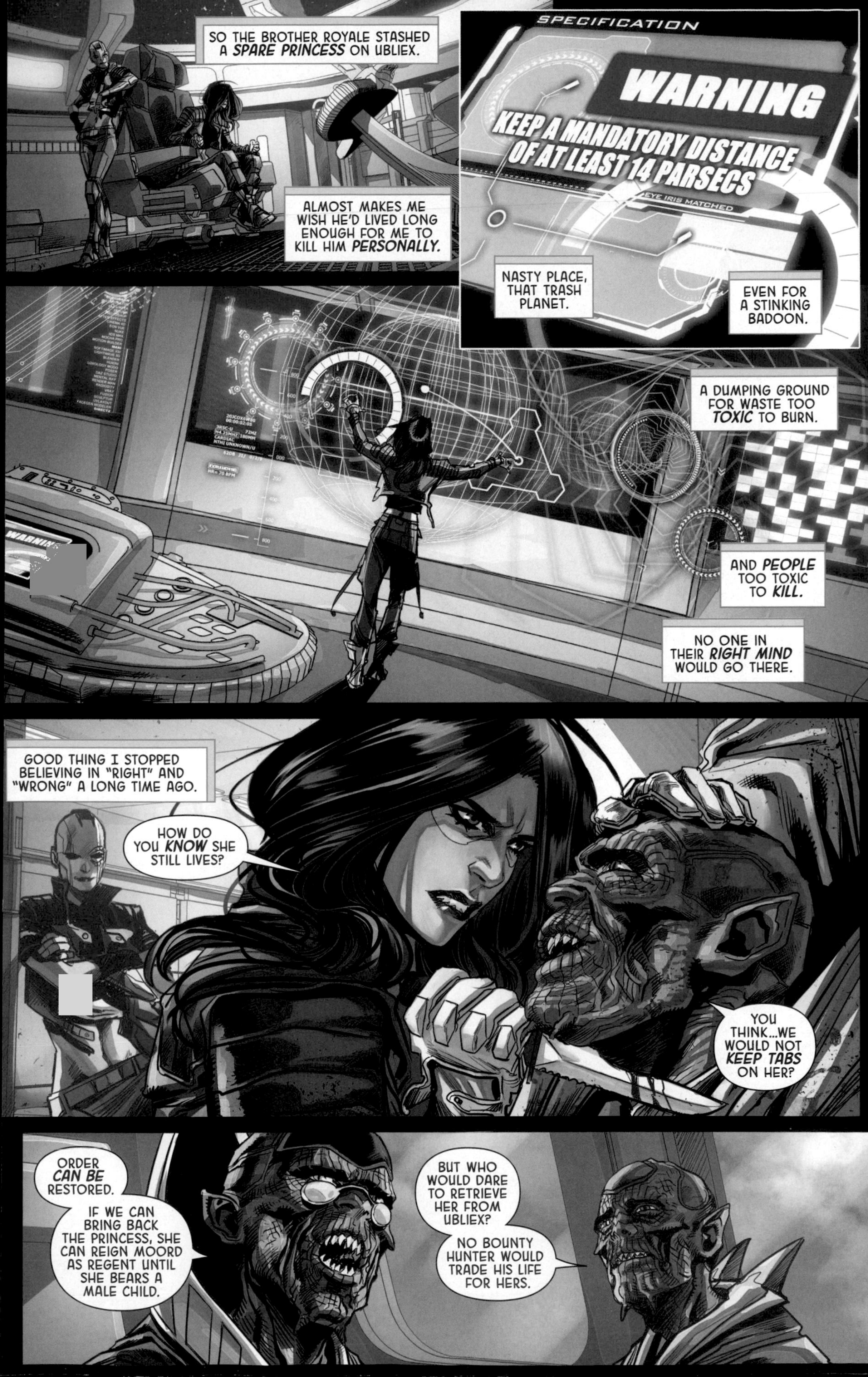
SO THE BROTHER ROYALE STASHED A SPARE PRINCESS ON UBLIEX.
ALMOST MAKES ME WISH HE'D LIVED LONG ENOUGH FOR ME TO KILL HIM PERSONALLY.
SPECIFICATION
WARNING
KEEP A MANDATORY DISTANCE OF AT LEAST 14 PARSECS
EYE IRIS MATCHED
NASTY PLACE, THAT TRASH PLANET.
EVEN FOR A STINKING BADOON.
A DUMPING GROUND FOR WASTE TOO TOXIC TO BURN.
AND PEOPLE TOO TOXIC TO KILL.
NO ONE IN THEIR RIGHT MIND WOULD GO THERE.
GOOD THING I STOPPED BELIEVING IN "RIGHT" AND "WRONG" A LONG TIME AGO.
HOW DO YOU KNOW SHE STILL LIVES?
YOU THINK...WE WOULD NOT KEEP TABS ON HER?
ORDER CAN BE RESTORED.
IF WE CAN BRING BACK THE PRINCESS, SHE CAN REIGN MOORD AS REGENT UNTIL SHE BEARS A MALE CHILD.
BUT WHO WOULD DARE TO RETRIEVE HER FROM UBLIEX?
NO BOUNTY HUNTER WOULD TRADE HIS LIFE FOR HERS.

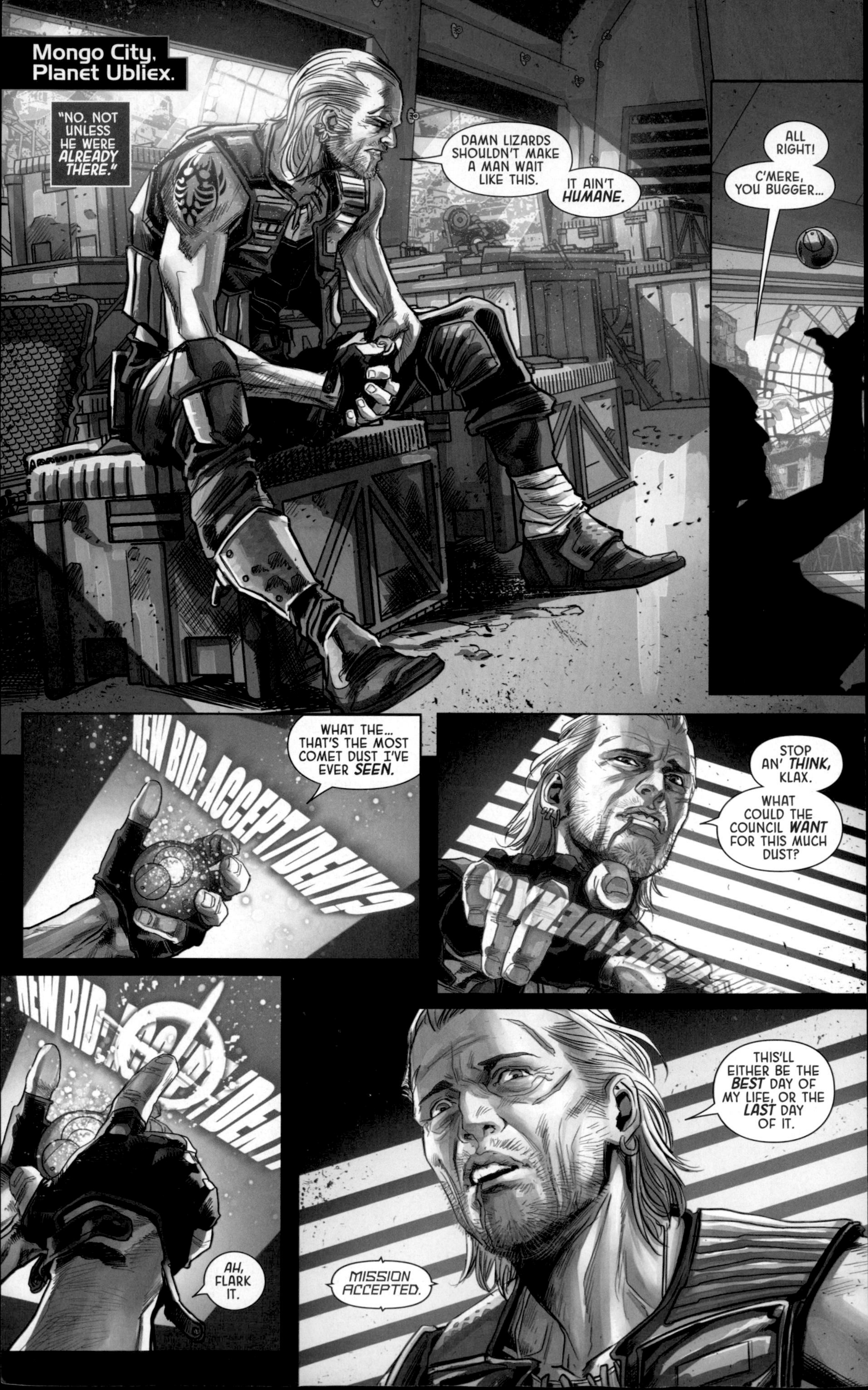

Mongo City, Planet Ubliex.
"NO. NOT UNLESS HE WERE ALREADY THERE."
DAMN LIZARDS SHOULDN'T MAKE A MAN WAIT LIKE THIS.
IT AIN'T HUMANE.
ALL RIGHT!
C'MERE, YOU BUGGER...
NEW BID: ACCEPT/DENY?
WHAT THE... THAT'S THE MOST COMET DUST I'VE EVER SEEN.
STOP AN' THINK, KLAX.
WHAT COULD THE COUNCIL WANT FOR THIS MUCH DUST?
NEW BID:
AH, FLARK IT.
THIS'LL EITHER BE THE BEST DAY OF MY LIFE, OR THE LAST DAY OF IT.
MISSION ACCEPTED.

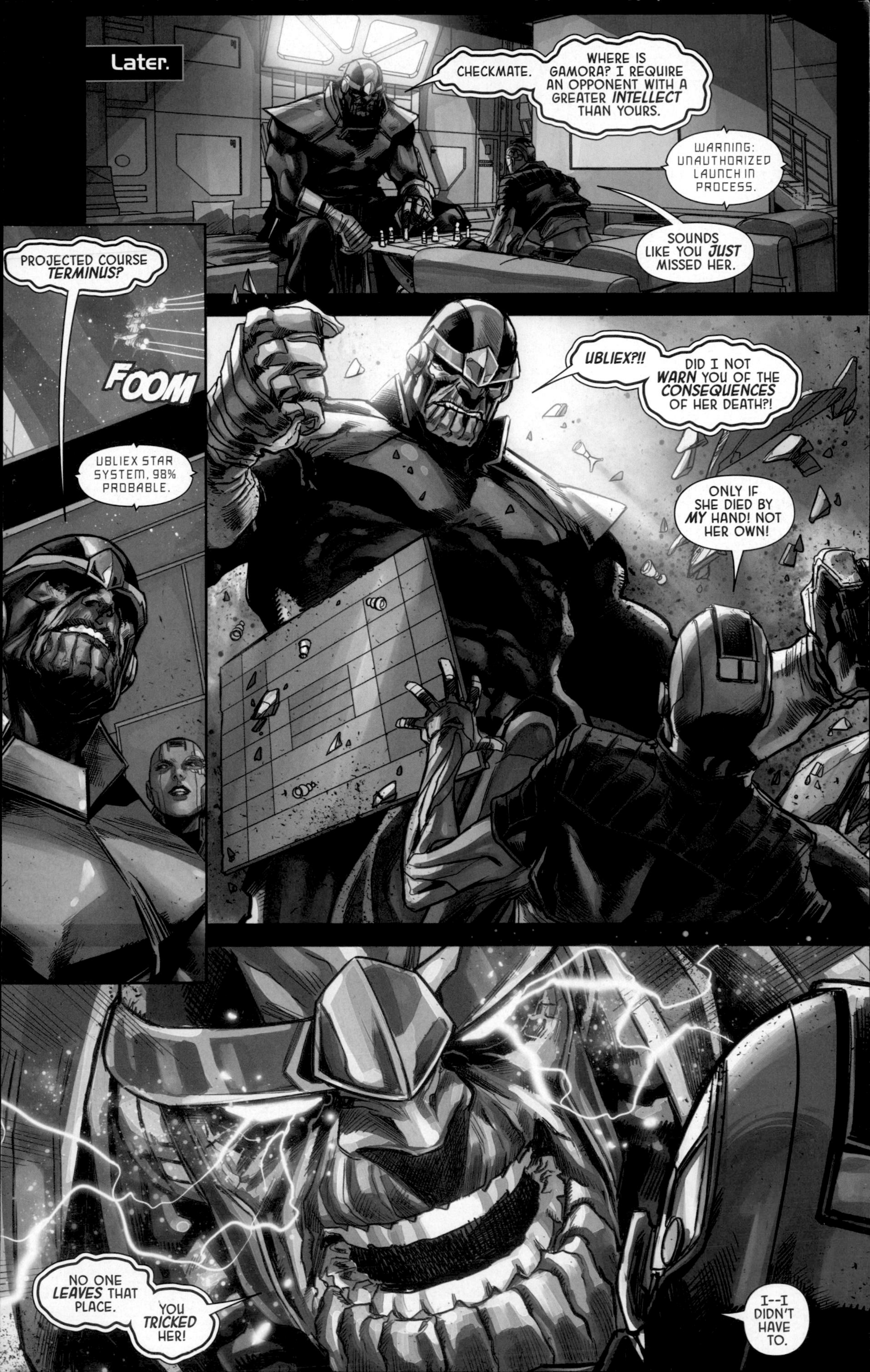
Later.
CHECKMATE.
WHERE IS GAMORA? I REQUIRE AN OPPONENT WITH A GREATER INTELLECT THAN YOURS.
WARNING: UNAUTHORIZED LAUNCH IN PROCESS.
SOUNDS LIKE YOU JUST MISSED HER.
PROJECTED COURSE TERMINUS?
FOOM
UBLIEX STAR SYSTEM, 98% PROBABLE.
UBLIEX?!!
DID I NOT WARN YOU OF THE CONSEQUENCES OF HER DEATH?!
ONLY IF SHE DIED BY MY HAND! NOT HER OWN!
NO ONE LEAVES THAT PLACE.
YOU TRICKED HER!
I--I DIDN'T HAVE TO.

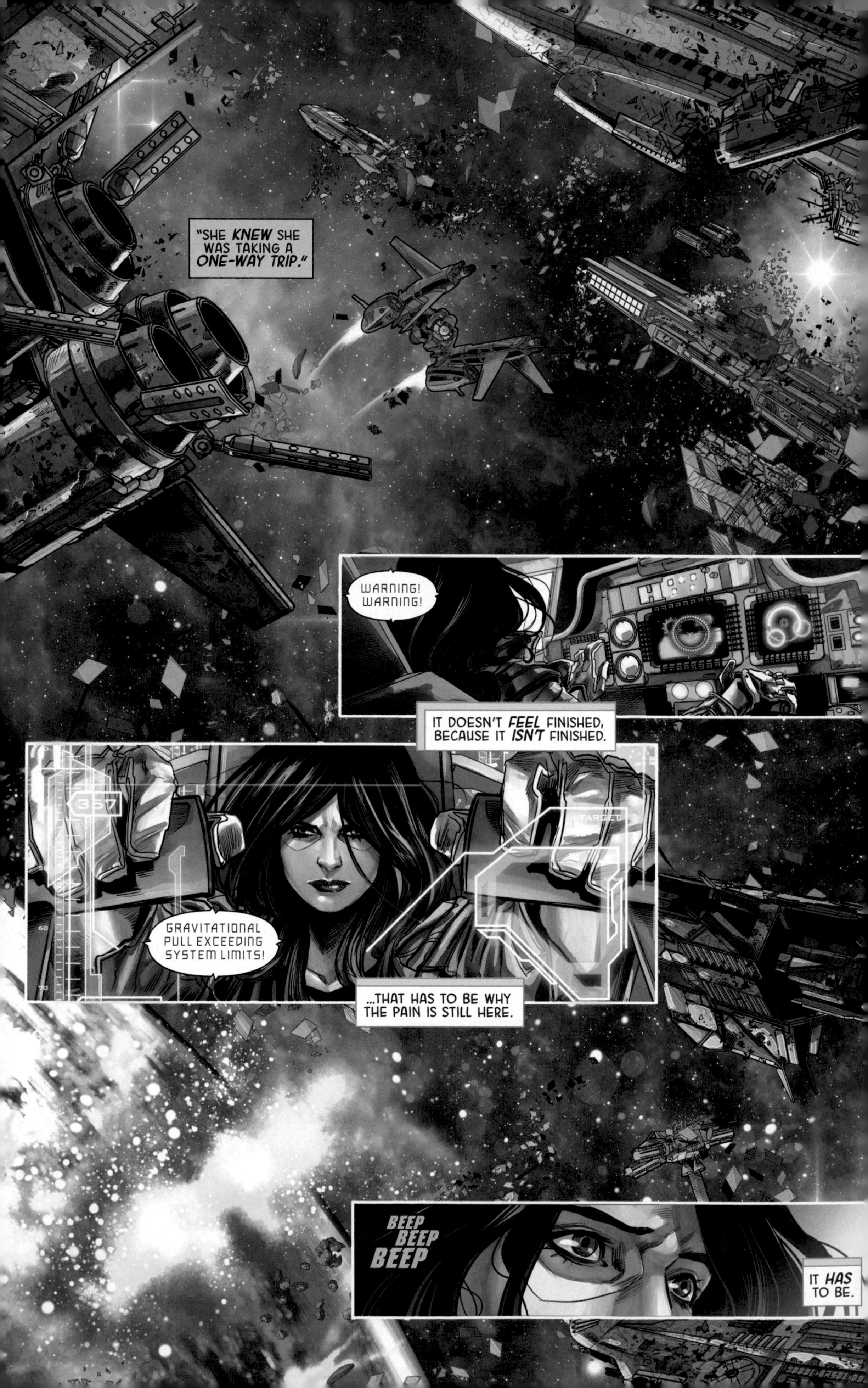
"SHE KNEW SHE WAS TAKING A ONE-WAY TRIP."
WARNING! WARNING!
IT DOESN'T FEEL FINISHED, BECAUSE IT ISN'T FINISHED.
357
TARGET
GRAVITATIONAL PULL EXCEEDING SYSTEM LIMITS!
...THAT HAS TO BE WHY THE PAIN IS STILL HERE.
BEEP BEEP BEEP
IT HAS TO BE.

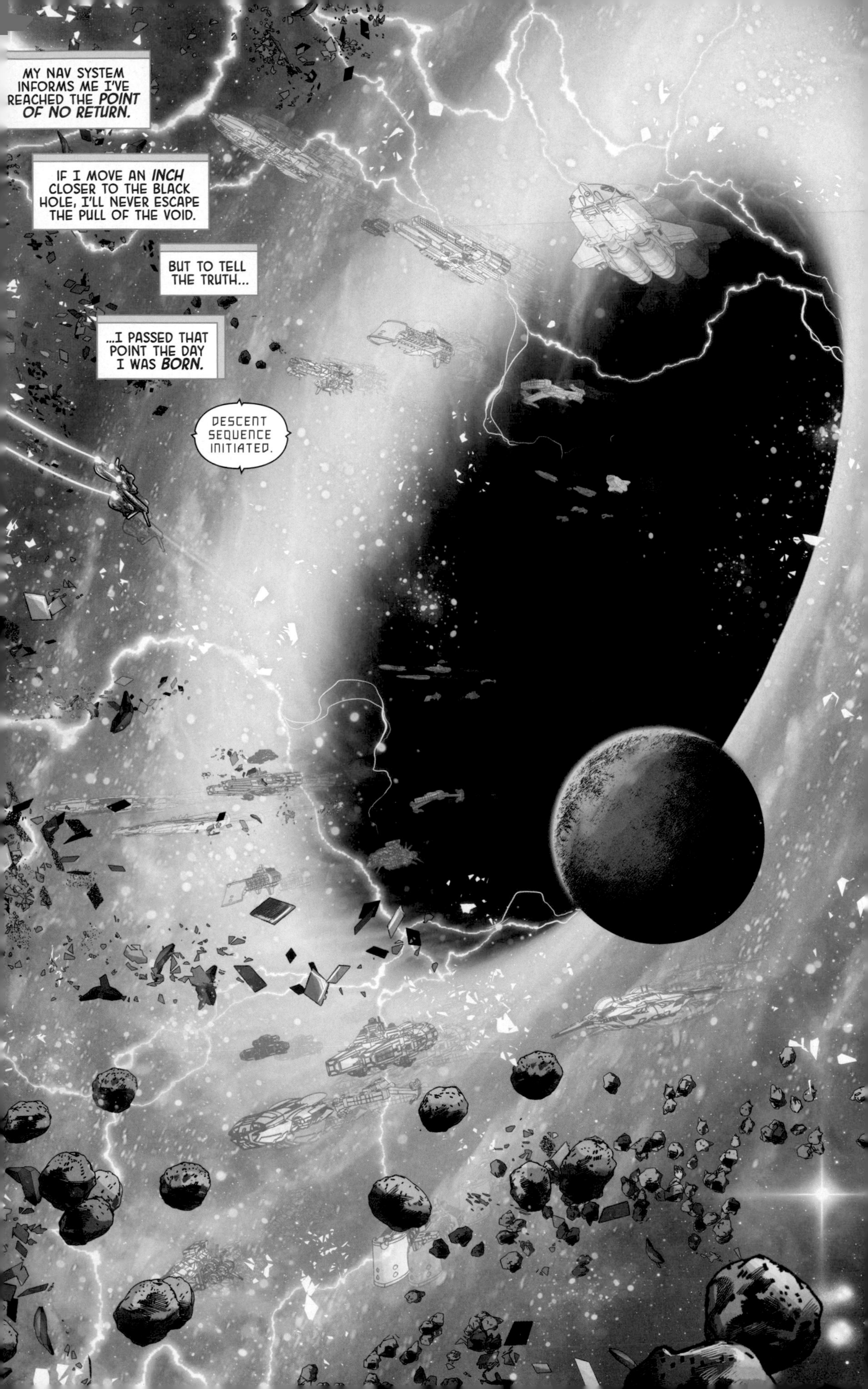
MY NAV SYSTEM INFORMS ME I'VE REACHED THE *POINT OF NO RETURN.*
IF I MOVE AN *INCH* CLOSER TO THE BLACK HOLE, I'LL NEVER ESCAPE THE PULL OF THE VOID.
BUT TO TELL THE TRUTH...
...I PASSED THAT POINT THE DAY I WAS *BORN.*
DESCENT SEQUENCE INITIATED.

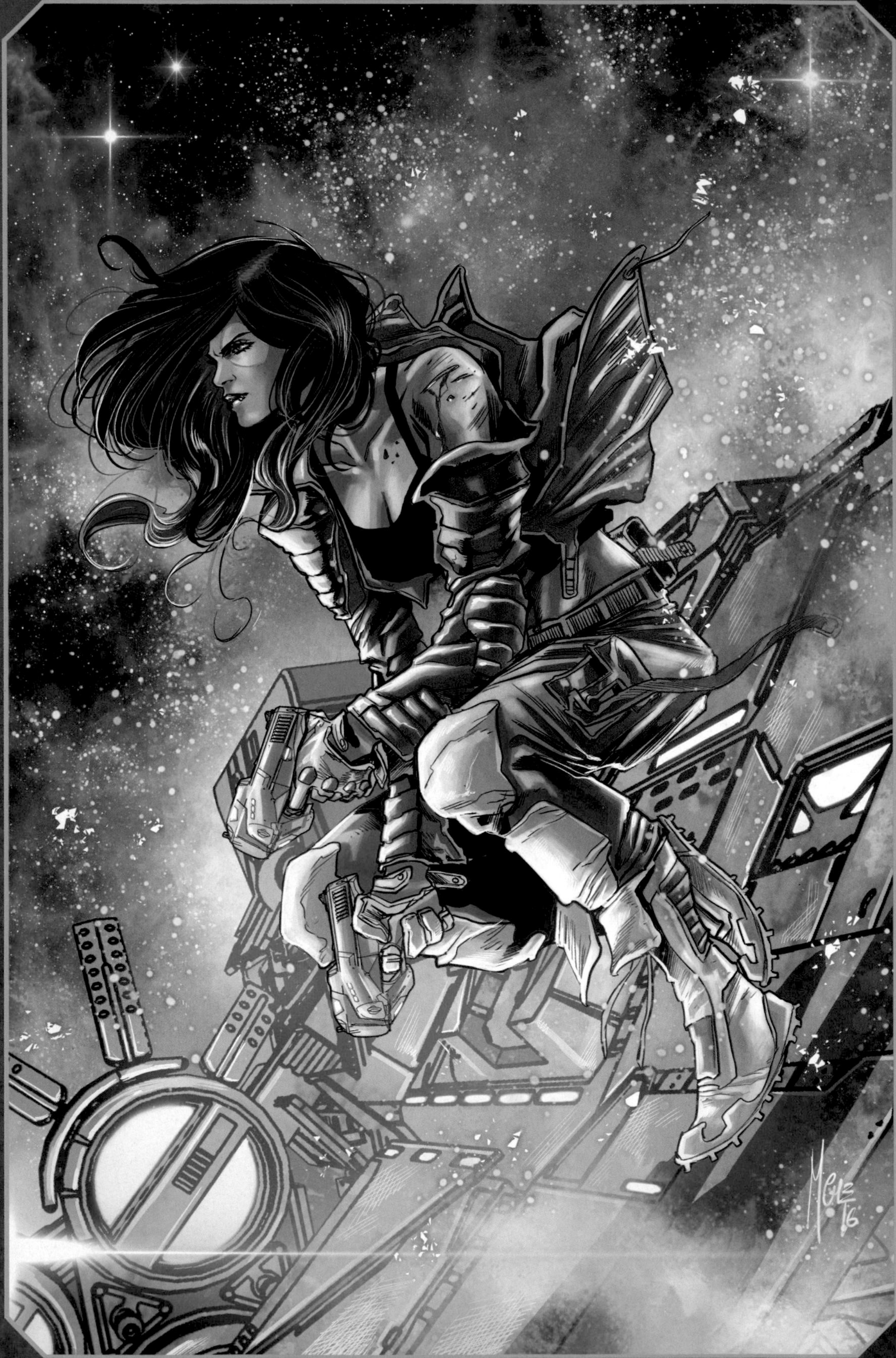
MCH2
'16

#1 VARIANT BY **MARCO CHECCHETTO**

2

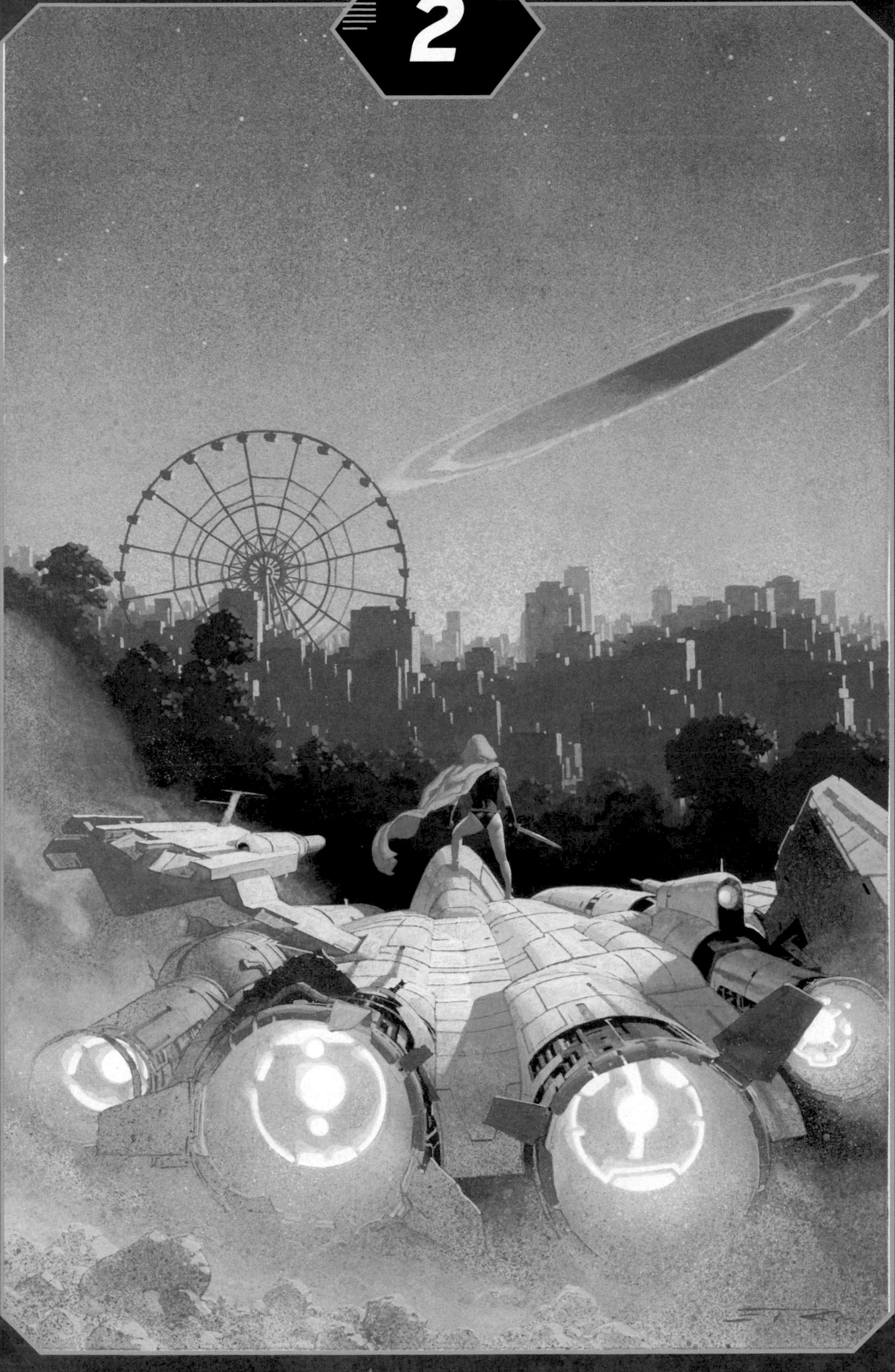

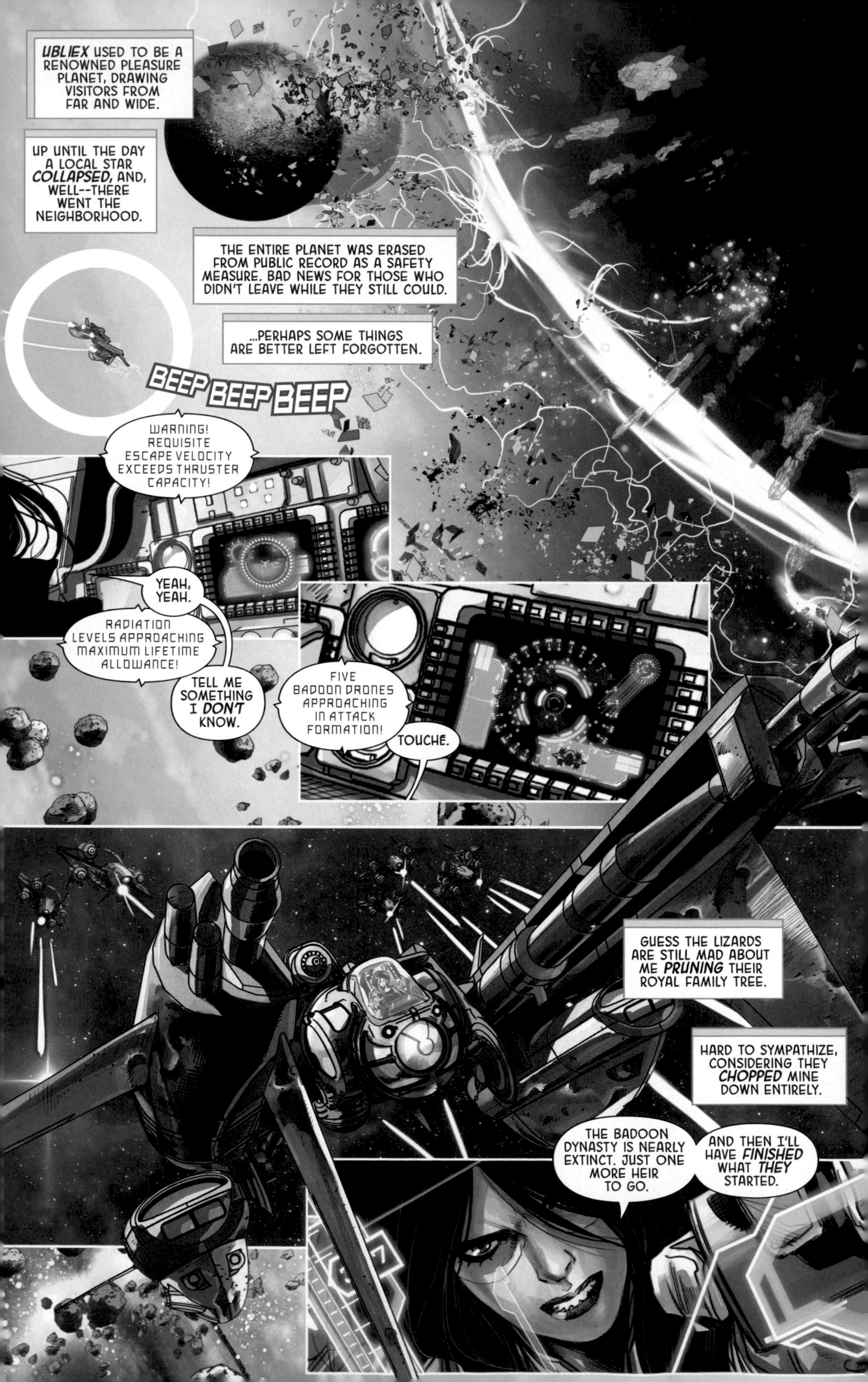
UBLIEX USED TO BE A RENOWNED PLEASURE PLANET, DRAWING VISITORS FROM FAR AND WIDE.
UP UNTIL THE DAY A LOCAL STAR COLLAPSED, AND, WELL--THERE WENT THE NEIGHBORHOOD.
THE ENTIRE PLANET WAS ERASED FROM PUBLIC RECORD AS A SAFETY MEASURE. BAD NEWS FOR THOSE WHO DIDN'T LEAVE WHILE THEY STILL COULD.
...PERHAPS SOME THINGS ARE BETTER LEFT FORGOTTEN.
BEEP BEEP BEEP
WARNING! REQUISITE ESCAPE VELOCITY EXCEEDS THRUSTER CAPACITY!
YEAH, YEAH.
RADIATION LEVELS APPROACHING MAXIMUM LIFETIME ALLOWANCE!
TELL ME SOMETHING I DON'T KNOW.
FIVE BADOON DRONES APPROACHING IN ATTACK FORMATION!
TOUCHÉ.
GUESS THE LIZARDS ARE STILL MAD ABOUT ME PRUNING THEIR ROYAL FAMILY TREE.
HARD TO SYMPATHIZE, CONSIDERING THEY CHOPPED MINE DOWN ENTIRELY.
THE BADOON DYNASTY IS NEARLY EXTINCT. JUST ONE MORE HEIR TO GO.
AND THEN I'LL HAVE FINISHED WHAT THEY STARTED.

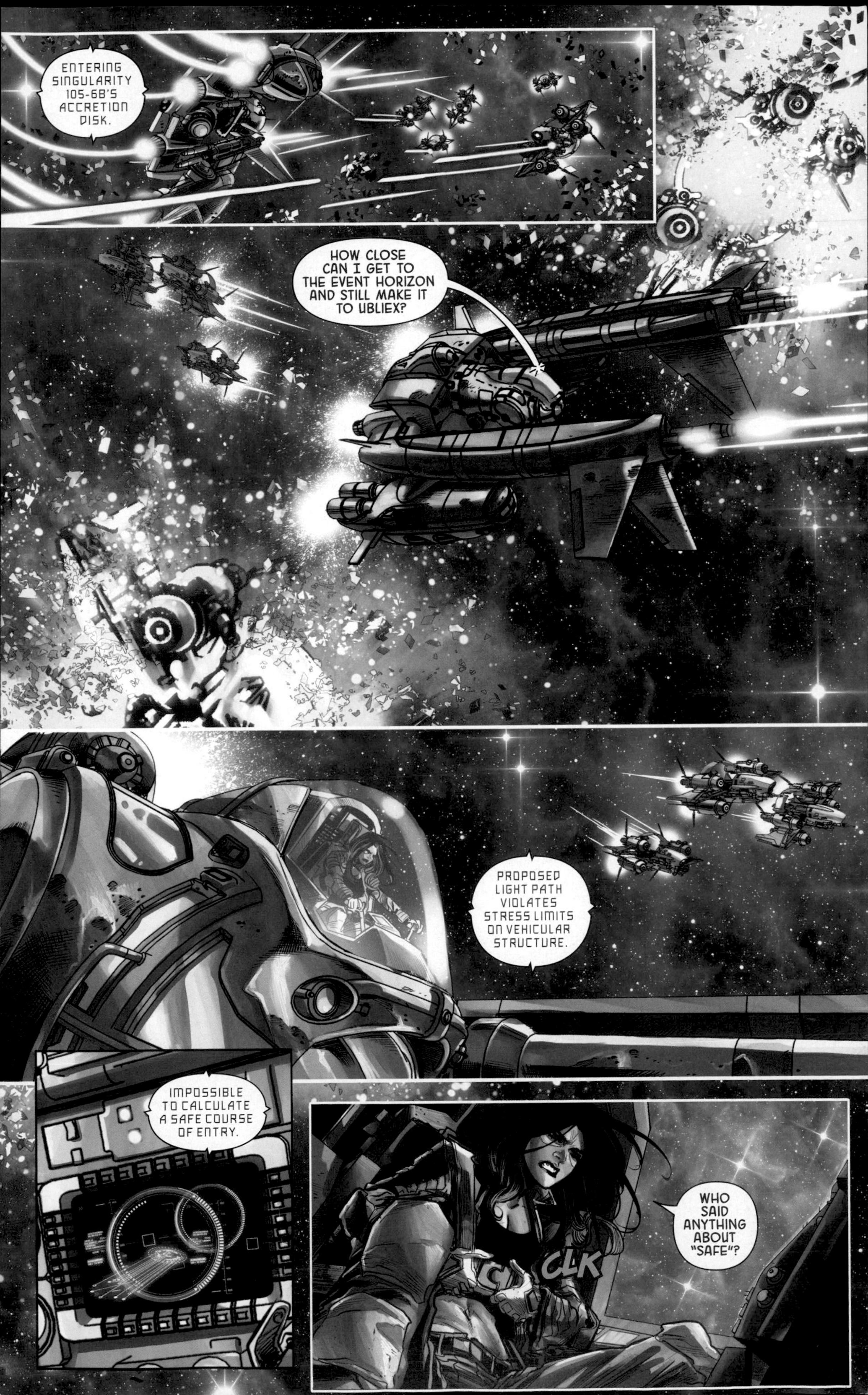
ENTERING SINGULARITY 105-6B'S ACCRETION DISK.
HOW CLOSE CAN I GET TO THE EVENT HORIZON AND STILL MAKE IT TO UBLIEX?
PROPOSED LIGHT PATH VIOLATES STRESS LIMITS ON VEHICULAR STRUCTURE.
IMPOSSIBLE TO CALCULATE A SAFE COURSE OF ENTRY.
CLK CLK
WHO SAID ANYTHING ABOUT "SAFE"?

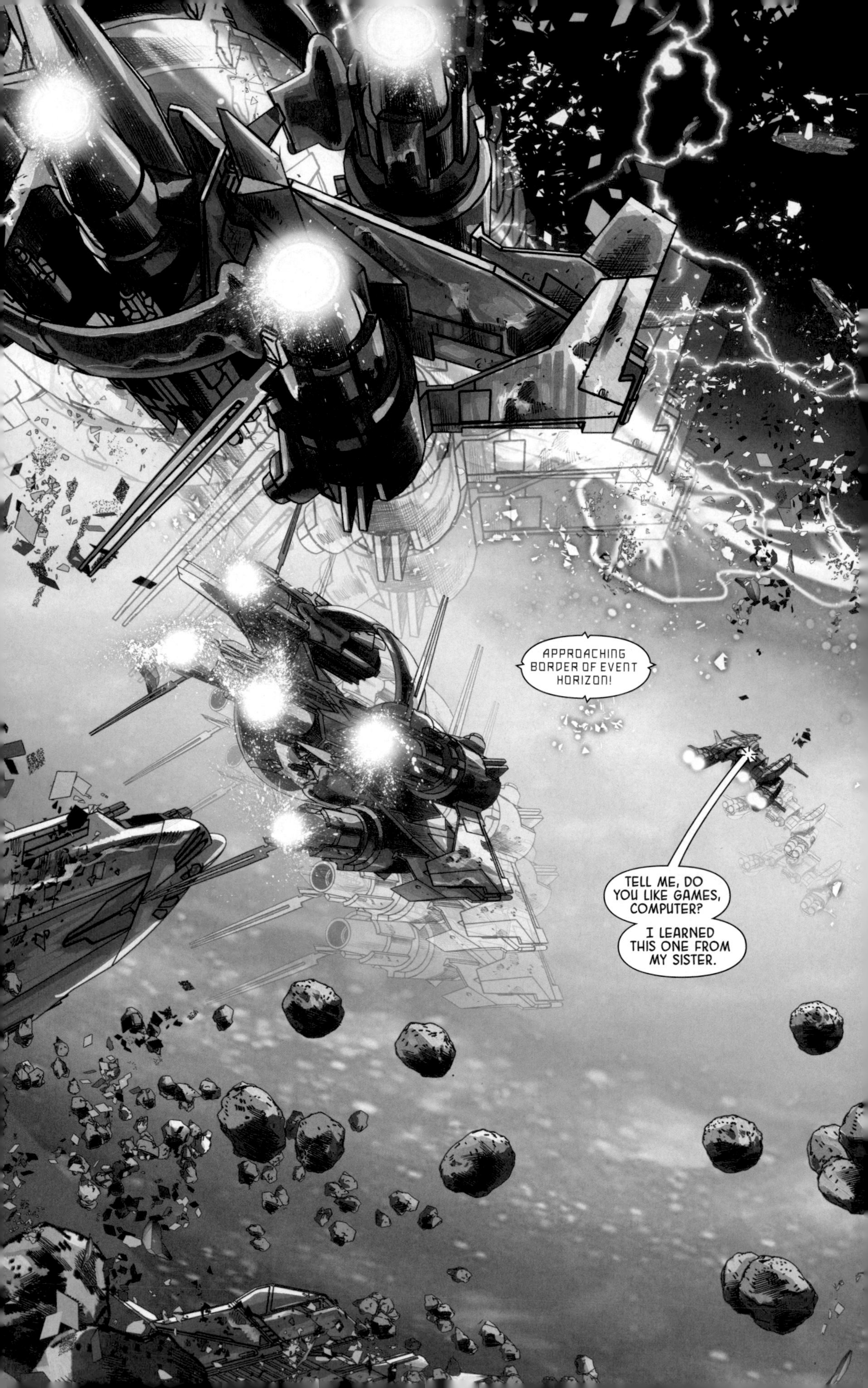
APPROACHING BORDER OF EVENT HORIZON!
TELL ME, DO YOU LIKE GAMES, COMPUTER?
I LEARNED THIS ONE FROM MY SISTER.

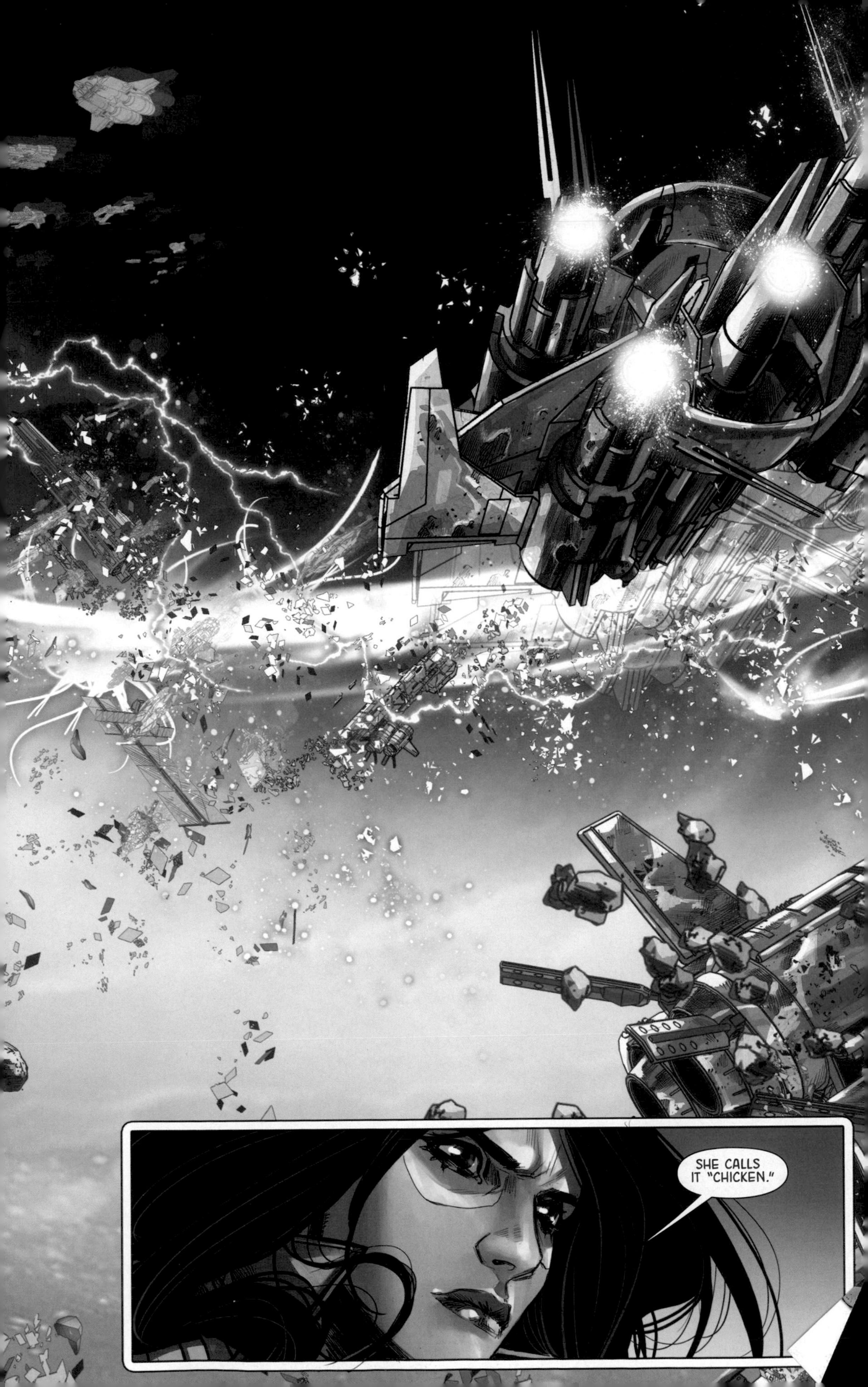
SHE CALLS IT "CHICKEN."

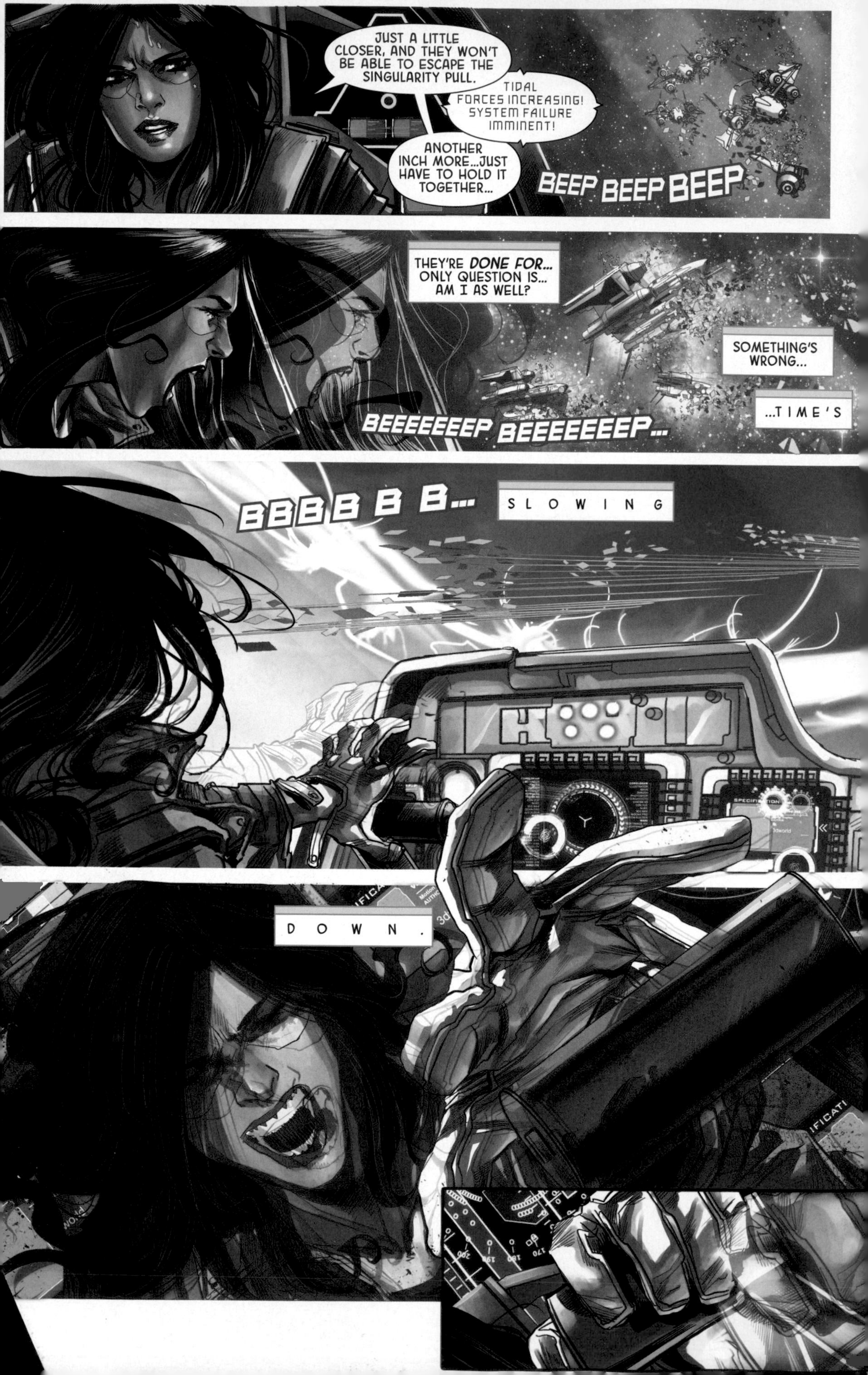

JUST A LITTLE CLOSER, AND THEY WON'T BE ABLE TO ESCAPE THE SINGULARITY PULL.
TIDAL FORCES INCREASING! SYSTEM FAILURE IMMINENT!
ANOTHER INCH MORE...JUST HAVE TO HOLD IT TOGETHER...
BEEP BEEP BEEP
THEY'RE DONE FOR... ONLY QUESTION IS... AM I AS WELL?
SOMETHING'S WRONG...
...TIME'S
BEEEEEEEP BEEEEEEEP...
BBBB B B...
S L O W I N G
D O W N .

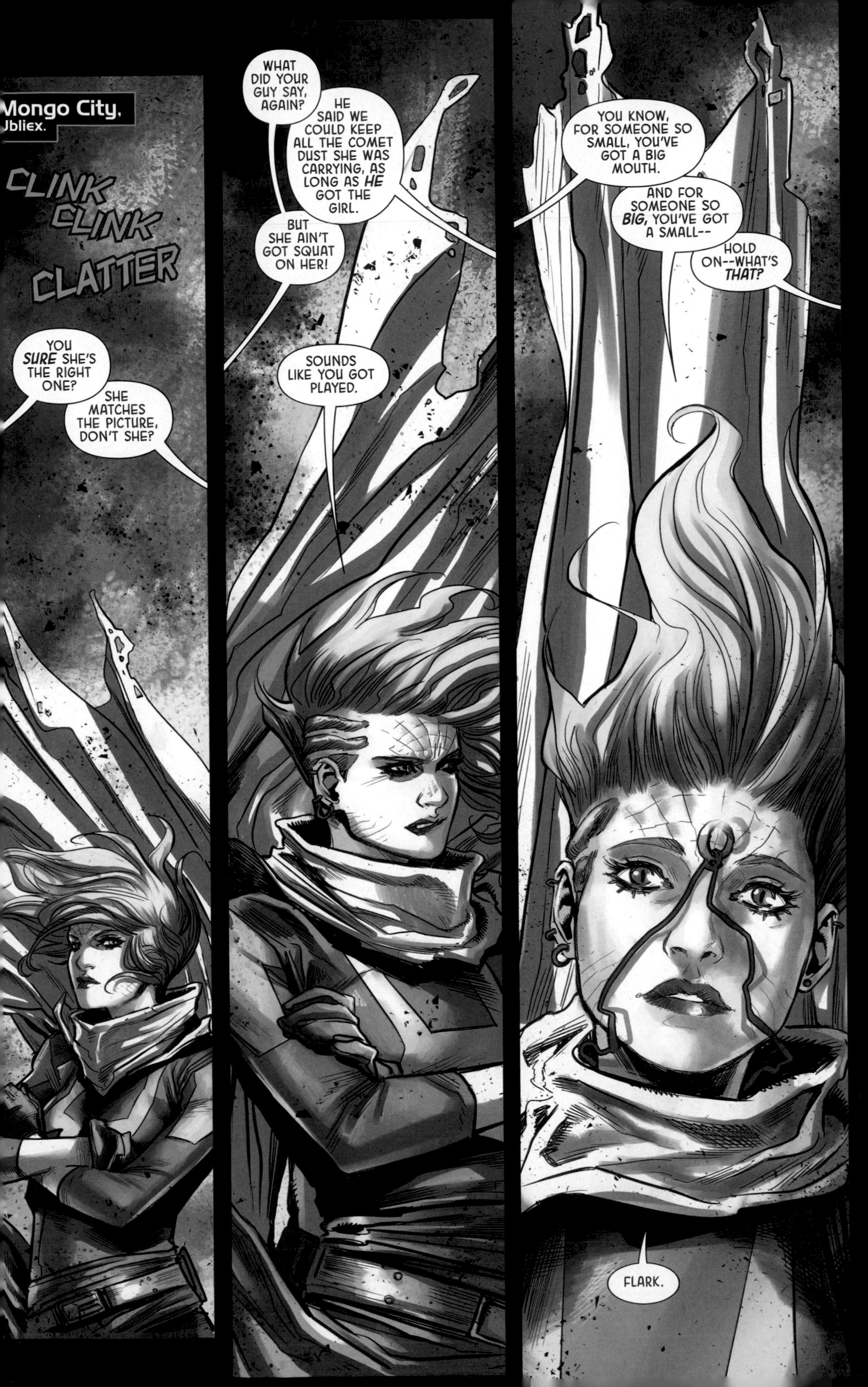
Mongo City,
Ubliex.
CLINK CLINK
CLATTER
YOU SURE SHE'S THE RIGHT ONE?
SHE MATCHES THE PICTURE, DON'T SHE?
WHAT DID YOUR GUY SAY, AGAIN?
HE SAID WE COULD KEEP ALL THE COMET DUST SHE WAS CARRYING, AS LONG AS HE GOT THE GIRL.
BUT SHE AIN'T GOT SQUAT ON HER!
SOUNDS LIKE YOU GOT PLAYED.
YOU KNOW, FOR SOMEONE SO SMALL, YOU'VE GOT A BIG MOUTH.
AND FOR SOMEONE SO BIG, YOU'VE GOT A SMALL--
HOLD ON--WHAT'S THAT?
FLARK.

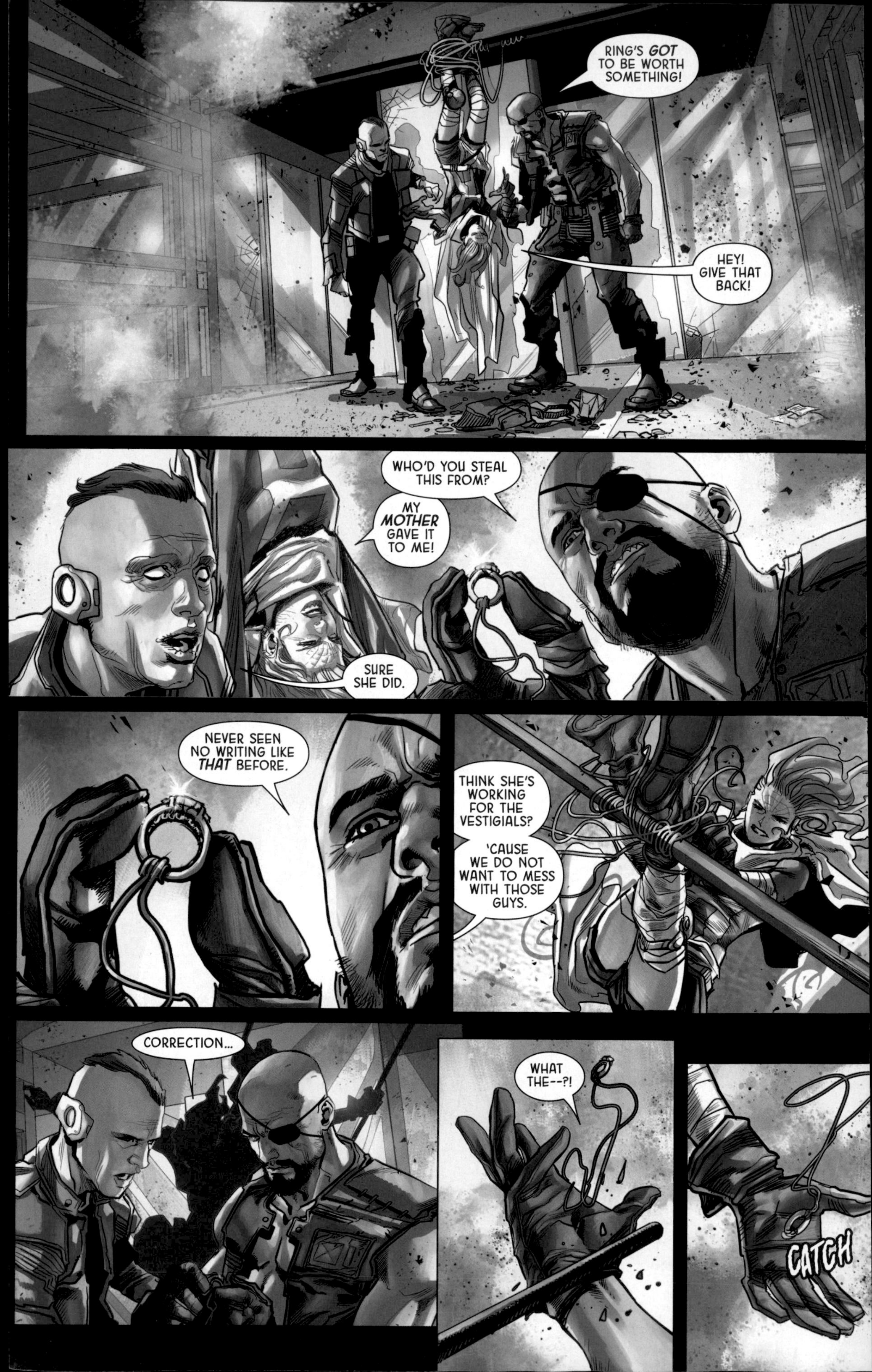
RING'S GOT TO BE WORTH SOMETHING!
HEY! GIVE THAT BACK!
WHO'D YOU STEAL THIS FROM?
MY MOTHER GAVE IT TO ME!
SURE SHE DID.
NEVER SEEN NO WRITING LIKE THAT BEFORE.
THINK SHE'S WORKING FOR THE VESTIGIALS?
'CAUSE WE DO NOT WANT TO MESS WITH THOSE GUYS.
CORRECTION...
WHAT THE--?!
CATCH

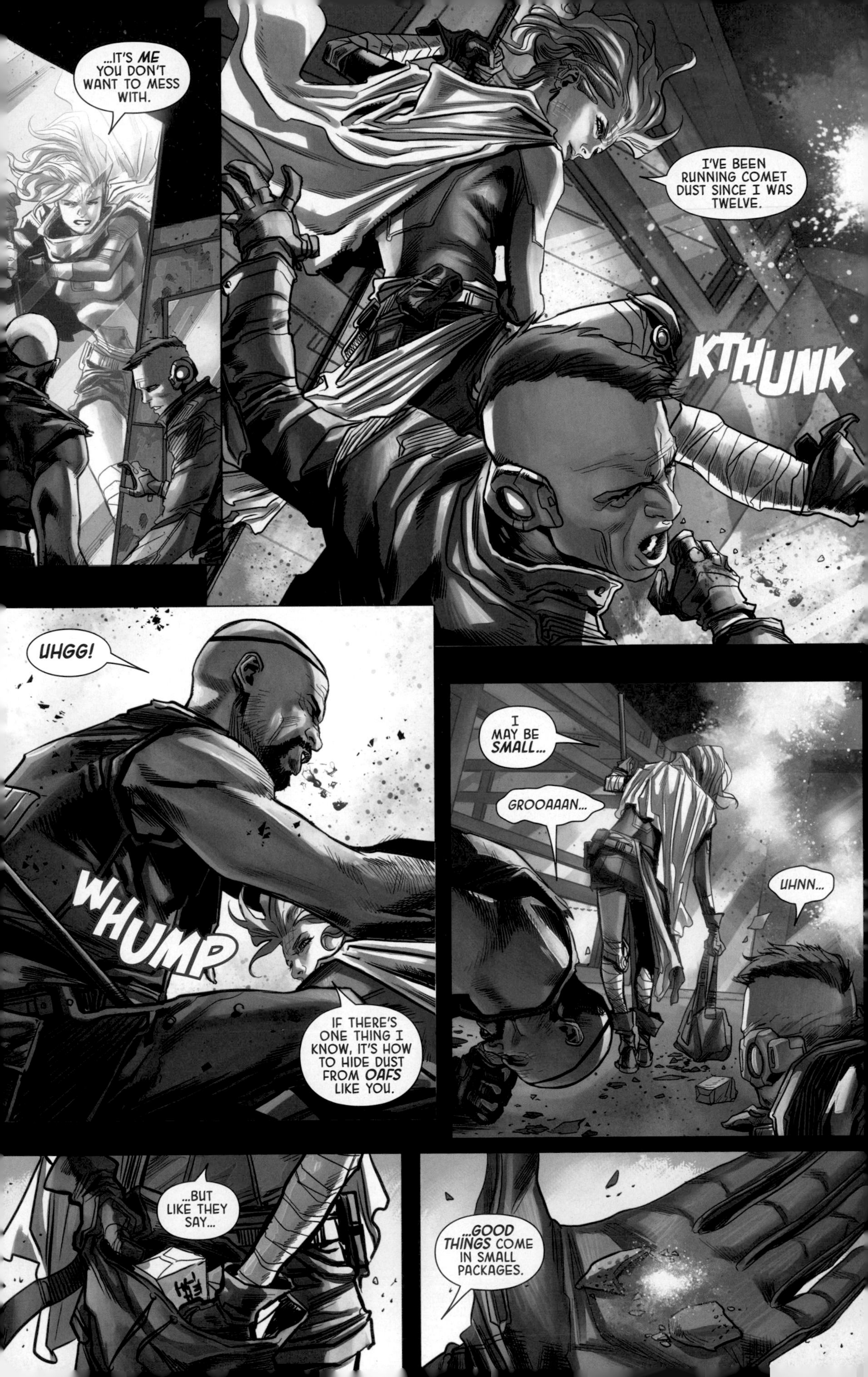
...IT'S ME YOU DON'T WANT TO MESS WITH.
I'VE BEEN RUNNING COMET DUST SINCE I WAS TWELVE.
KTHUNK
UHGG!
WHUMP
IF THERE'S ONE THING I KNOW, IT'S HOW TO HIDE DUST FROM OAFS LIKE YOU.
I MAY BE SMALL...
GROOAAAN...
UHNN...
...BUT LIKE THEY SAY...
...GOOD THINGS COME IN SMALL PACKAGES.

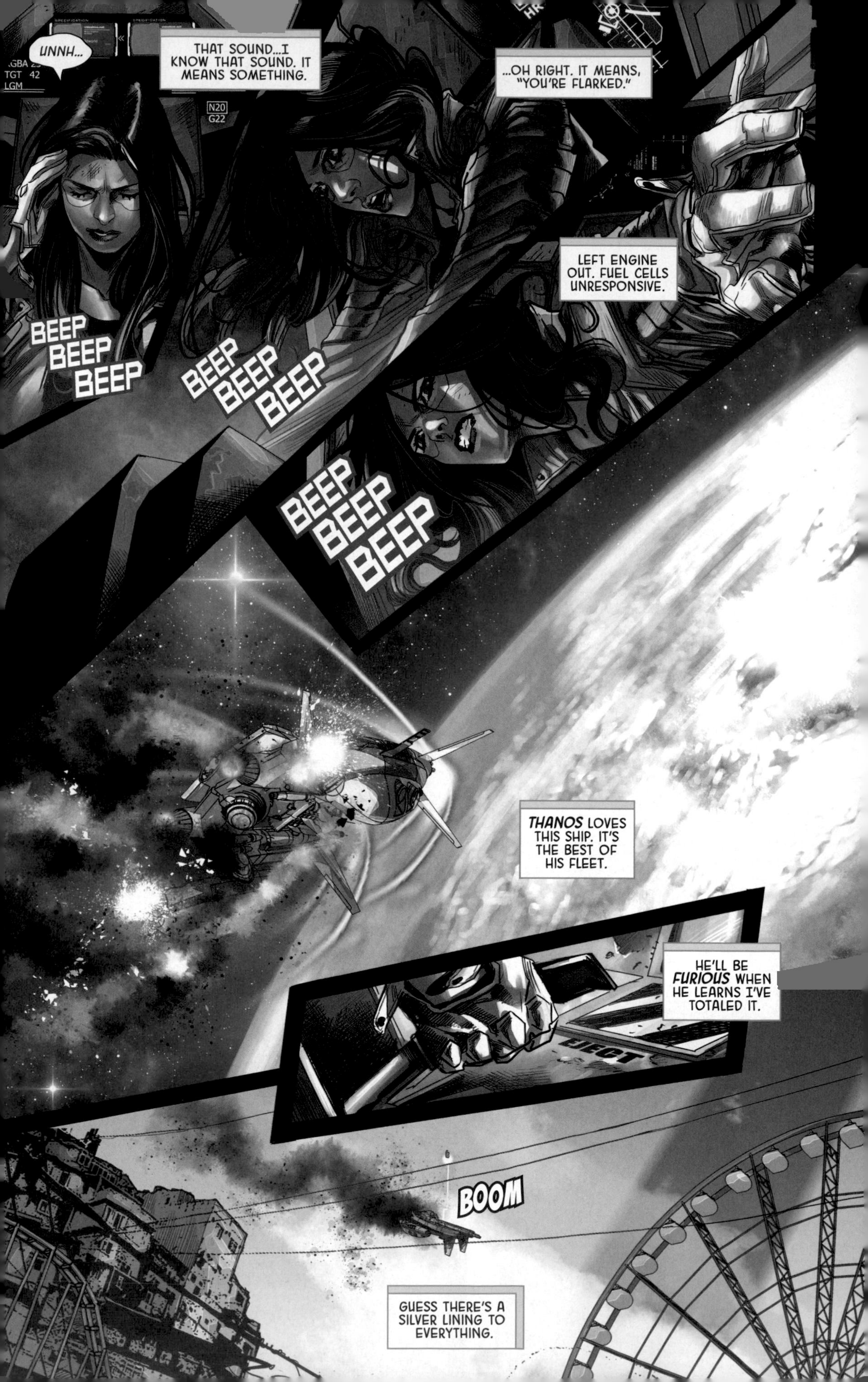

UNNH...
THAT SOUND...I KNOW THAT SOUND. IT MEANS SOMETHING.
...OH RIGHT. IT MEANS, "YOU'RE FLARKED."
LEFT ENGINE OUT. FUEL CELLS UNRESPONSIVE.
BEEP BEEP BEEP
BEEP BEEP BEEP
BEEP BEEP BEEP
THANOS LOVES THIS SHIP. IT'S THE BEST OF HIS FLEET.
HE'LL BE FURIOUS WHEN HE LEARNS I'VE TOTALED IT.
EJECT
BOOM
GUESS THERE'S A SILVER LINING TO EVERYTHING.

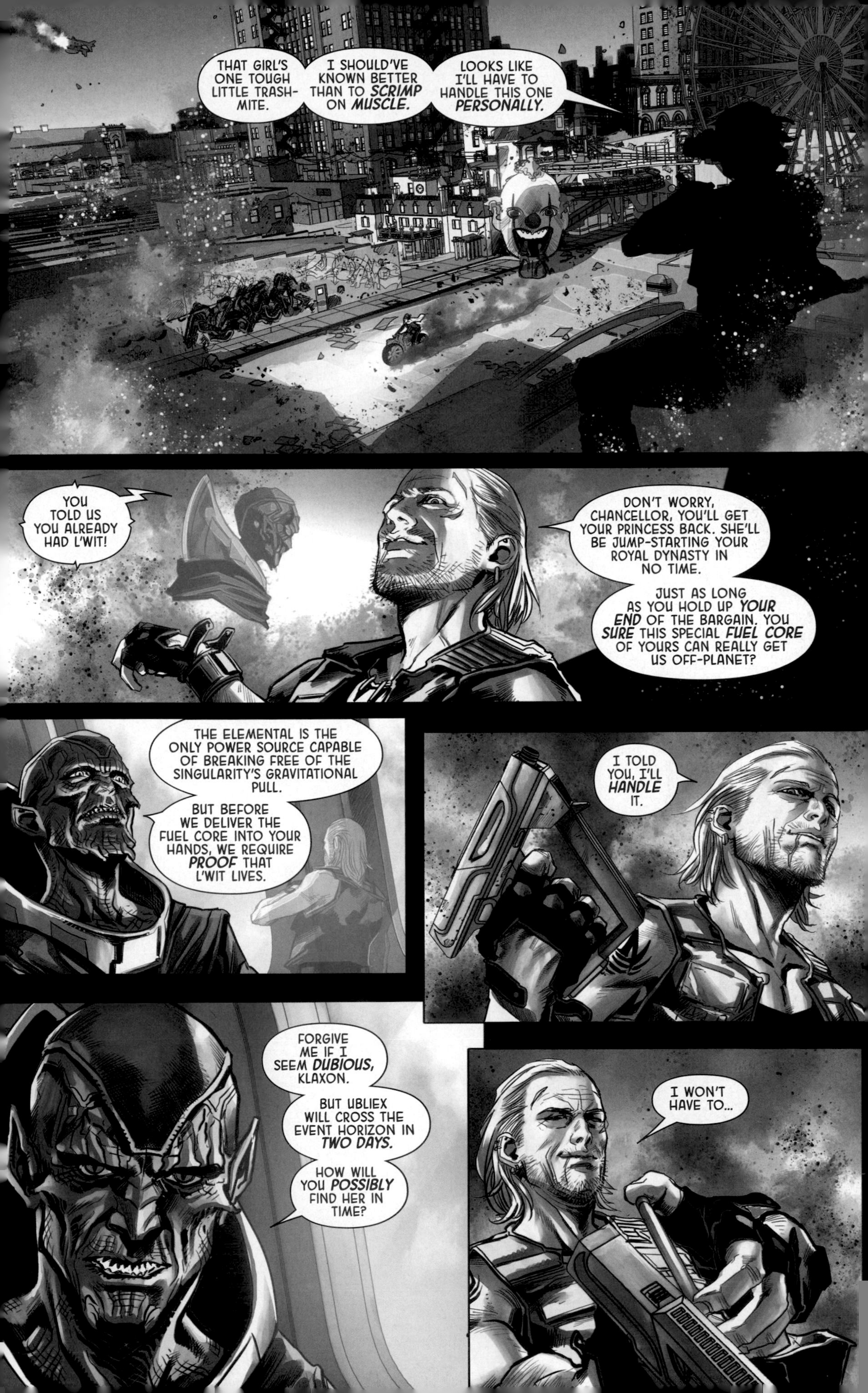
THAT GIRL'S ONE TOUGH LITTLE TRASH-MITE.
I SHOULD'VE KNOWN BETTER THAN TO SCRIMP ON MUSCLE.
LOOKS LIKE I'LL HAVE TO HANDLE THIS ONE PERSONALLY.
YOU TOLD US YOU ALREADY HAD L'WIT!
DON'T WORRY, CHANCELLOR, YOU'LL GET YOUR PRINCESS BACK. SHE'LL BE JUMP-STARTING YOUR ROYAL DYNASTY IN NO TIME.
JUST AS LONG AS YOU HOLD UP YOUR END OF THE BARGAIN. YOU SURE THIS SPECIAL FUEL CORE OF YOURS CAN REALLY GET US OFF-PLANET?
THE ELEMENTAL IS THE ONLY POWER SOURCE CAPABLE OF BREAKING FREE OF THE SINGULARITY'S GRAVITATIONAL PULL.
BUT BEFORE WE DELIVER THE FUEL CORE INTO YOUR HANDS, WE REQUIRE PROOF THAT L'WIT LIVES.
I TOLD YOU, I'LL HANDLE IT.
FORGIVE ME IF I SEEM DUBIOUS, KLAXON.
BUT UBLIEX WILL CROSS THE EVENT HORIZON IN TWO DAYS.
HOW WILL YOU POSSIBLY FIND HER IN TIME?
I WON'T HAVE TO...

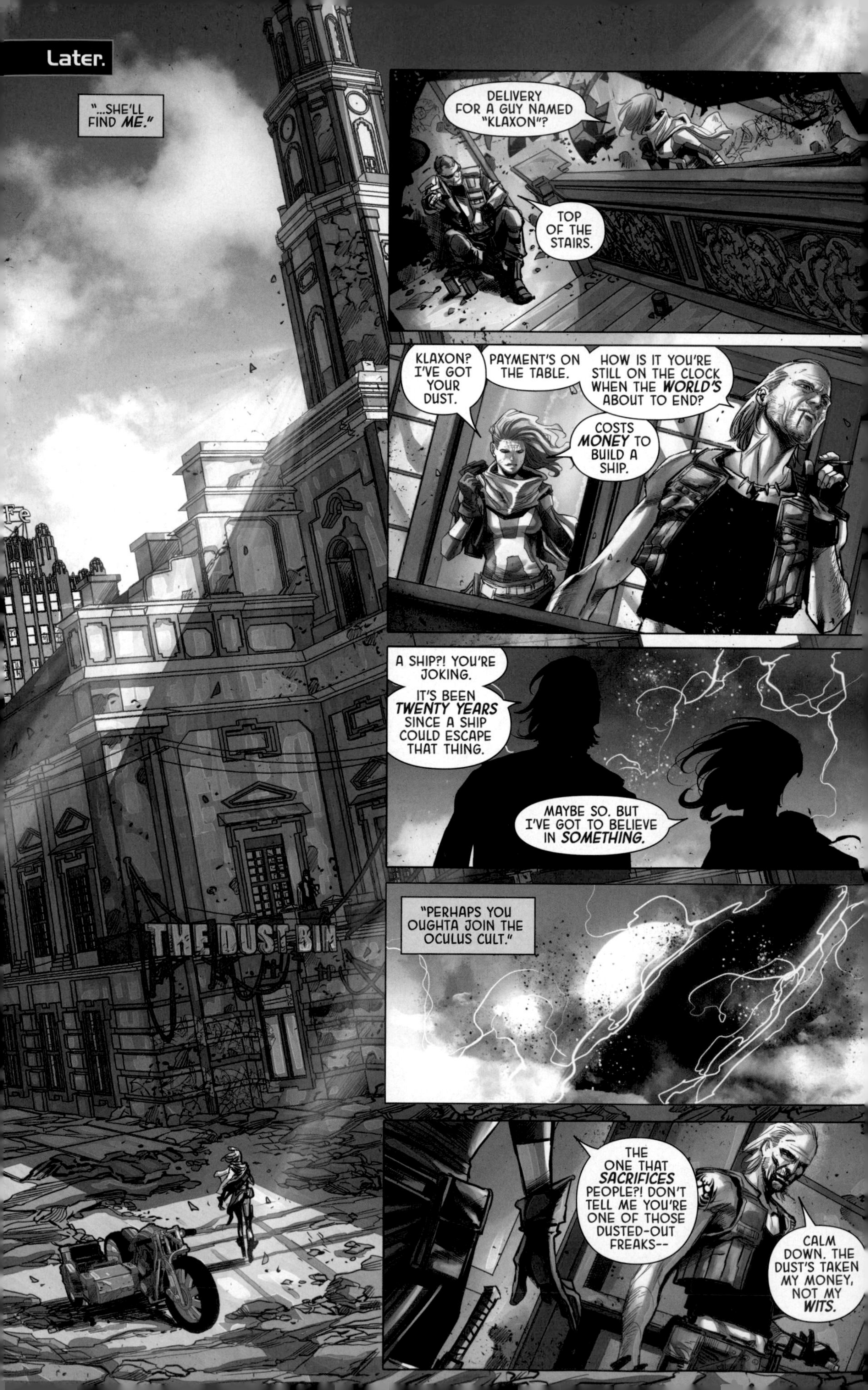
Later.
"...SHE'LL FIND ME."
THE DUST BIN
DELIVERY FOR A GUY NAMED "KLAXON"?
TOP OF THE STAIRS.
KLAXON? I'VE GOT YOUR DUST.
PAYMENT'S ON THE TABLE.
HOW IS IT YOU'RE STILL ON THE CLOCK WHEN THE WORLD'S ABOUT TO END?
COSTS MONEY TO BUILD A SHIP.
A SHIP?! YOU'RE JOKING.
IT'S BEEN TWENTY YEARS SINCE A SHIP COULD ESCAPE THAT THING.
MAYBE SO. BUT I'VE GOT TO BELIEVE IN SOMETHING.
"PERHAPS YOU OUGHTA JOIN THE OCULUS CULT."
THE ONE THAT SACRIFICES PEOPLE?! DON'T TELL ME YOU'RE ONE OF THOSE DUSTED-OUT FREAKS--
CALM DOWN. THE DUST'S TAKEN MY MONEY, NOT MY WITS.

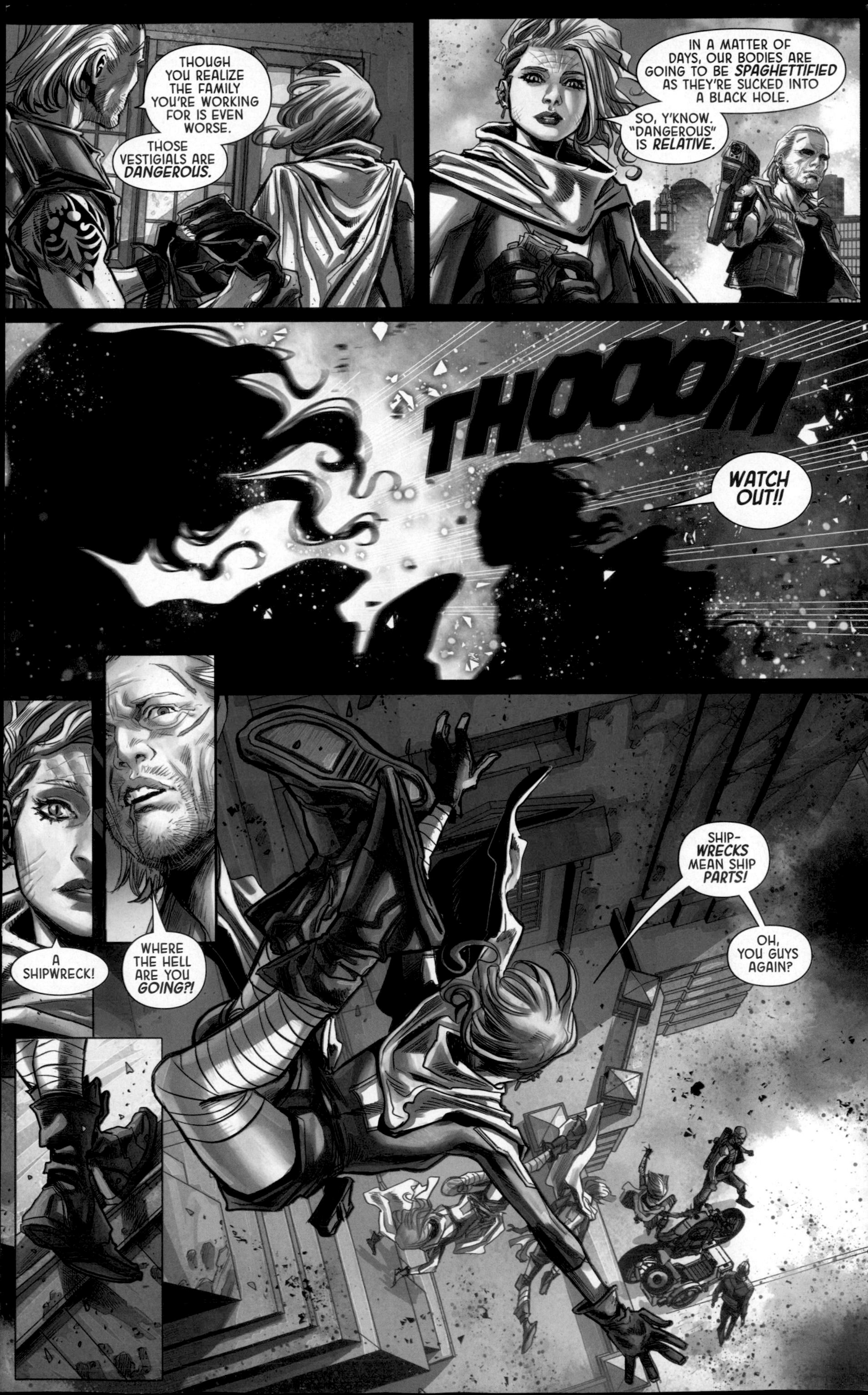
THOUGH YOU REALIZE THE FAMILY YOU'RE WORKING FOR IS EVEN WORSE.
THOSE VESTIGIALS ARE DANGEROUS.
IN A MATTER OF DAYS, OUR BODIES ARE GOING TO BE SPAGHETTIFIED AS THEY'RE SUCKED INTO A BLACK HOLE.
SO, Y'KNOW. "DANGEROUS" IS RELATIVE.
THOOOM
WATCH OUT!!
A SHIPWRECK!
WHERE THE HELL ARE YOU GOING?!
SHIP-WRECKS MEAN SHIP PARTS!
OH, YOU GUYS AGAIN?

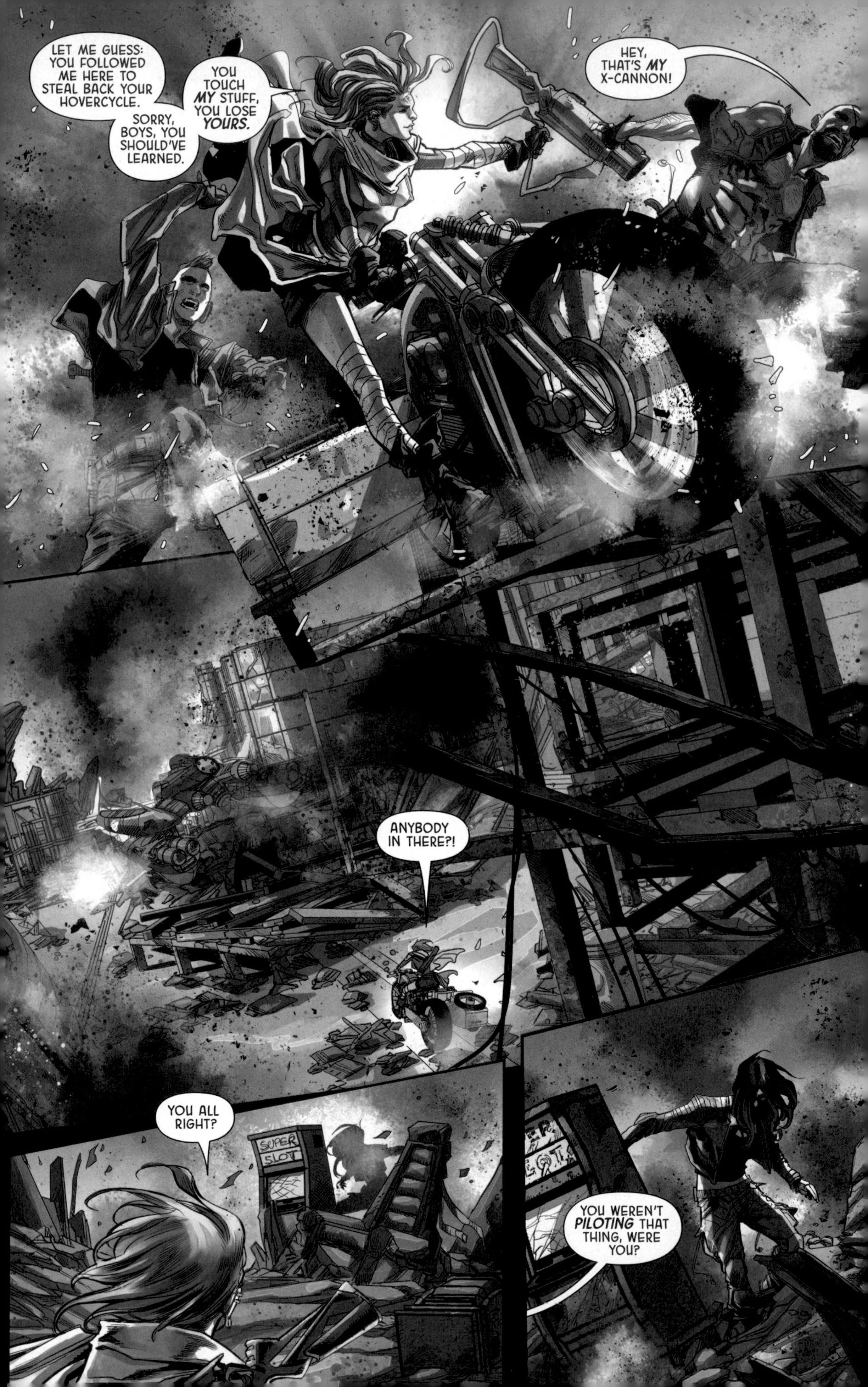
LET ME GUESS: YOU FOLLOWED ME HERE TO STEAL BACK YOUR HOVERCYCLE.
SORRY, BOYS, YOU SHOULD'VE LEARNED.
YOU TOUCH MY STUFF, YOU LOSE YOURS.
HEY, THAT'S MY X-CANNON!
ANYBODY IN THERE?!
YOU ALL RIGHT?
SUPER SLOT
YOU WEREN'T PILOTING THAT THING, WERE YOU?

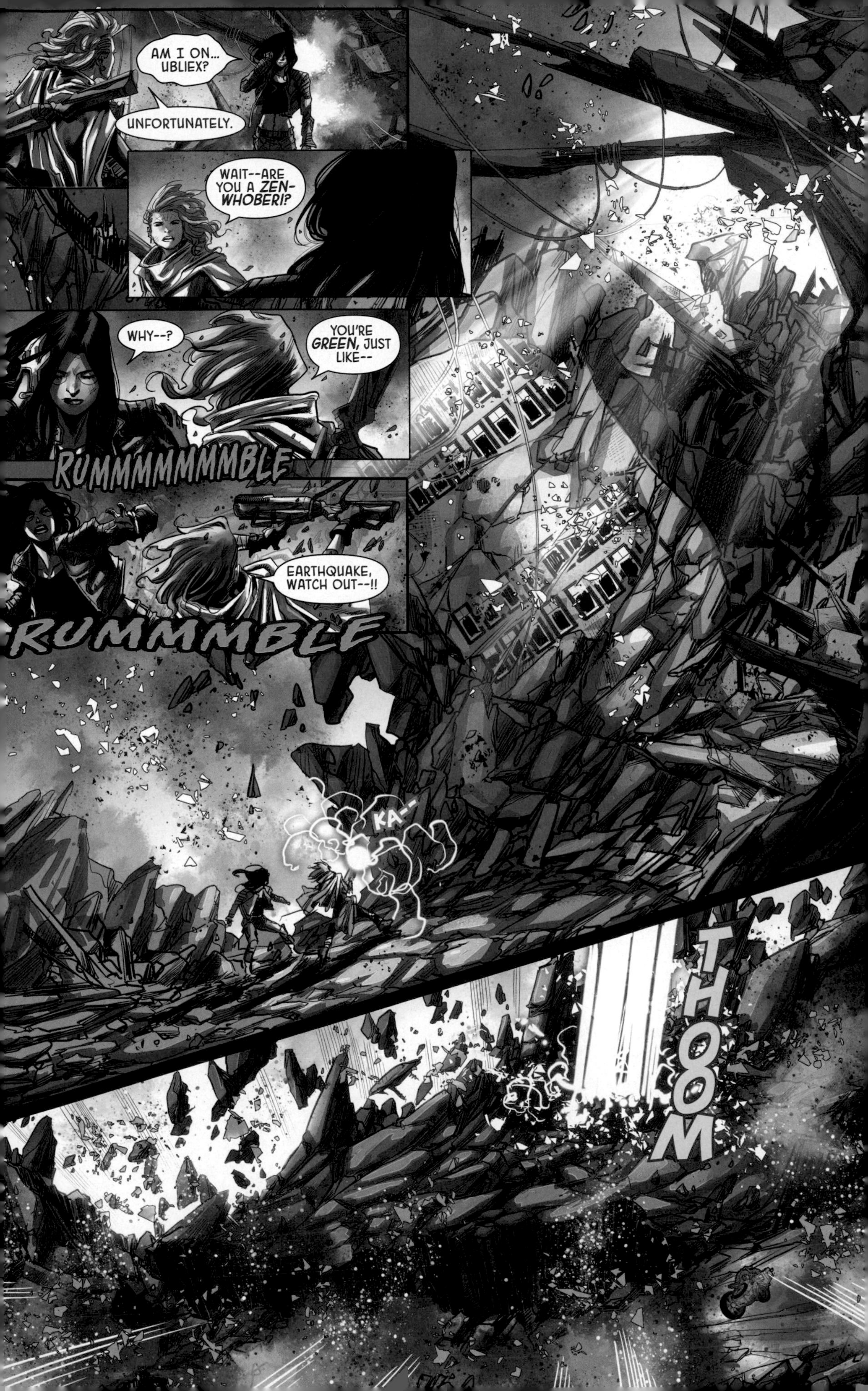

AM I ON... UBLIEX?
UNFORTUNATELY.
WAIT--ARE YOU A ZEN-WHOBERI?
WHY--?
YOU'RE GREEN, JUST LIKE--
RUMMMMMMMBLE
EARTHQUAKE, WATCH OUT--!!
RUMMMBLE
KA-
THOOM

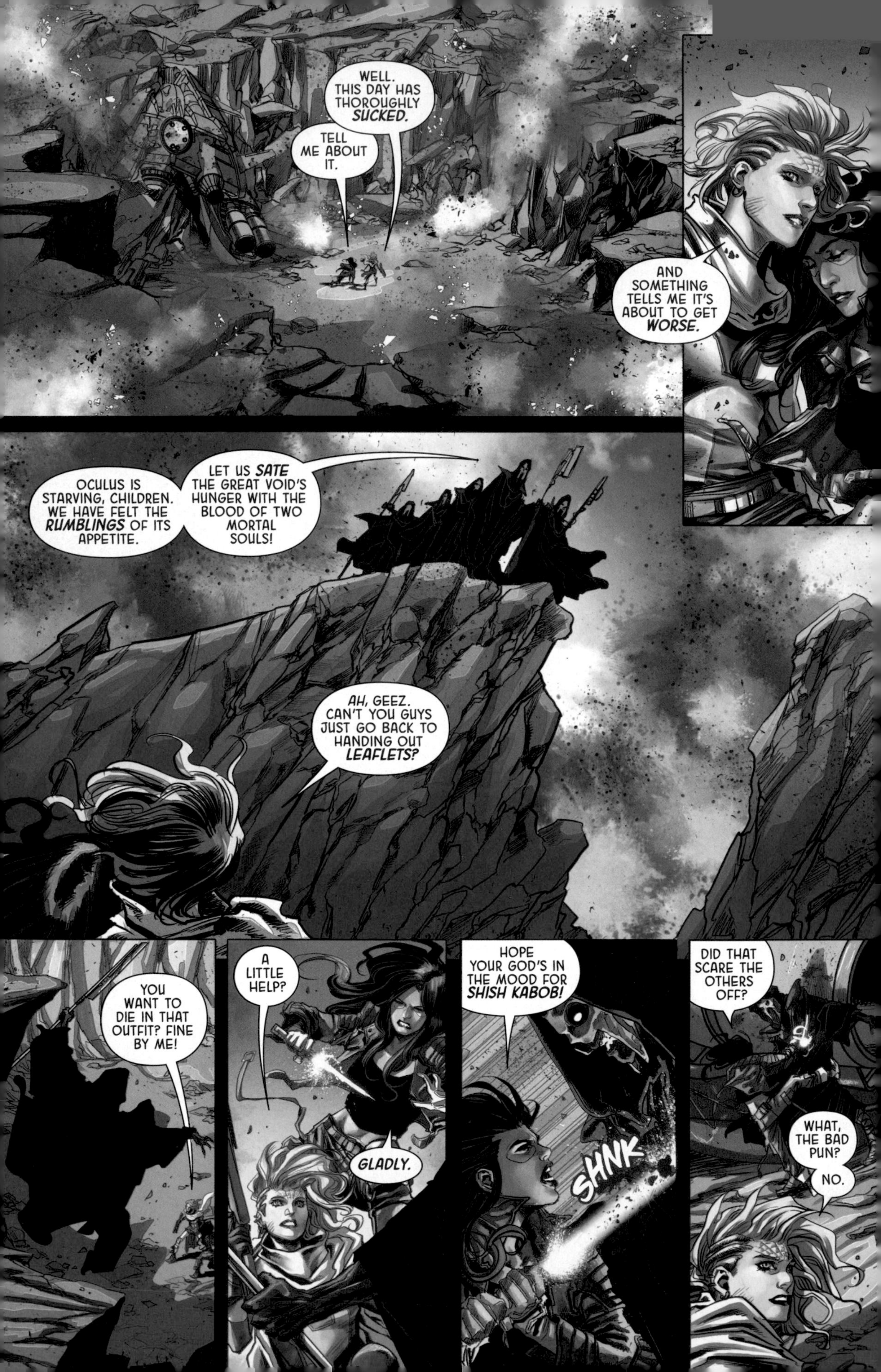
WELL. THIS DAY HAS THOROUGHLY SUCKED.
TELL ME ABOUT IT.
AND SOMETHING TELLS ME IT'S ABOUT TO GET WORSE.
OCULUS IS STARVING, CHILDREN. WE HAVE FELT THE RUMBLINGS OF ITS APPETITE.
LET US SATE THE GREAT VOID'S HUNGER WITH THE BLOOD OF TWO MORTAL SOULS!
AH, GEEZ. CAN'T YOU GUYS JUST GO BACK TO HANDING OUT LEAFLETS?
YOU WANT TO DIE IN THAT OUTFIT? FINE BY ME!
A LITTLE HELP?
GLADLY.
HOPE YOUR GOD'S IN THE MOOD FOR SHISH KABOB!
SHNK
DID THAT SCARE THE OTHERS OFF?
WHAT, THE BAD PUN?
NO.

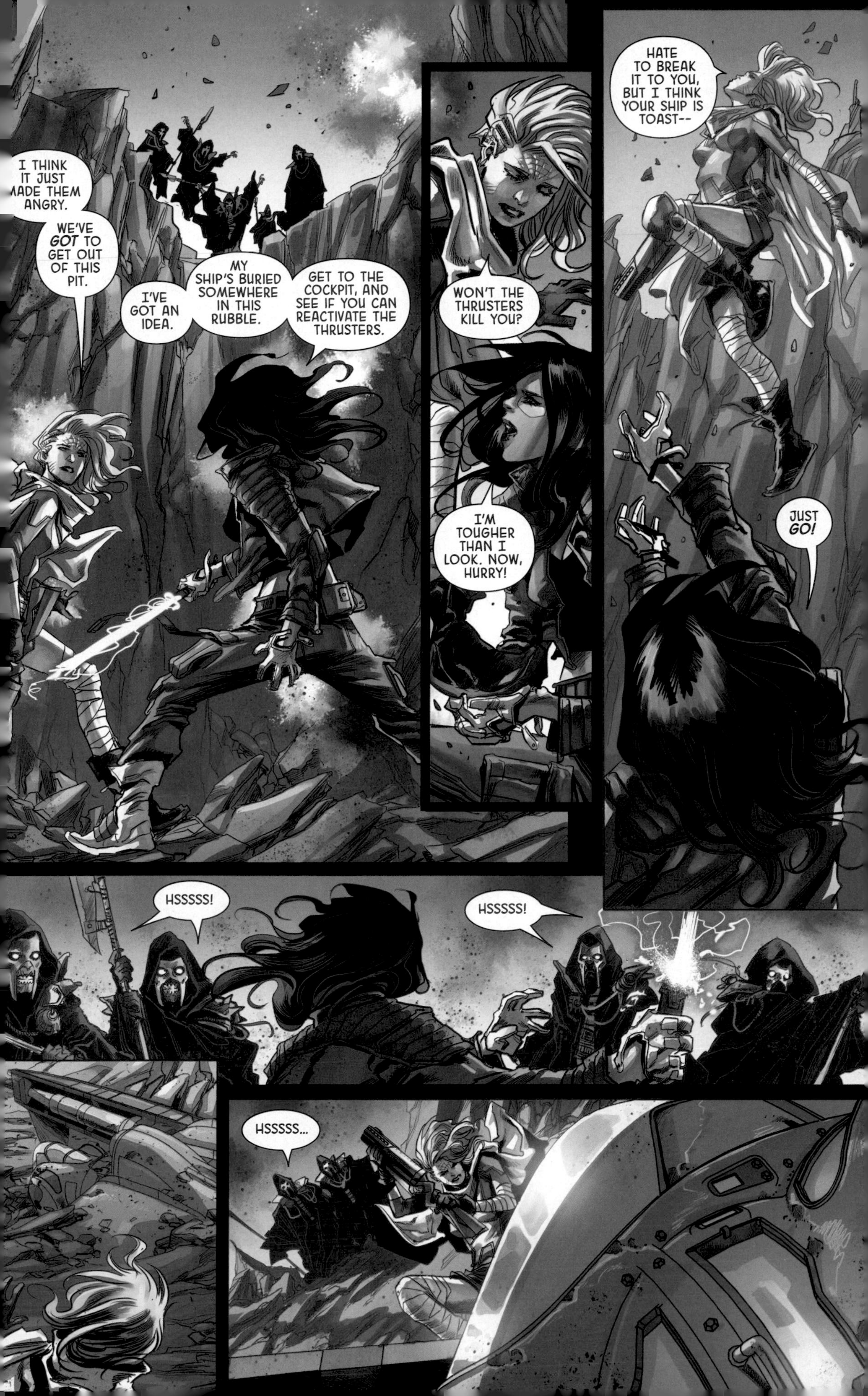
I THINK IT JUST MADE THEM ANGRY.
WE'VE *GOT* TO GET OUT OF THIS PIT.
I'VE GOT AN IDEA.
MY SHIP'S BURIED SOMEWHERE IN THIS RUBBLE.
GET TO THE COCKPIT, AND SEE IF YOU CAN REACTIVATE THE THRUSTERS.
WON'T THE THRUSTERS KILL YOU?
I'M TOUGHER THAN I LOOK. NOW, HURRY!
HATE TO BREAK IT TO YOU, BUT I THINK YOUR SHIP IS TOAST--
JUST *GO!*
HSSSSS!
HSSSSS!
HSSSSS...

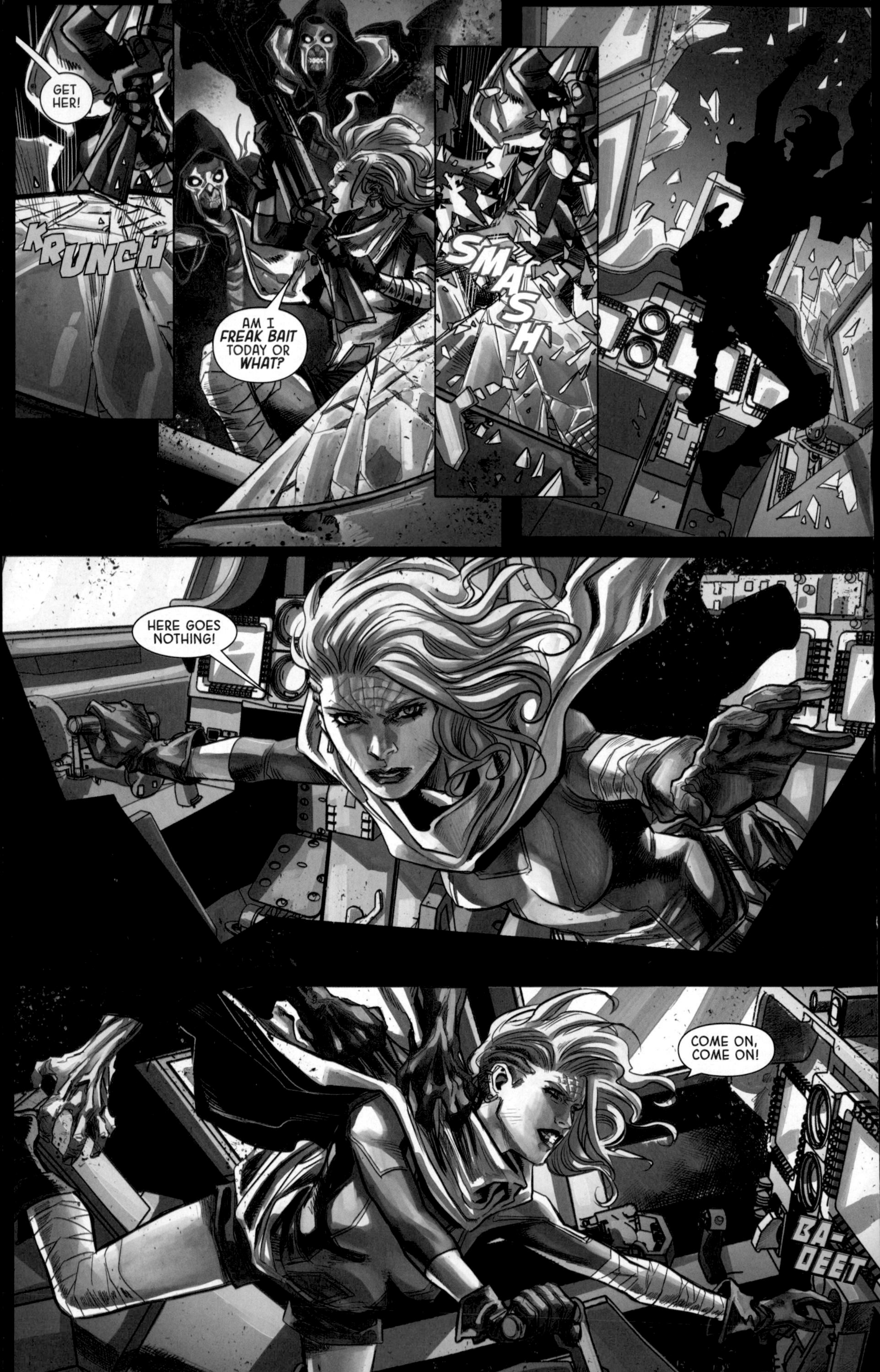
GET HER!
KRUNCH
AM I FREAK BAIT TODAY OR WHAT?
SMASH
HERE GOES NOTHING!
COME ON, COME ON!
BA-DEET

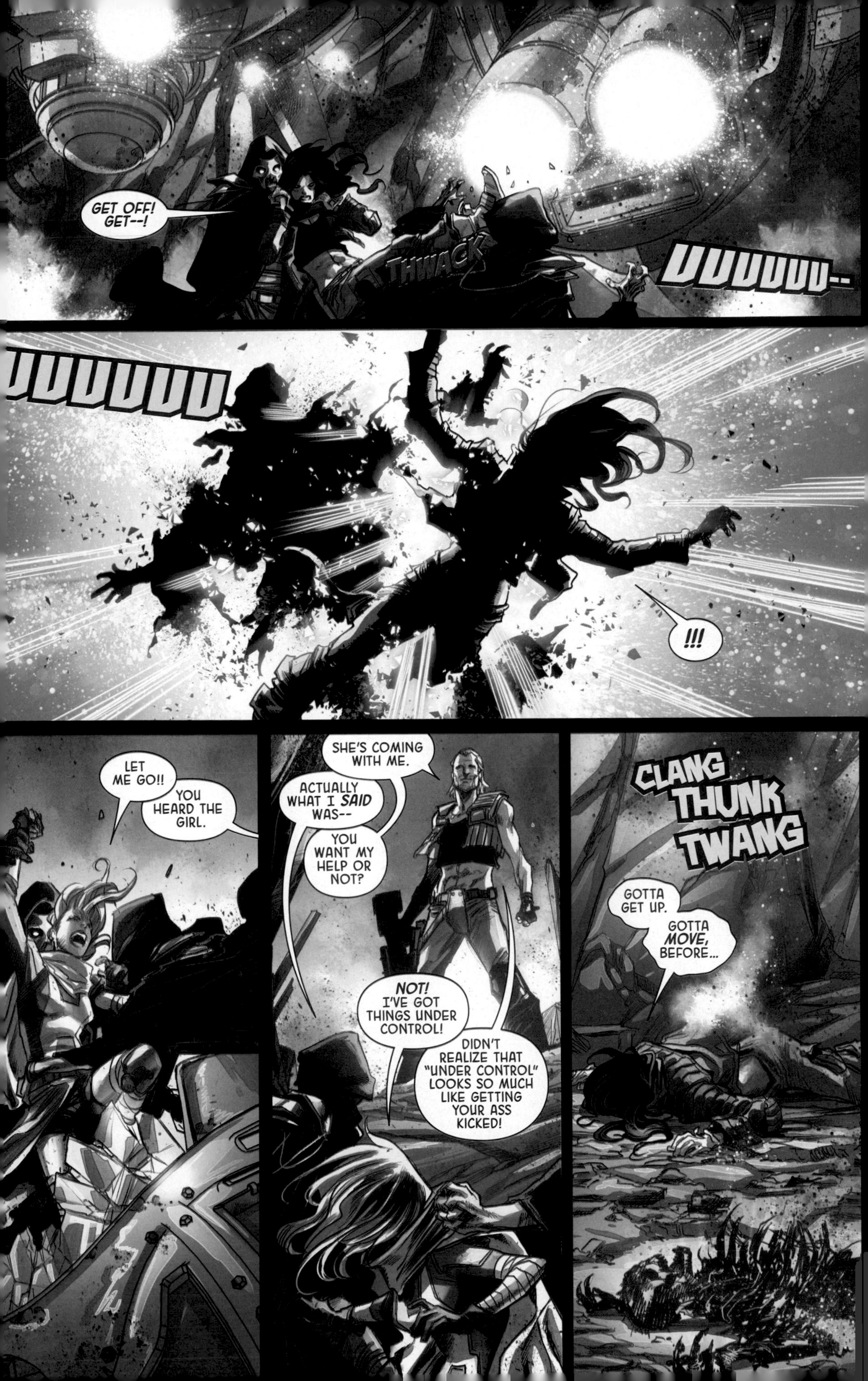
GET OFF! GET--!
THWACK
UUUUUU--
UUUUUUU
!!!
LET ME GO!!
YOU HEARD THE GIRL.
SHE'S COMING WITH ME.
ACTUALLY WHAT I *SAID* WAS--
YOU WANT MY HELP OR NOT?
NOT! I'VE GOT THINGS UNDER CONTROL!
DIDN'T REALIZE THAT "UNDER CONTROL" LOOKS SO MUCH LIKE GETTING YOUR ASS KICKED!
CLANG THUNK TWANG
GOTTA GET UP.
GOTTA *MOVE,* BEFORE...

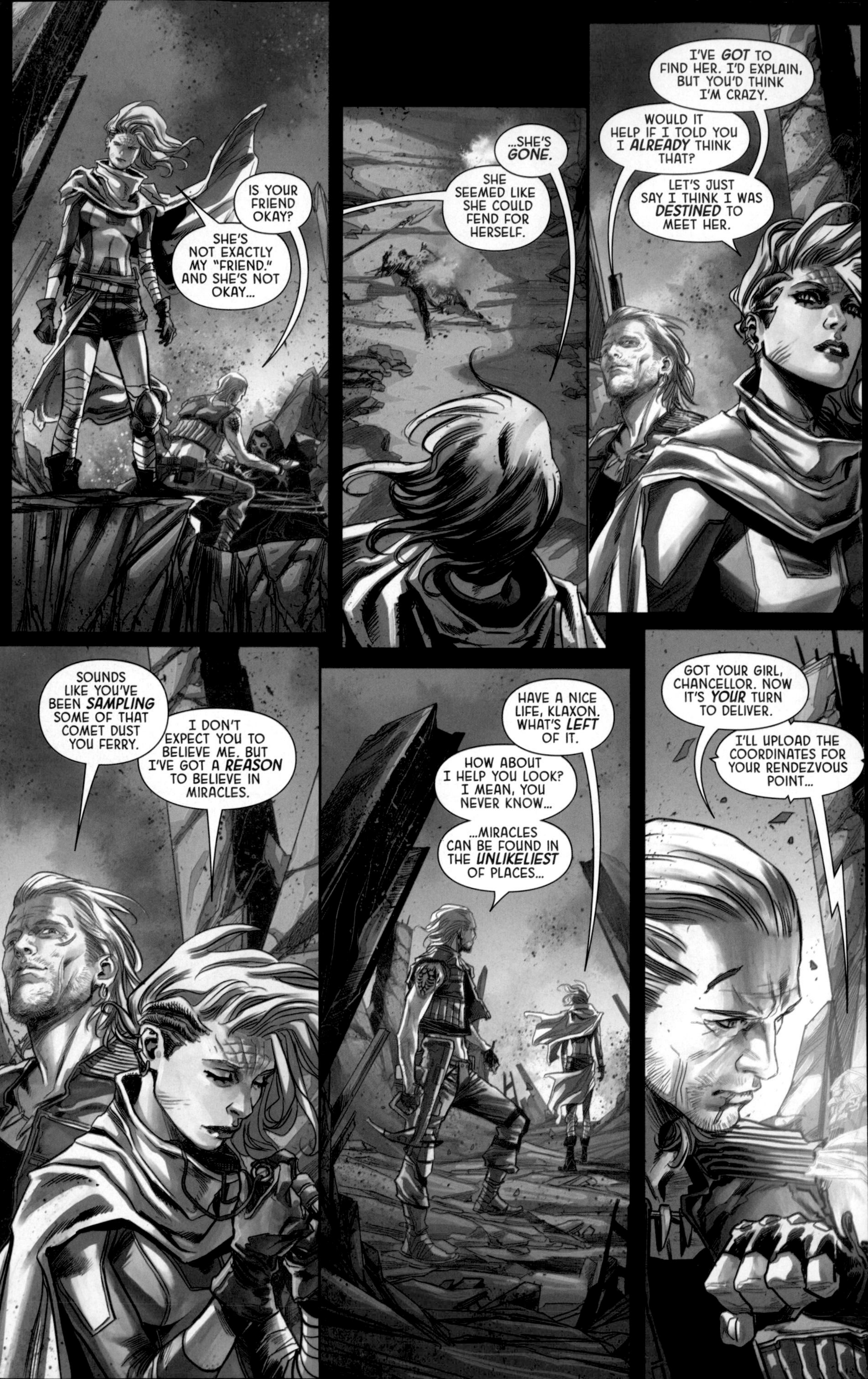
IS YOUR FRIEND OKAY?
SHE'S NOT EXACTLY MY "FRIEND." AND SHE'S NOT OKAY...
...SHE'S GONE.
SHE SEEMED LIKE SHE COULD FEND FOR HERSELF.
I'VE GOT TO FIND HER. I'D EXPLAIN, BUT YOU'D THINK I'M CRAZY.
WOULD IT HELP IF I TOLD YOU I ALREADY THINK THAT?
LET'S JUST SAY I THINK I WAS DESTINED TO MEET HER.
SOUNDS LIKE YOU'VE BEEN SAMPLING SOME OF THAT COMET DUST YOU FERRY.
I DON'T EXPECT YOU TO BELIEVE ME. BUT I'VE GOT A REASON TO BELIEVE IN MIRACLES.
HAVE A NICE LIFE, KLAXON. WHAT'S LEFT OF IT.
HOW ABOUT I HELP YOU LOOK? I MEAN, YOU NEVER KNOW...
...MIRACLES CAN BE FOUND IN THE UNLIKELIEST OF PLACES...
GOT YOUR GIRL, CHANCELLOR. NOW IT'S YOUR TURN TO DELIVER.
I'LL UPLOAD THE COORDINATES FOR YOUR RENDEZVOUS POINT...

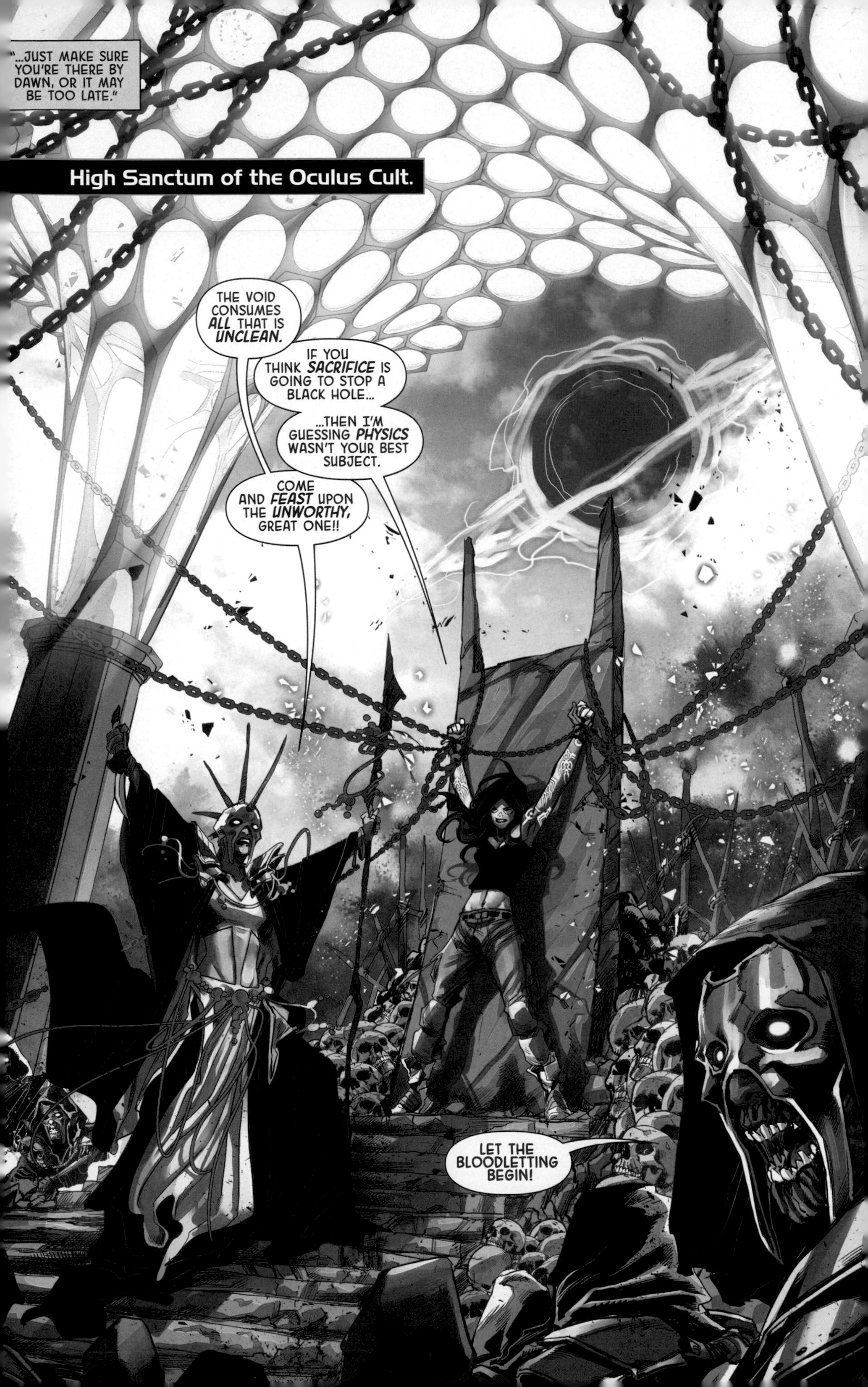
"...JUST MAKE SURE YOU'RE THERE BY DAWN, OR IT MAY BE TOO LATE."
High Sanctum of the Oculus Cult.
THE VOID CONSUMES ALL THAT IS UNCLEAN.
IF YOU THINK SACRIFICE IS GOING TO STOP A BLACK HOLE...
...THEN I'M GUESSING PHYSICS WASN'T YOUR BEST SUBJECT.
COME AND FEAST UPON THE UNWORTHY, GREAT ONE!!
LET THE BLOODLETTING BEGIN!

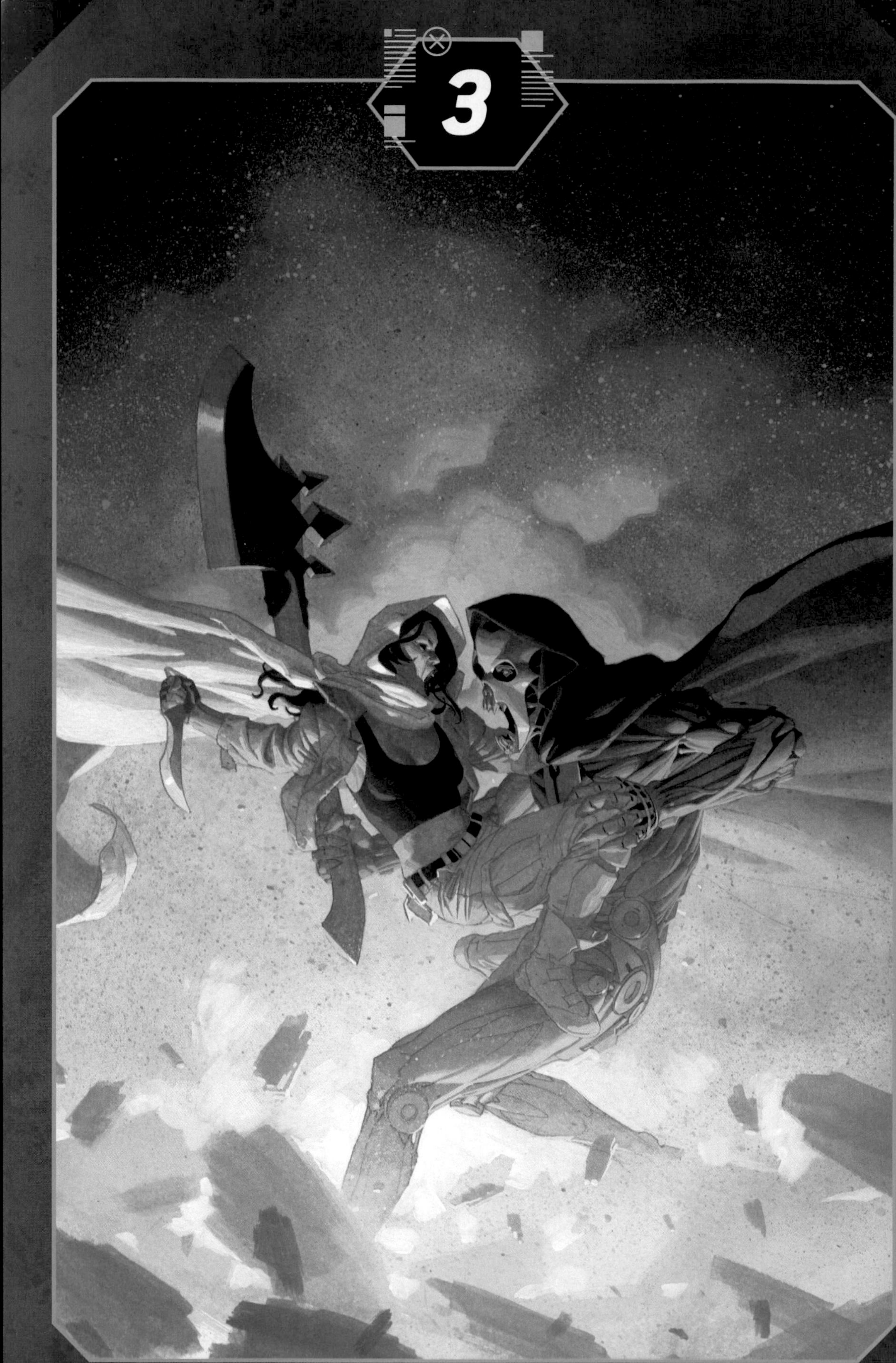
3

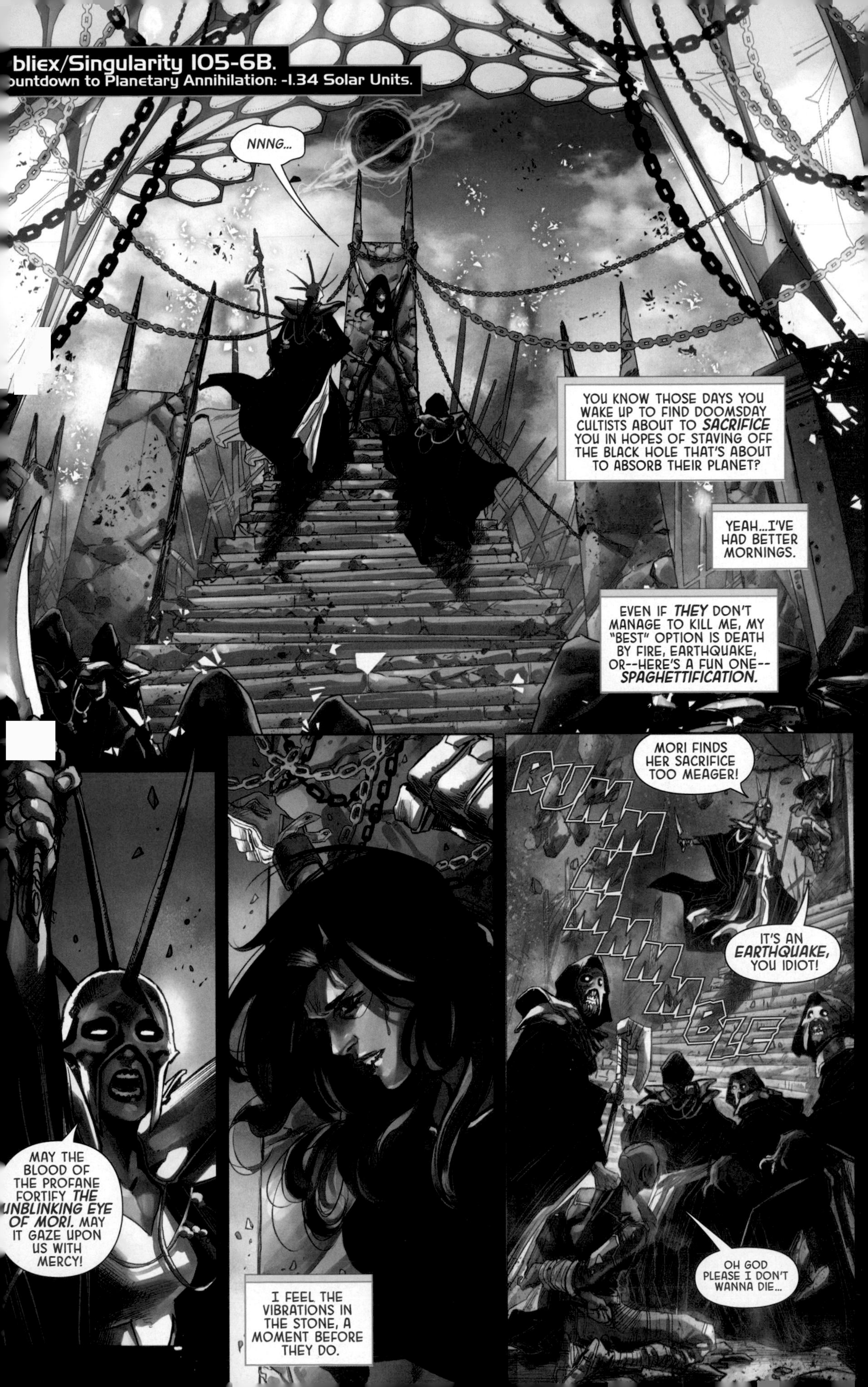
bliex/Singularity 105-6B.
ountdown to Planetary Annihilation: -1.34 Solar Units.
NNNG...
YOU KNOW THOSE DAYS YOU WAKE UP TO FIND DOOMSDAY CULTISTS ABOUT TO SACRIFICE YOU IN HOPES OF STAVING OFF THE BLACK HOLE THAT'S ABOUT TO ABSORB THEIR PLANET?
YEAH...I'VE HAD BETTER MORNINGS.
EVEN IF THEY DON'T MANAGE TO KILL ME, MY "BEST" OPTION IS DEATH BY FIRE, EARTHQUAKE, OR--HERE'S A FUN ONE-- SPAGHETTIFICATION.
MAY THE BLOOD OF THE PROFANE FORTIFY THE UNBLINKING EYE OF MORI. MAY IT GAZE UPON US WITH MERCY!
I FEEL THE VIBRATIONS IN THE STONE, A MOMENT BEFORE THEY DO.
RUMMMMMMMMBLE
MORI FINDS HER SACRIFICE TOO MEAGER!
IT'S AN EARTHQUAKE, YOU IDIOT!
OH GOD PLEASE I DON'T WANNA DIE...

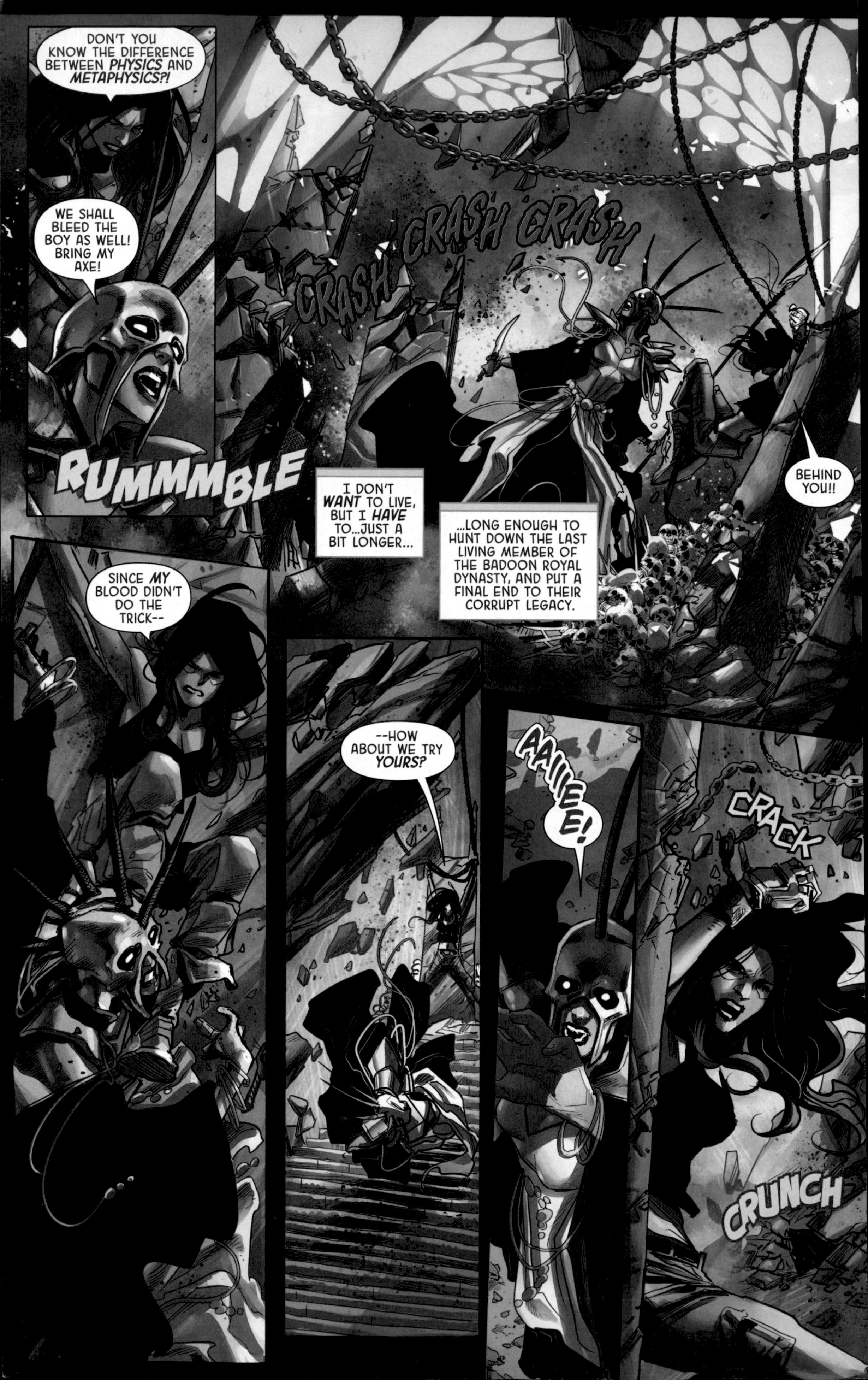

DON'T YOU KNOW THE DIFFERENCE BETWEEN PHYSICS AND METAPHYSICS?!
WE SHALL BLEED THE BOY AS WELL! BRING MY AXE!
RUMMMBLE
CRASH CRASH CRASH
I DON'T WANT TO LIVE, BUT I HAVE TO...JUST A BIT LONGER...
...LONG ENOUGH TO HUNT DOWN THE LAST LIVING MEMBER OF THE BADOON ROYAL DYNASTY, AND PUT A FINAL END TO THEIR CORRUPT LEGACY.
BEHIND YOU!!
SINCE MY BLOOD DIDN'T DO THE TRICK--
--HOW ABOUT WE TRY YOURS?
AAIIIEEE!
CRACK
CRUNCH

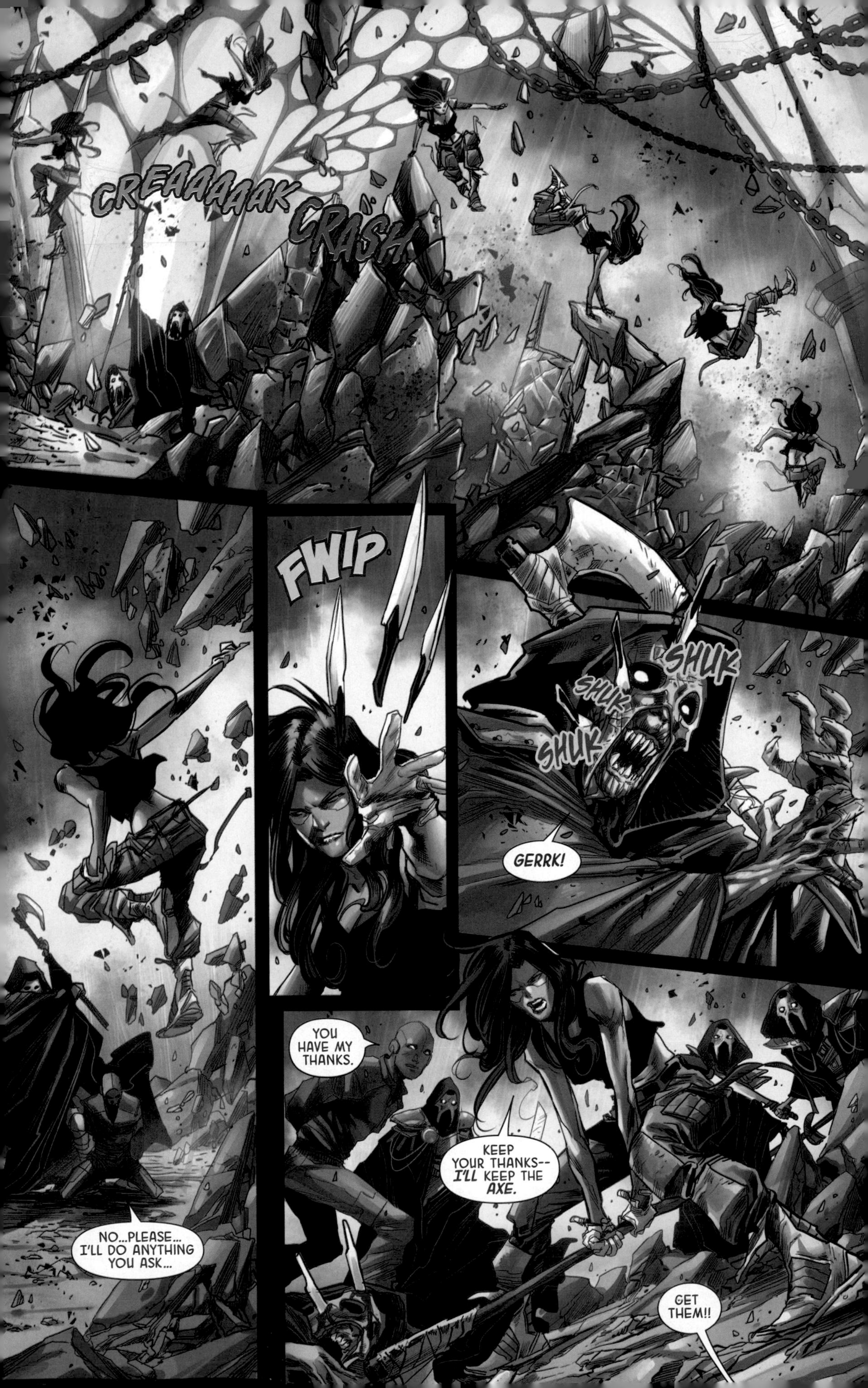
CREAAAAAK
CRASH
FWIP
SHUK
SHUK
SHUK
GERRK!
NO...PLEASE... I'LL DO ANYTHING YOU ASK...
YOU HAVE MY THANKS.
KEEP YOUR THANKS-- I'LL KEEP THE AXE.
GET THEM!!

STAY DOWN.

SLICE

SLICE

AUGHH!

!!

AAA! EUH!

YOU--YOU SAVED MY LIFE.

NO. I DELAYED YOUR DEATH.

BEHEADING'S A BETTER WAY TO GO.

I'D RATHER DIE TOMORROW THAN AT THE HANDS OF THESE *FREAKS.* THEY'VE BEEN PICKING THE WEAKEST OF US OFF, ONE BY ONE.

"US"?

ORPHANS. ANYONE WITHOUT A *FAMILY* TO PROTECT THEM.

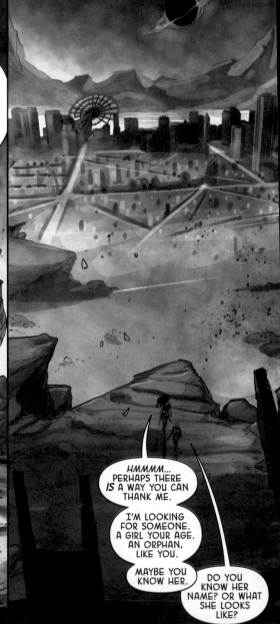

HMMMM... PERHAPS THERE *IS* A WAY YOU CAN THANK ME.

I'M LOOKING FOR SOMEONE. A GIRL YOUR AGE. AN ORPHAN, LIKE YOU.

MAYBE YOU KNOW HER.

DO YOU KNOW HER NAME? OR WHAT SHE LOOKS LIKE?

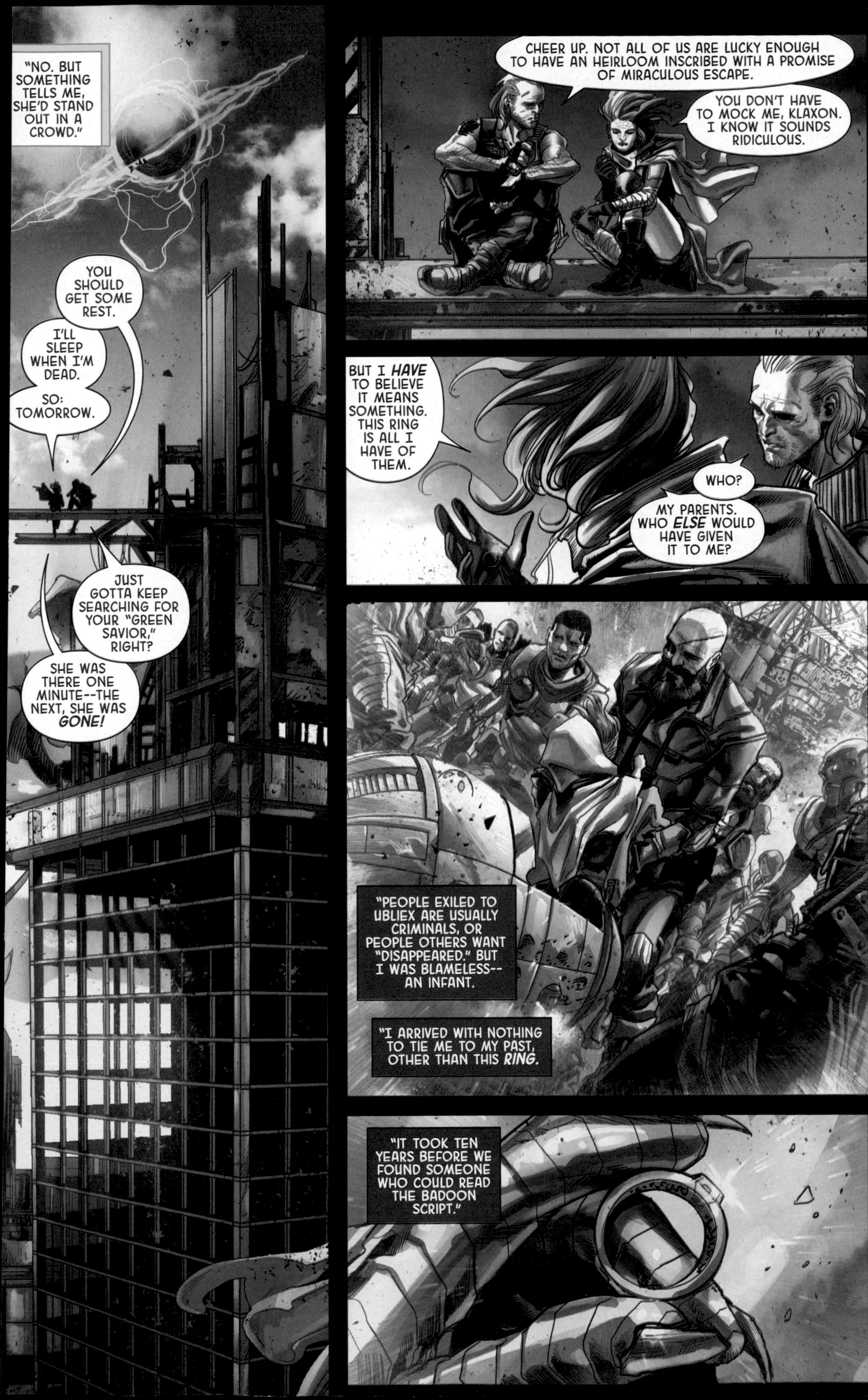
"NO. BUT SOMETHING TELLS ME, SHE'D STAND OUT IN A CROWD."
YOU SHOULD GET SOME REST.
I'LL SLEEP WHEN I'M DEAD.
SO: TOMORROW.
JUST GOTTA KEEP SEARCHING FOR YOUR "GREEN SAVIOR," RIGHT?
SHE WAS THERE ONE MINUTE--THE NEXT, SHE WAS *GONE!*
CHEER UP. NOT ALL OF US ARE LUCKY ENOUGH TO HAVE AN HEIRLOOM INSCRIBED WITH A PROMISE OF MIRACULOUS ESCAPE.
YOU DON'T HAVE TO MOCK ME, KLAXON. I KNOW IT SOUNDS RIDICULOUS.
BUT I *HAVE* TO BELIEVE IT MEANS SOMETHING. THIS RING IS ALL I HAVE OF THEM.
WHO?
MY PARENTS. WHO *ELSE* WOULD HAVE GIVEN IT TO ME?
"PEOPLE EXILED TO UBLIEX ARE USUALLY CRIMINALS, OR PEOPLE OTHERS WANT "DISAPPEARED." BUT I WAS BLAMELESS--AN INFANT.
"I ARRIVED WITH NOTHING TO TIE ME TO MY PAST, OTHER THAN THIS *RING.*
"IT TOOK TEN YEARS BEFORE WE FOUND SOMEONE WHO COULD READ THE BADOON SCRIPT."

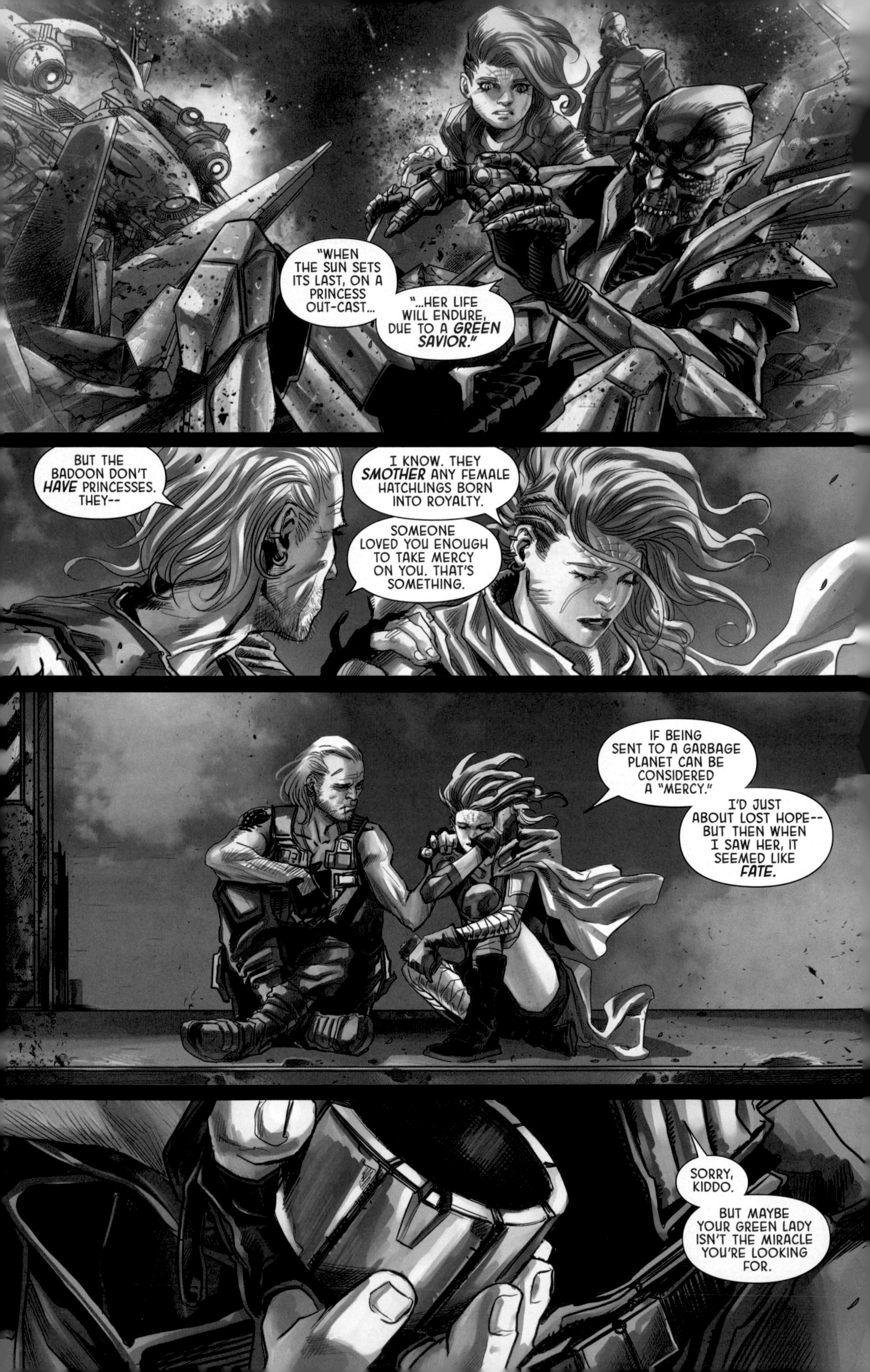
"WHEN THE SUN SETS ITS LAST, ON A PRINCESS OUT-CAST...
"...HER LIFE WILL ENDURE, DUE TO A GREEN SAVIOR."
BUT THE BADOON DON'T HAVE PRINCESSES. THEY--
I KNOW. THEY SMOTHER ANY FEMALE HATCHLINGS BORN INTO ROYALTY.
SOMEONE LOVED YOU ENOUGH TO TAKE MERCY ON YOU. THAT'S SOMETHING.
IF BEING SENT TO A GARBAGE PLANET CAN BE CONSIDERED A "MERCY."
I'D JUST ABOUT LOST HOPE-- BUT THEN WHEN I SAW HER, IT SEEMED LIKE FATE.
SORRY, KIDDO.
BUT MAYBE YOUR GREEN LADY ISN'T THE MIRACLE YOU'RE LOOKING FOR.

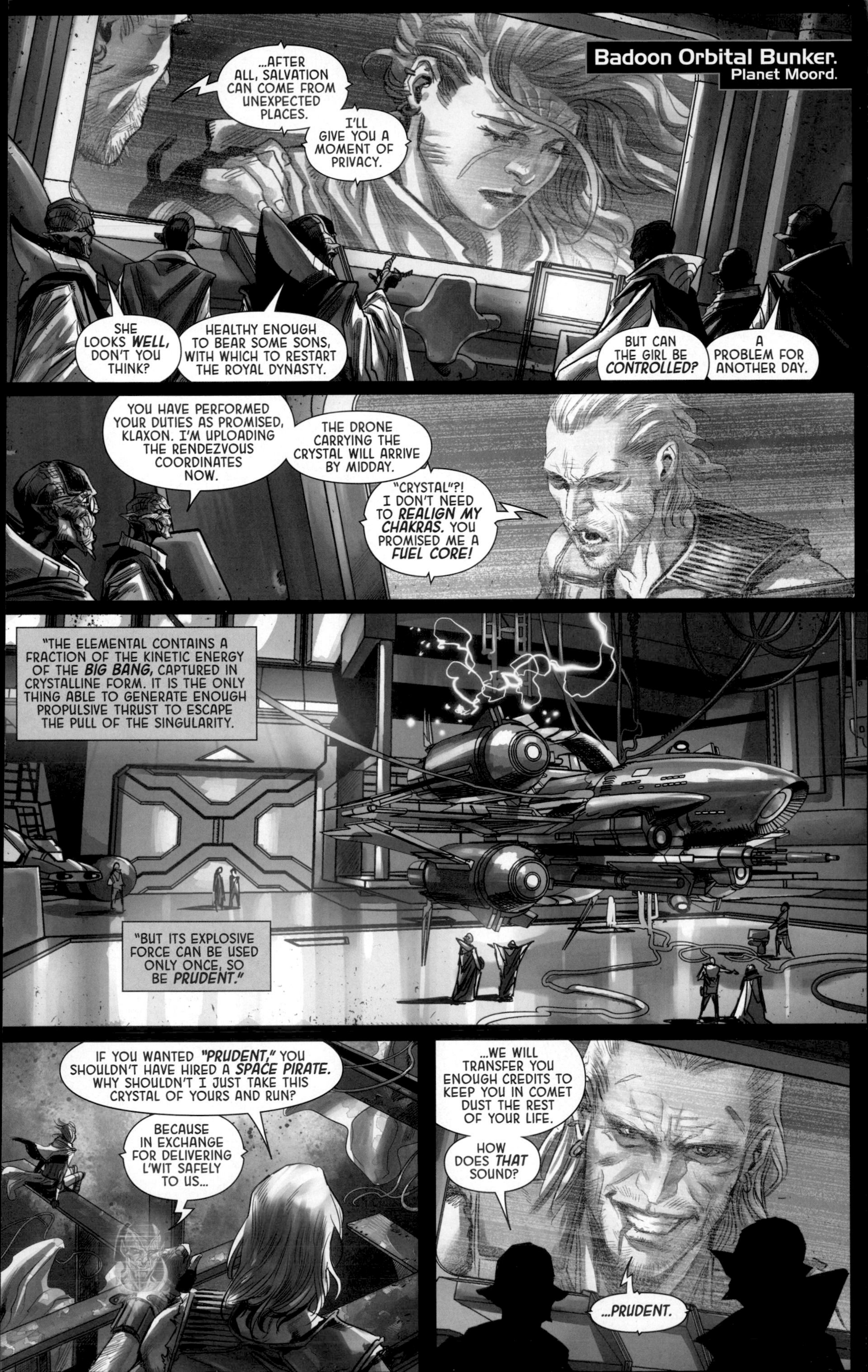
Badoon Orbital Bunker.
Planet Moord.
...AFTER ALL, SALVATION CAN COME FROM UNEXPECTED PLACES.
I'LL GIVE YOU A MOMENT OF PRIVACY.
SHE LOOKS WELL, DON'T YOU THINK?
HEALTHY ENOUGH TO BEAR SOME SONS, WITH WHICH TO RESTART THE ROYAL DYNASTY.
BUT CAN THE GIRL BE CONTROLLED?
A PROBLEM FOR ANOTHER DAY.
YOU HAVE PERFORMED YOUR DUTIES AS PROMISED, KLAXON. I'M UPLOADING THE RENDEZVOUS COORDINATES NOW.
THE DRONE CARRYING THE CRYSTAL WILL ARRIVE BY MIDDAY.
"CRYSTAL"?! I DON'T NEED TO REALIGN MY CHAKRAS. YOU PROMISED ME A FUEL CORE!
"THE ELEMENTAL CONTAINS A FRACTION OF THE KINETIC ENERGY OF THE BIG BANG, CAPTURED IN CRYSTALLINE FORM. IT IS THE ONLY THING ABLE TO GENERATE ENOUGH PROPULSIVE THRUST TO ESCAPE THE PULL OF THE SINGULARITY.
"BUT ITS EXPLOSIVE FORCE CAN BE USED ONLY ONCE, SO BE PRUDENT."
IF YOU WANTED "PRUDENT," YOU SHOULDN'T HAVE HIRED A SPACE PIRATE. WHY SHOULDN'T I JUST TAKE THIS CRYSTAL OF YOURS AND RUN?
BECAUSE IN EXCHANGE FOR DELIVERING L'WIT SAFELY TO US...
...WE WILL TRANSFER YOU ENOUGH CREDITS TO KEEP YOU IN COMET DUST THE REST OF YOUR LIFE.
HOW DOES THAT SOUND?
...PRUDENT.

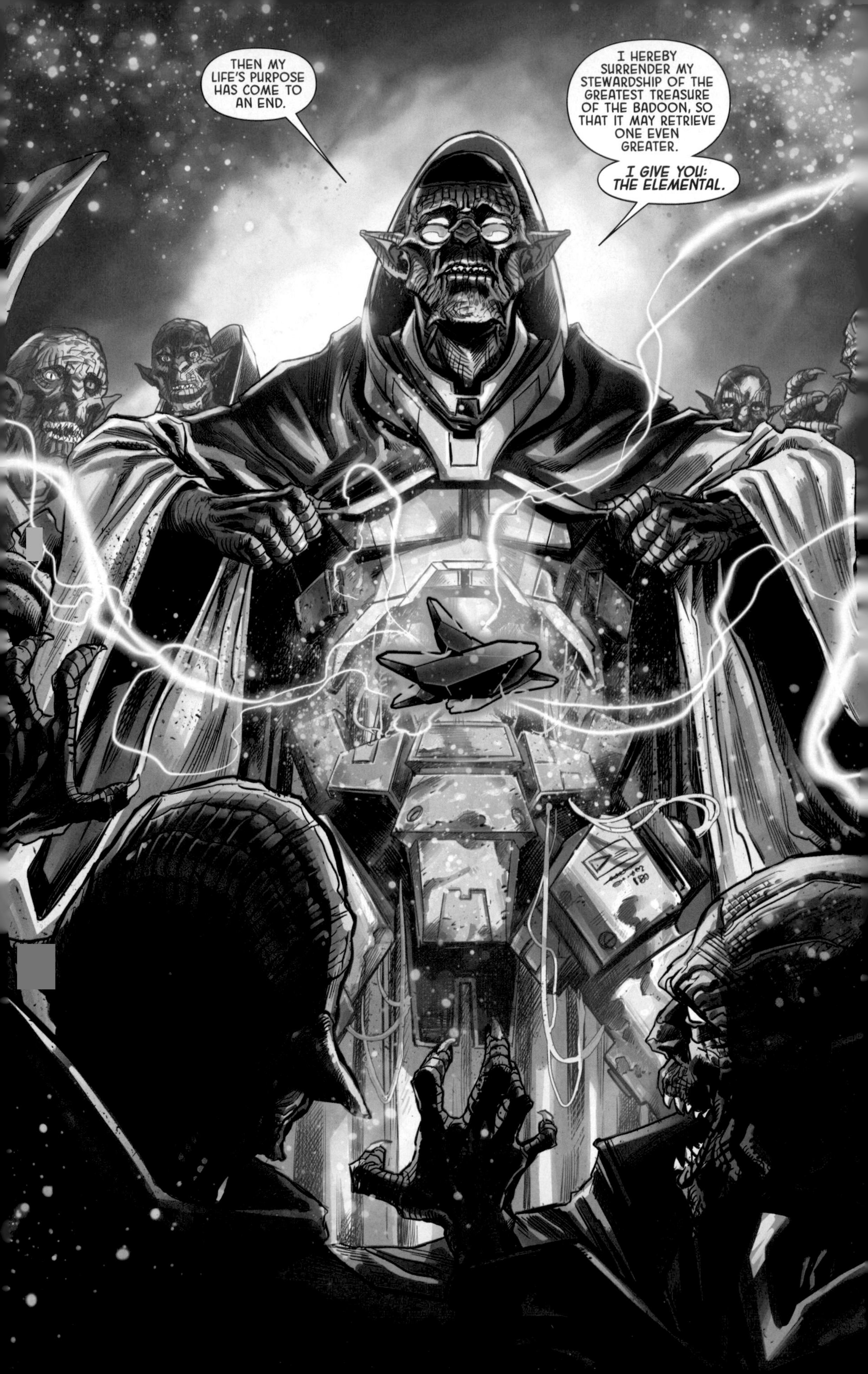
THEN MY LIFE'S PURPOSE HAS COME TO AN END.
I HEREBY SURRENDER MY STEWARDSHIP OF THE GREATEST TREASURE OF THE BADOON, SO THAT IT MAY RETRIEVE ONE EVEN GREATER.
I GIVE YOU: THE ELEMENTAL.

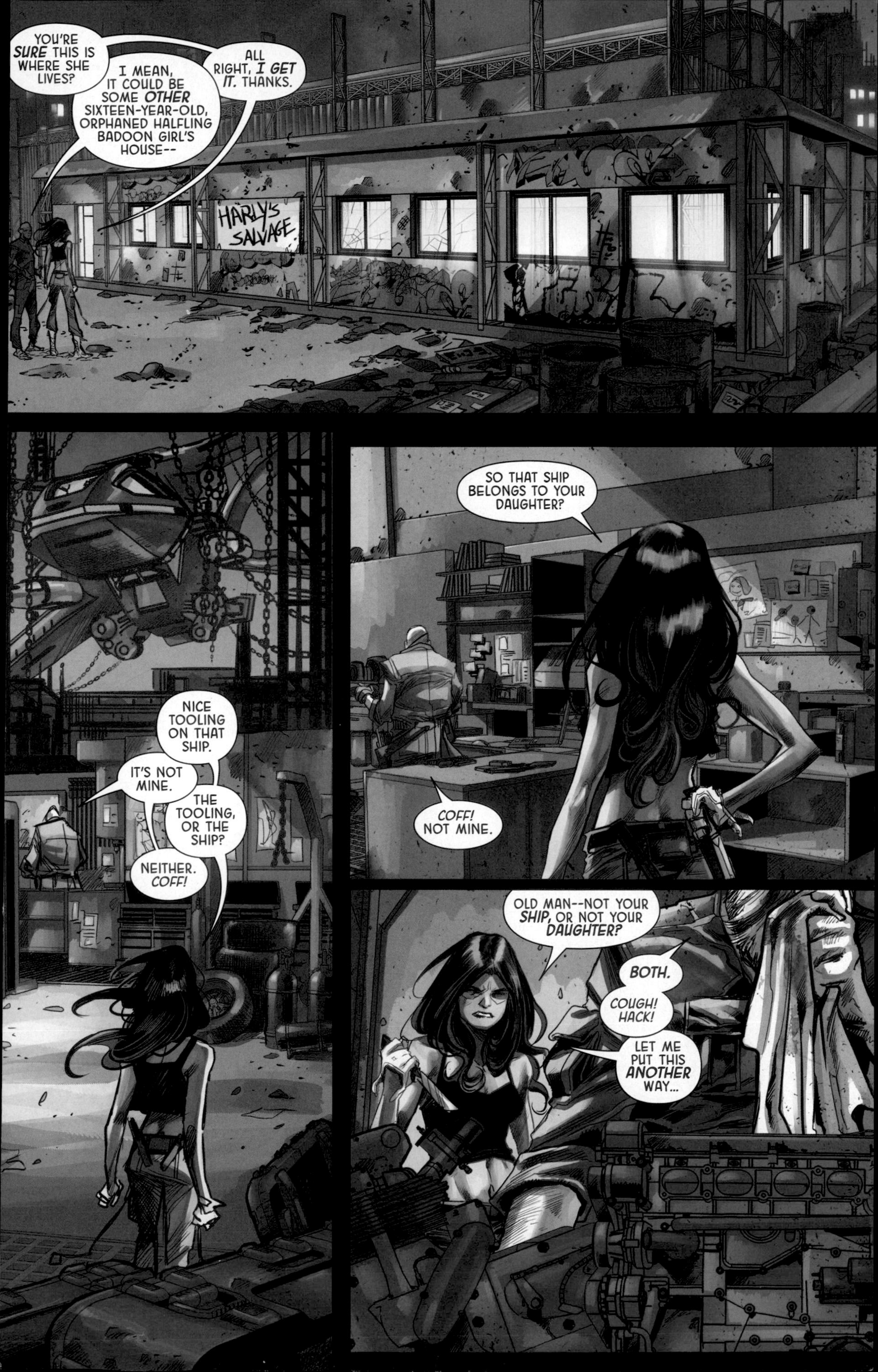
YOU'RE SURE THIS IS WHERE SHE LIVES?
I MEAN, IT COULD BE SOME OTHER SIXTEEN-YEAR-OLD, ORPHANED HALFLING BADOON GIRL'S HOUSE--
ALL RIGHT, I GET IT. THANKS.
HARLY'S SALVAGE
NICE TOOLING ON THAT SHIP.
IT'S NOT MINE.
THE TOOLING, OR THE SHIP?
NEITHER. COFF!
SO THAT SHIP BELONGS TO YOUR DAUGHTER?
COFF! NOT MINE.
OLD MAN--NOT YOUR SHIP, OR NOT YOUR DAUGHTER?
BOTH.
COUGH! HACK!
LET ME PUT THIS ANOTHER WAY...

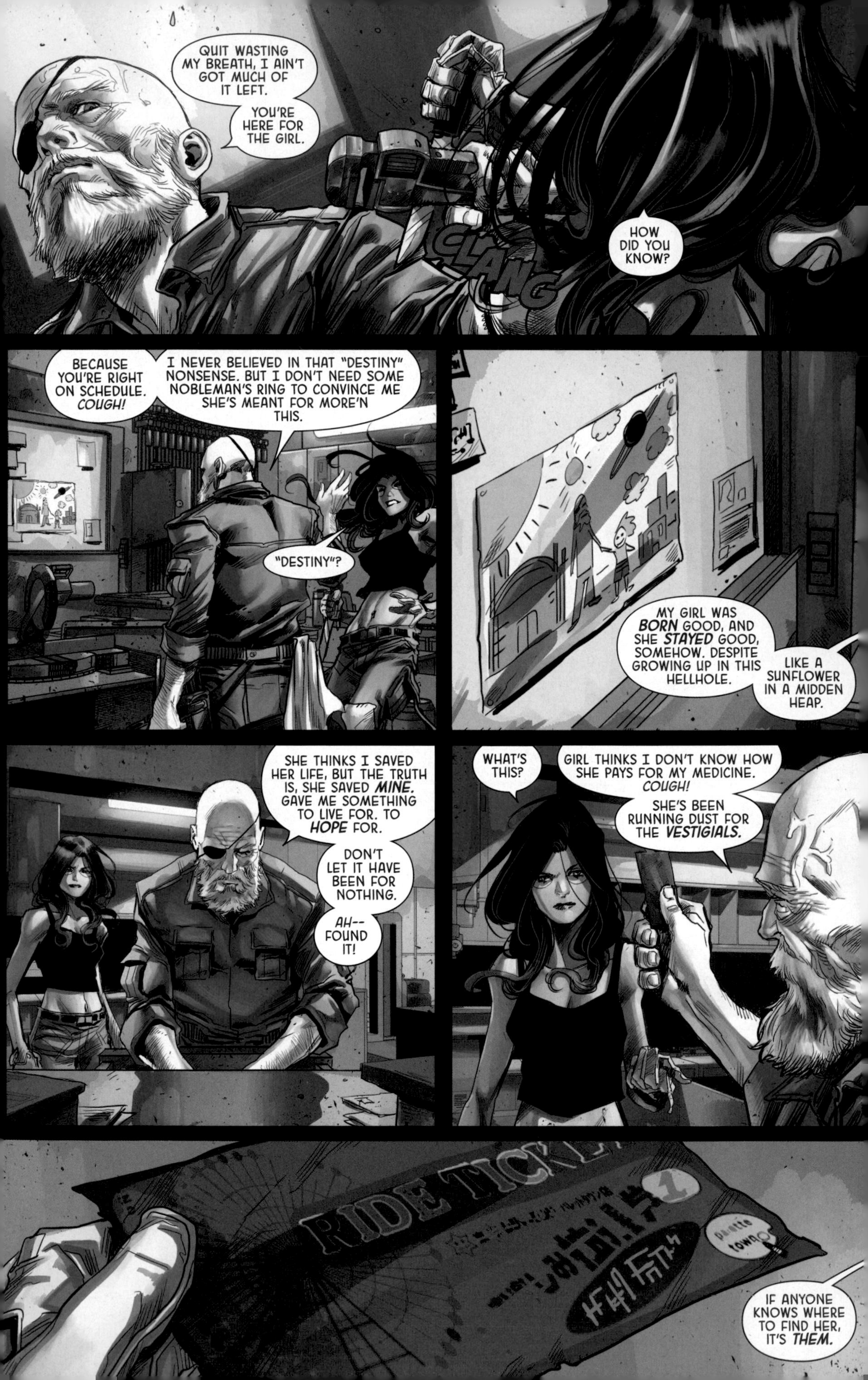
QUIT WASTING MY BREATH, I AIN'T GOT MUCH OF IT LEFT.
YOU'RE HERE FOR THE GIRL.
CLANG
HOW DID YOU KNOW?
BECAUSE YOU'RE RIGHT ON SCHEDULE. *COUGH!*
I NEVER BELIEVED IN THAT "DESTINY" NONSENSE. BUT I DON'T NEED SOME NOBLEMAN'S RING TO CONVINCE ME SHE'S MEANT FOR MORE'N THIS.
"DESTINY"?
MY GIRL WAS **BORN** GOOD, AND SHE **STAYED** GOOD, SOMEHOW. DESPITE GROWING UP IN THIS HELLHOLE.
LIKE A SUNFLOWER IN A MIDDEN HEAP.
SHE THINKS I SAVED HER LIFE, BUT THE TRUTH IS, SHE SAVED **MINE.** GAVE ME SOMETHING TO LIVE FOR. TO **HOPE** FOR.
DON'T LET IT HAVE BEEN FOR NOTHING.
AH-- FOUND IT!
WHAT'S THIS?
GIRL THINKS I DON'T KNOW HOW SHE PAYS FOR MY MEDICINE. *COUGH!*
SHE'S BEEN RUNNING DUST FOR THE **VESTIGIALS.**
RIDE TICKET
IF ANYONE KNOWS WHERE TO FIND HER, IT'S **THEM.**

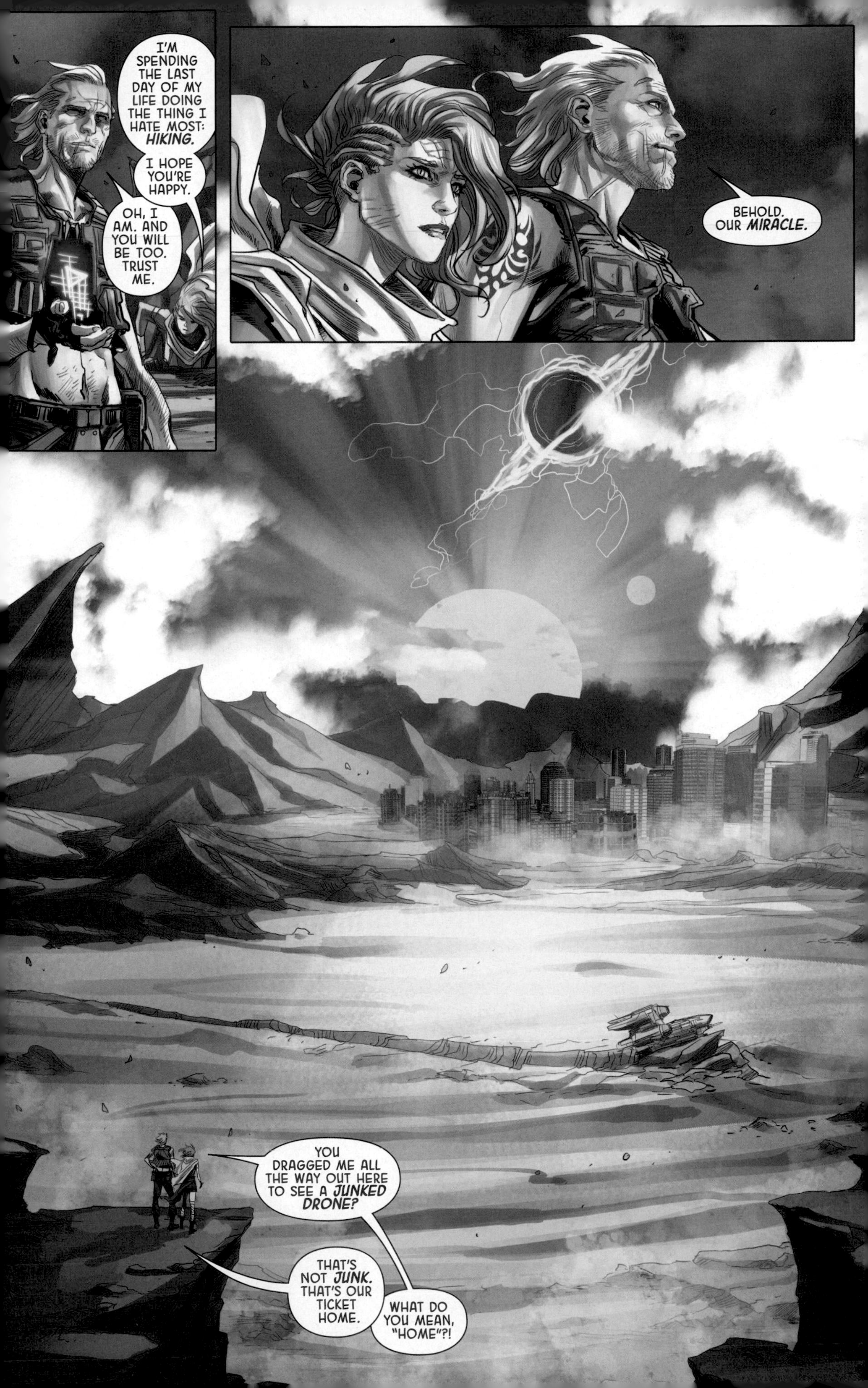
I'M SPENDING THE LAST DAY OF MY LIFE DOING THE THING I HATE MOST: HIKING.
I HOPE YOU'RE HAPPY.
OH, I AM. AND YOU WILL BE TOO. TRUST ME.
BEHOLD. OUR MIRACLE.
YOU DRAGGED ME ALL THE WAY OUT HERE TO SEE A JUNKED DRONE?
THAT'S NOT JUNK. THAT'S OUR TICKET HOME.
WHAT DO YOU MEAN, "HOME"?!

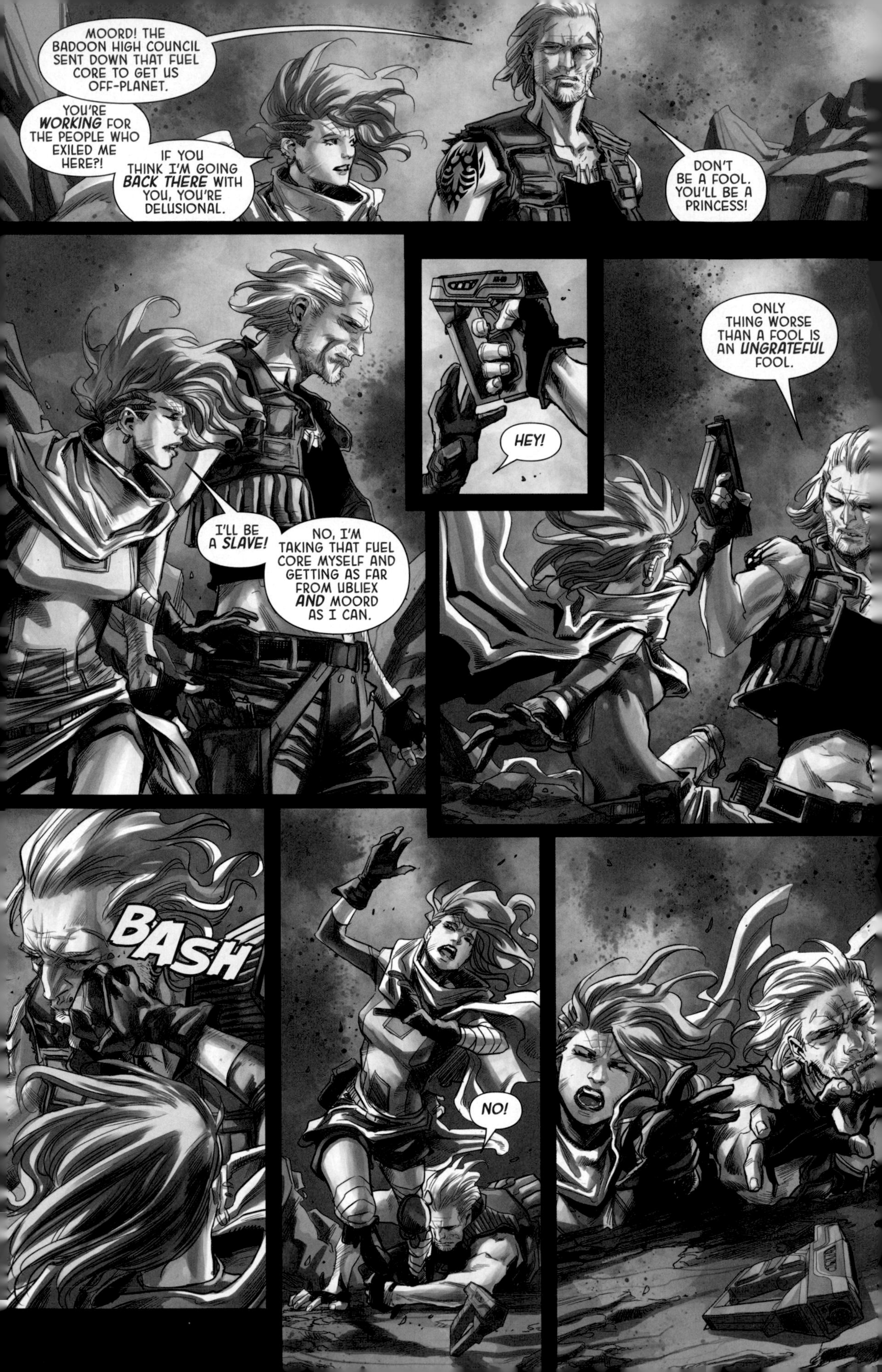
MOORD! THE BADOON HIGH COUNCIL SENT DOWN THAT FUEL CORE TO GET US OFF-PLANET.
YOU'RE WORKING FOR THE PEOPLE WHO EXILED ME HERE?!
IF YOU THINK I'M GOING BACK THERE WITH YOU, YOU'RE DELUSIONAL.
DON'T BE A FOOL. YOU'LL BE A PRINCESS!
I'LL BE A SLAVE!
NO, I'M TAKING THAT FUEL CORE MYSELF AND GETTING AS FAR FROM UBLIEX AND MOORD AS I CAN.
HEY!
ONLY THING WORSE THAN A FOOL IS AN UNGRATEFUL FOOL.
BASH
NO!

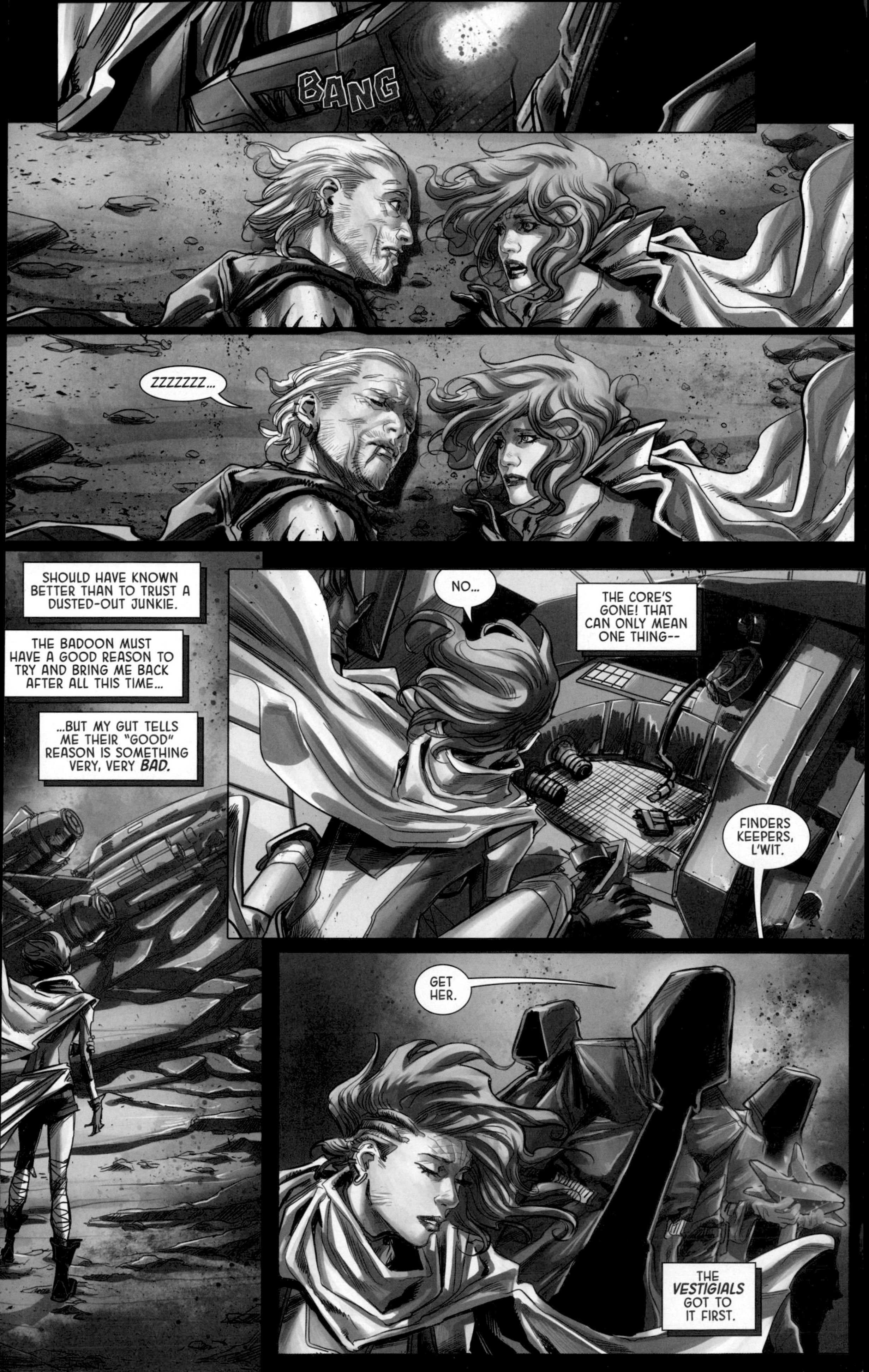
BANG
ZZZZZZZ...
SHOULD HAVE KNOWN BETTER THAN TO TRUST A DUSTED-OUT JUNKIE.
THE BADOON MUST HAVE A GOOD REASON TO TRY AND BRING ME BACK AFTER ALL THIS TIME...
...BUT MY GUT TELLS ME THEIR "GOOD" REASON IS SOMETHING VERY, VERY BAD.
NO...
THE CORE'S GONE! THAT CAN ONLY MEAN ONE THING--
FINDERS KEEPERS, L'WIT.
GET HER.
THE VESTIGIALS GOT TO IT FIRST.

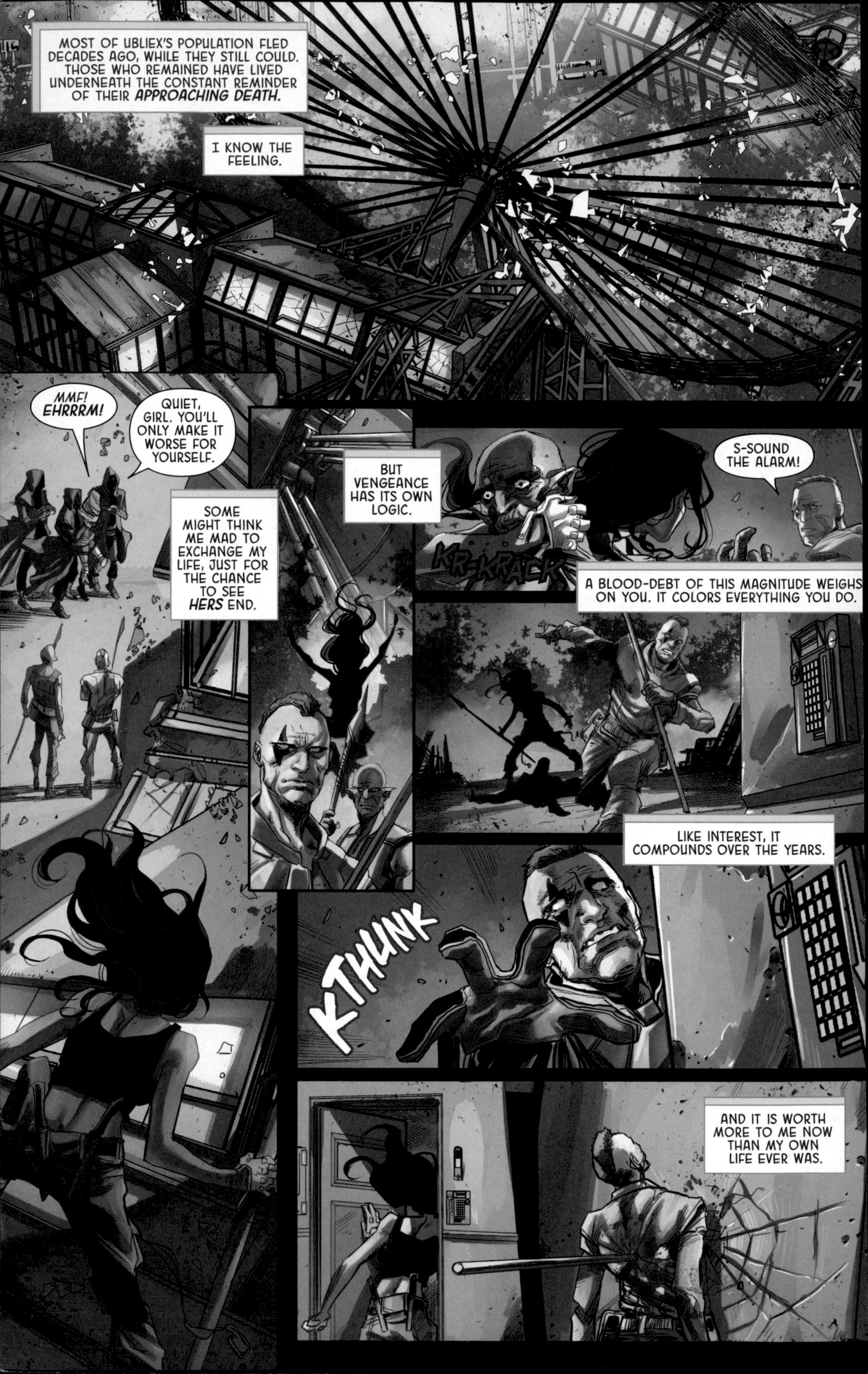
MOST OF UBLIEX'S POPULATION FLED DECADES AGO, WHILE THEY STILL COULD. THOSE WHO REMAINED HAVE LIVED UNDERNEATH THE CONSTANT REMINDER OF THEIR APPROACHING DEATH.
I KNOW THE FEELING.
MMF! EHRRRM!
QUIET, GIRL. YOU'LL ONLY MAKE IT WORSE FOR YOURSELF.
SOME MIGHT THINK ME MAD TO EXCHANGE MY LIFE, JUST FOR THE CHANCE TO SEE HERS END.
BUT VENGEANCE HAS ITS OWN LOGIC.
KR-KRACK
S-SOUND THE ALARM!
A BLOOD-DEBT OF THIS MAGNITUDE WEIGHS ON YOU. IT COLORS EVERYTHING YOU DO.
LIKE INTEREST, IT COMPOUNDS OVER THE YEARS.
KTHUNK
AND IT IS WORTH MORE TO ME NOW THAN MY OWN LIFE EVER WAS.

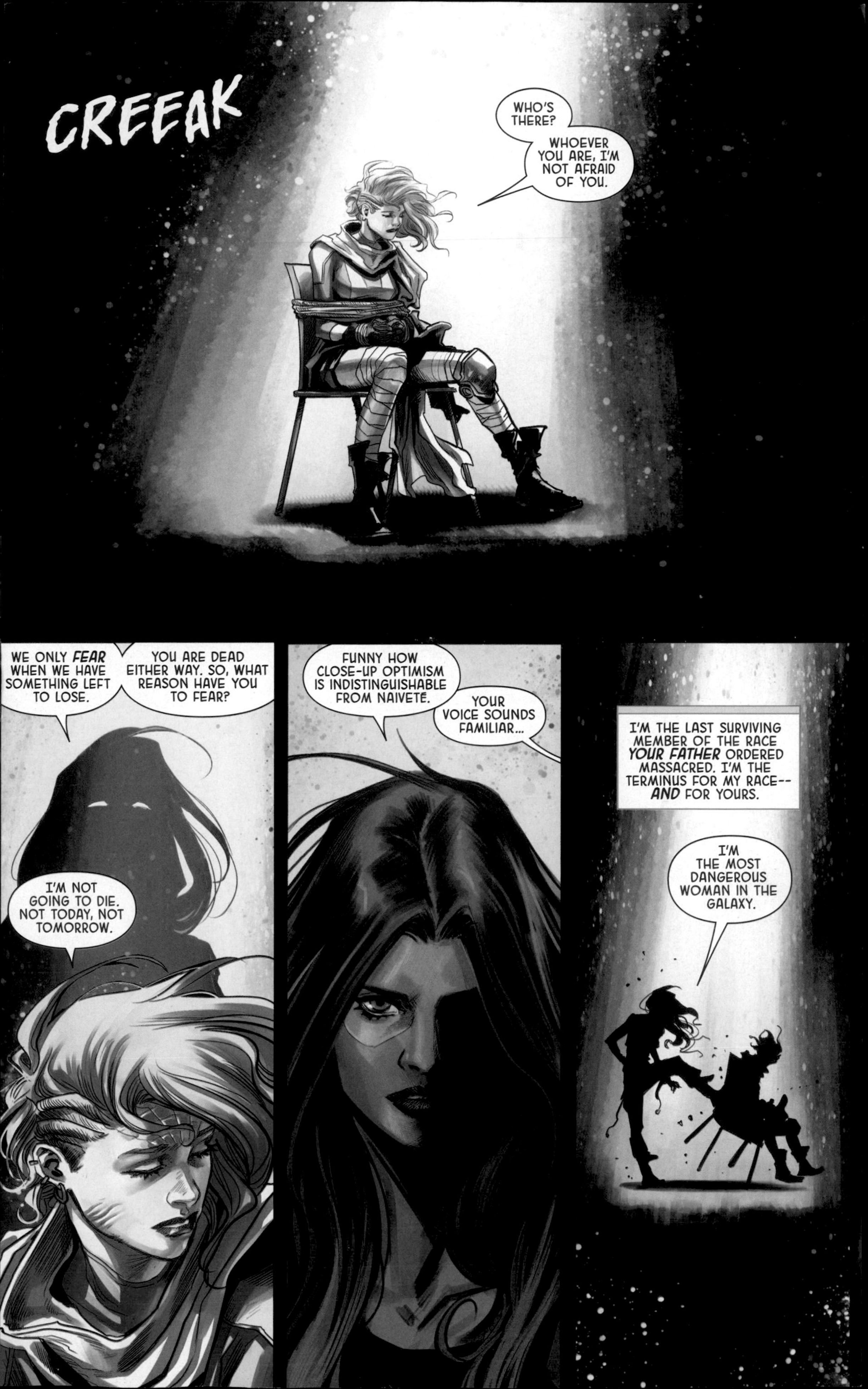
CREEAK
WHO'S THERE?
WHOEVER YOU ARE, I'M NOT AFRAID OF YOU.
WE ONLY FEAR WHEN WE HAVE SOMETHING LEFT TO LOSE.
YOU ARE DEAD EITHER WAY. SO, WHAT REASON HAVE YOU TO FEAR?
I'M NOT GOING TO DIE. NOT TODAY, NOT TOMORROW.
FUNNY HOW CLOSE-UP OPTIMISM IS INDISTINGUISHABLE FROM NAIVETE.
YOUR VOICE SOUNDS FAMILIAR...
I'M THE LAST SURVIVING MEMBER OF THE RACE YOUR FATHER ORDERED MASSACRED. I'M THE TERMINUS FOR MY RACE--AND FOR YOURS.
I'M THE MOST DANGEROUS WOMAN IN THE GALAXY.

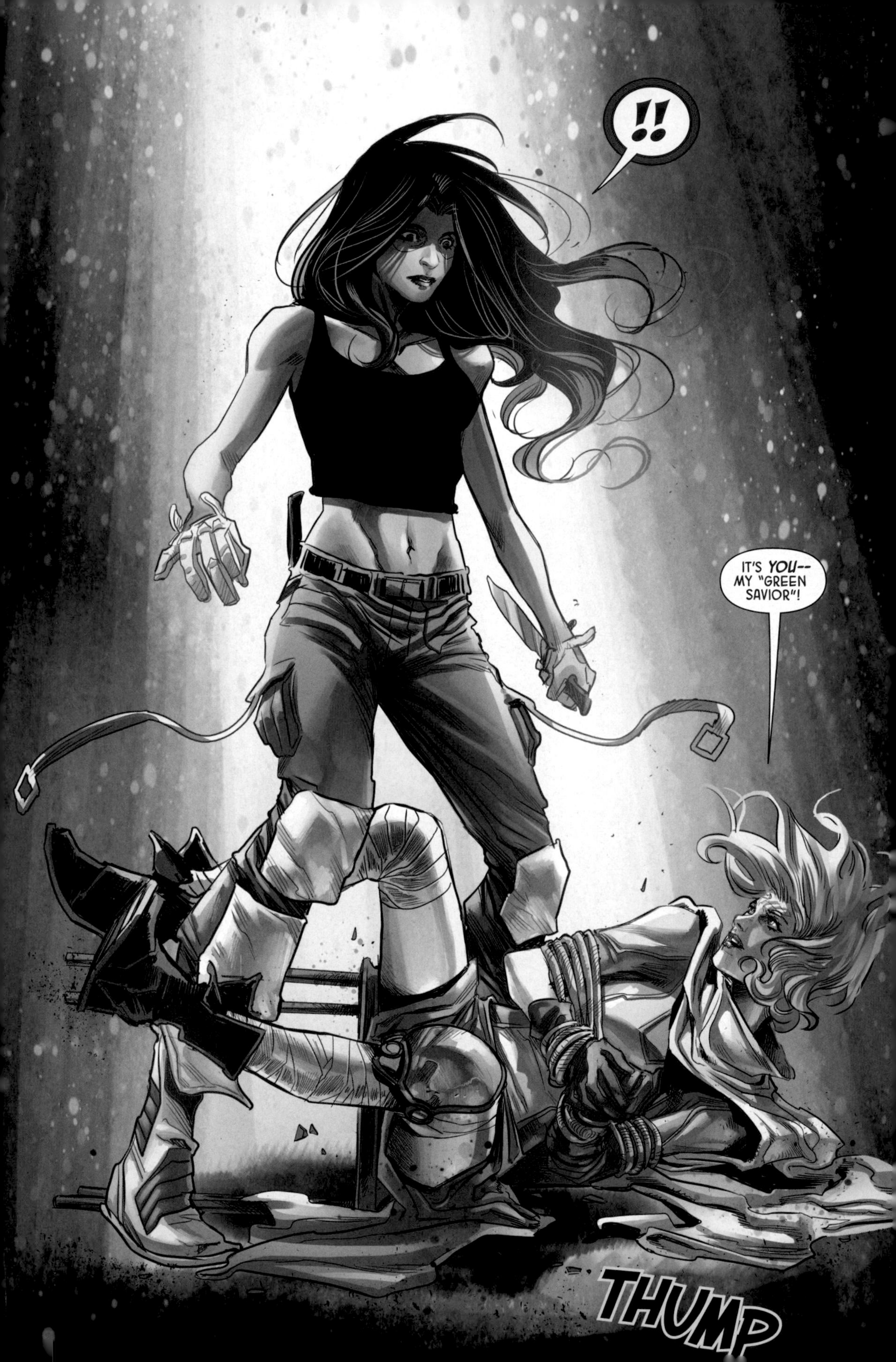
!!
IT'S YOU--
MY "GREEN
SAVIOR"!
THUMP

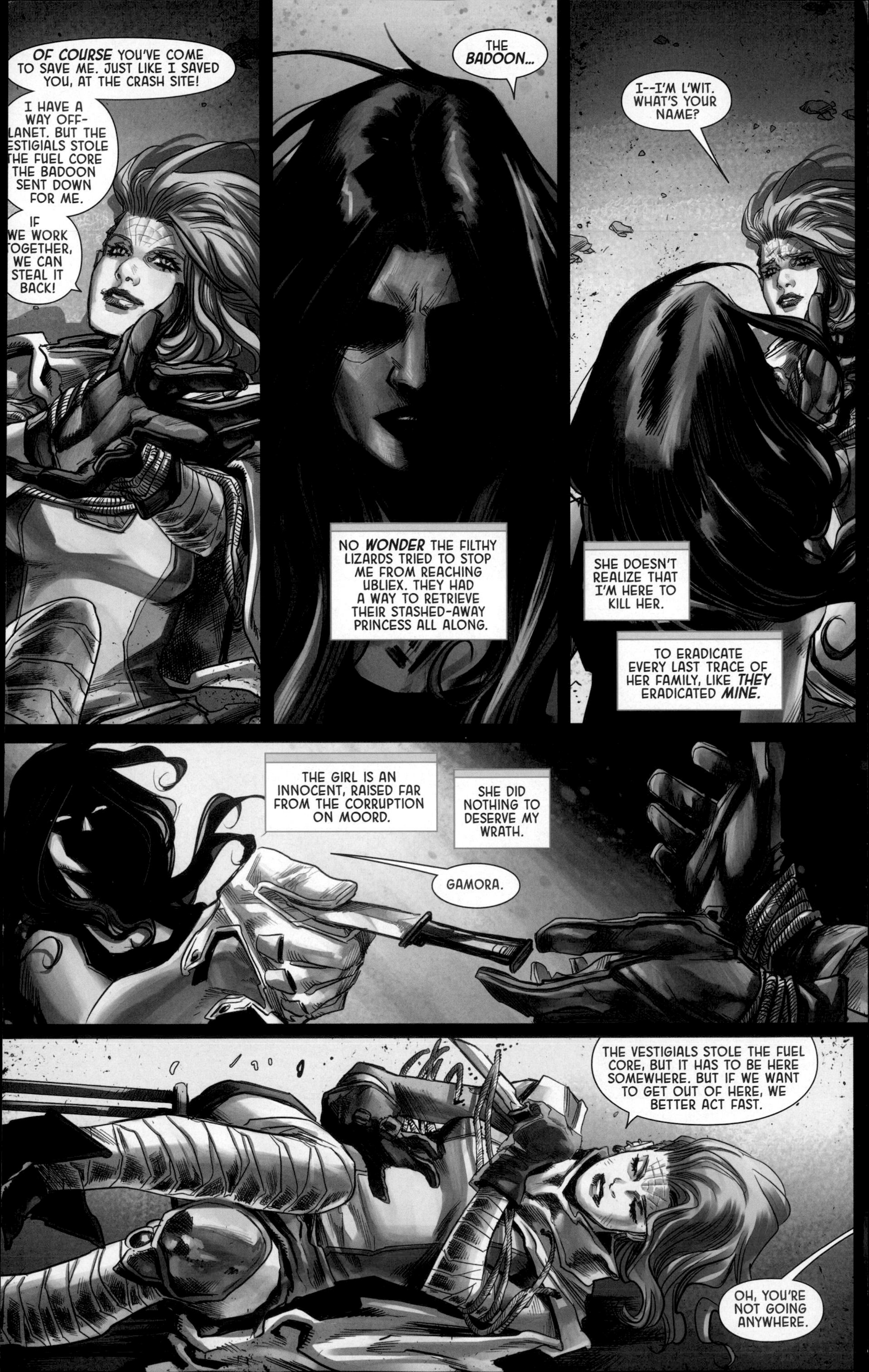
OF COURSE YOU'VE COME TO SAVE ME. JUST LIKE I SAVED YOU, AT THE CRASH SITE!
I HAVE A WAY OFF-PLANET. BUT THE VESTIGIALS STOLE THE FUEL CORE THE BADOON SENT DOWN FOR ME.
IF WE WORK TOGETHER, WE CAN STEAL IT BACK!
THE BADOON...
NO WONDER THE FILTHY LIZARDS TRIED TO STOP ME FROM REACHING UBLIEX. THEY HAD A WAY TO RETRIEVE THEIR STASHED-AWAY PRINCESS ALL ALONG.
I--I'M L'WIT. WHAT'S YOUR NAME?
SHE DOESN'T REALIZE THAT I'M HERE TO KILL HER.
TO ERADICATE EVERY LAST TRACE OF HER FAMILY, LIKE THEY ERADICATED MINE.
THE GIRL IS AN INNOCENT, RAISED FAR FROM THE CORRUPTION ON MOORD.
SHE DID NOTHING TO DESERVE MY WRATH.
GAMORA.
THE VESTIGIALS STOLE THE FUEL CORE, BUT IT HAS TO BE HERE SOMEWHERE. BUT IF WE WANT TO GET OUT OF HERE, WE BETTER ACT FAST.
OH, YOU'RE NOT GOING ANYWHERE.

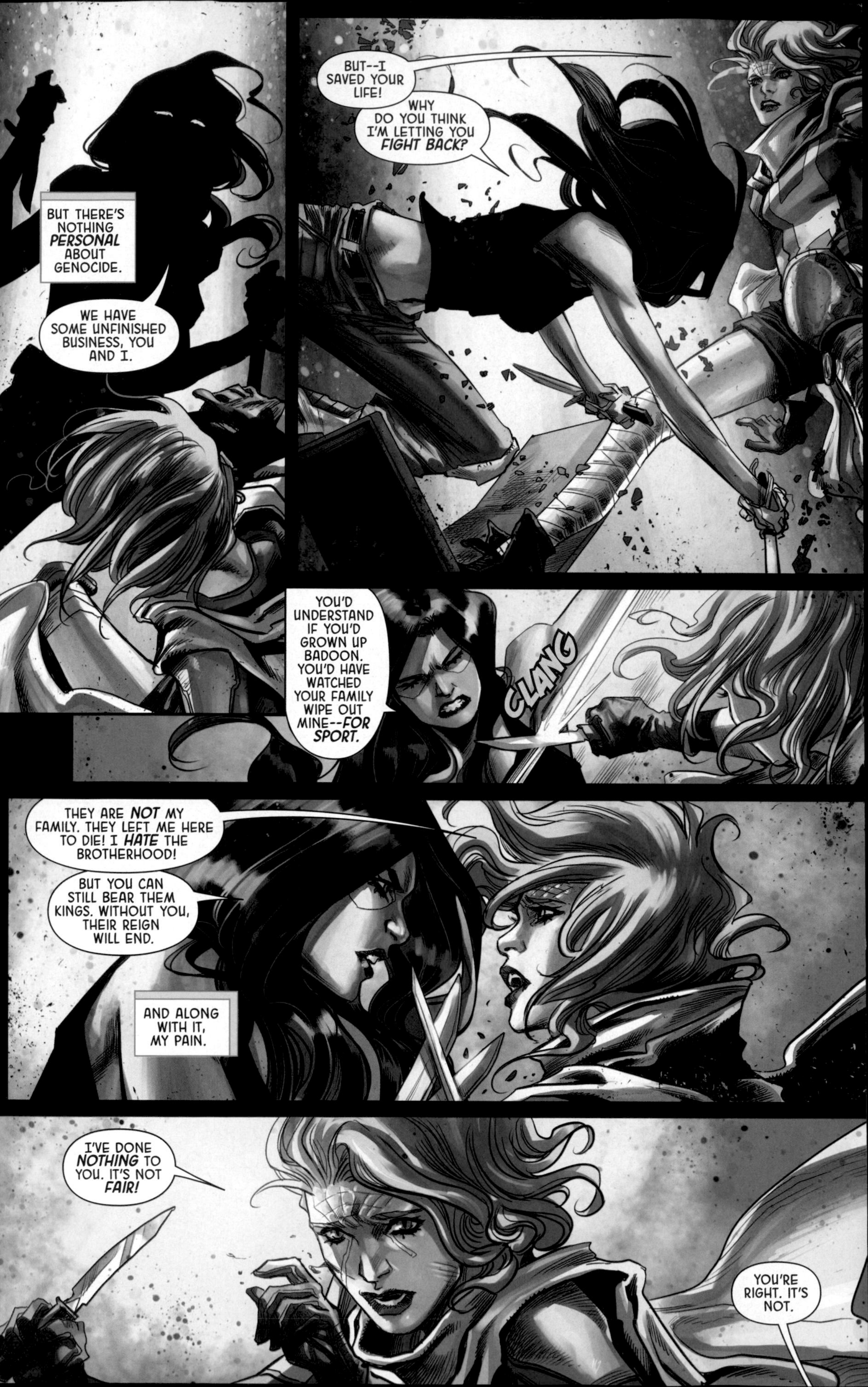
BUT THERE'S NOTHING PERSONAL ABOUT GENOCIDE.
WE HAVE SOME UNFINISHED BUSINESS, YOU AND I.
BUT--I SAVED YOUR LIFE!
WHY DO YOU THINK I'M LETTING YOU FIGHT BACK?
YOU'D UNDERSTAND IF YOU'D GROWN UP BADOON. YOU'D HAVE WATCHED YOUR FAMILY WIPE OUT MINE--FOR SPORT.
CLANG
THEY ARE NOT MY FAMILY. THEY LEFT ME HERE TO DIE! I HATE THE BROTHERHOOD!
BUT YOU CAN STILL BEAR THEM KINGS. WITHOUT YOU, THEIR REIGN WILL END.
AND ALONG WITH IT, MY PAIN.
I'VE DONE NOTHING TO YOU. IT'S NOT FAIR!
YOU'RE RIGHT. IT'S NOT.

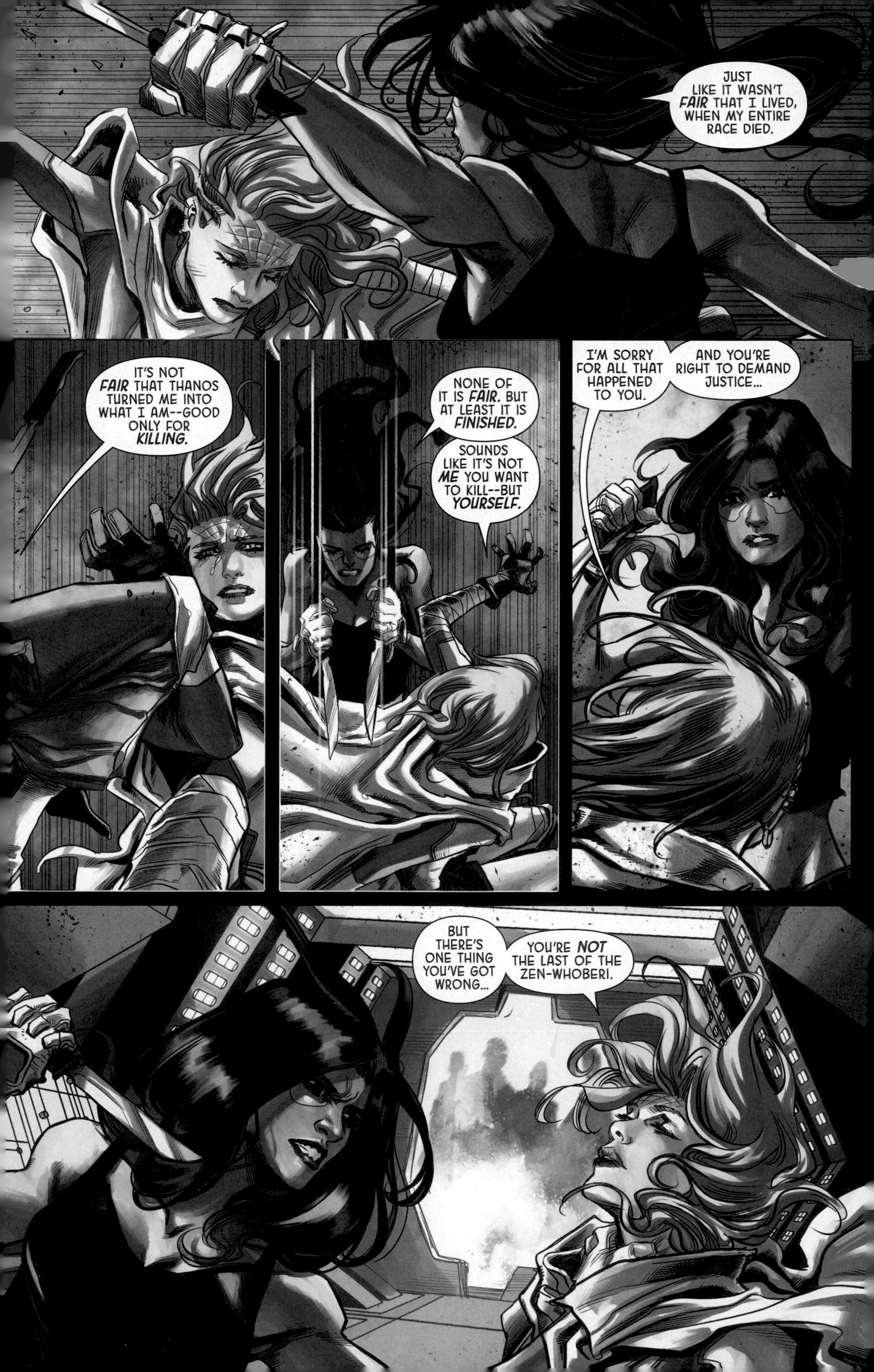
JUST LIKE IT WASN'T FAIR THAT I LIVED, WHEN MY ENTIRE RACE DIED.
IT'S NOT FAIR THAT THANOS TURNED ME INTO WHAT I AM--GOOD ONLY FOR KILLING.
NONE OF IT IS FAIR. BUT AT LEAST IT IS FINISHED.
SOUNDS LIKE IT'S NOT ME YOU WANT TO KILL--BUT YOURSELF.
I'M SORRY FOR ALL THAT HAPPENED TO YOU.
AND YOU'RE RIGHT TO DEMAND JUSTICE...
BUT THERE'S ONE THING YOU'VE GOT WRONG...
YOU'RE NOT THE LAST OF THE ZEN-WHOBERI.

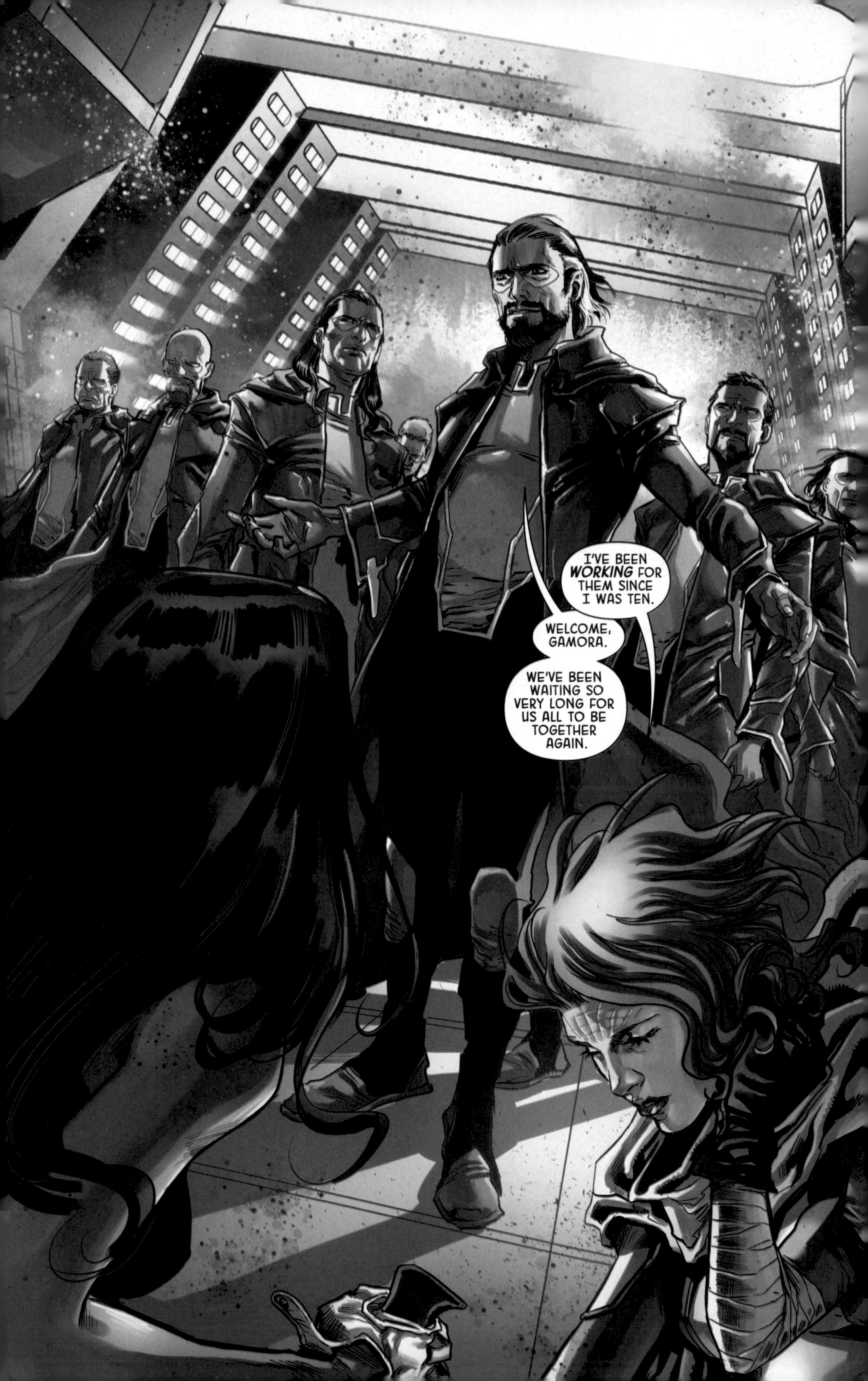
I'VE BEEN WORKING FOR THEM SINCE I WAS TEN.
WELCOME, GAMORA.
WE'VE BEEN WAITING SO VERY LONG FOR US ALL TO BE TOGETHER AGAIN.

4

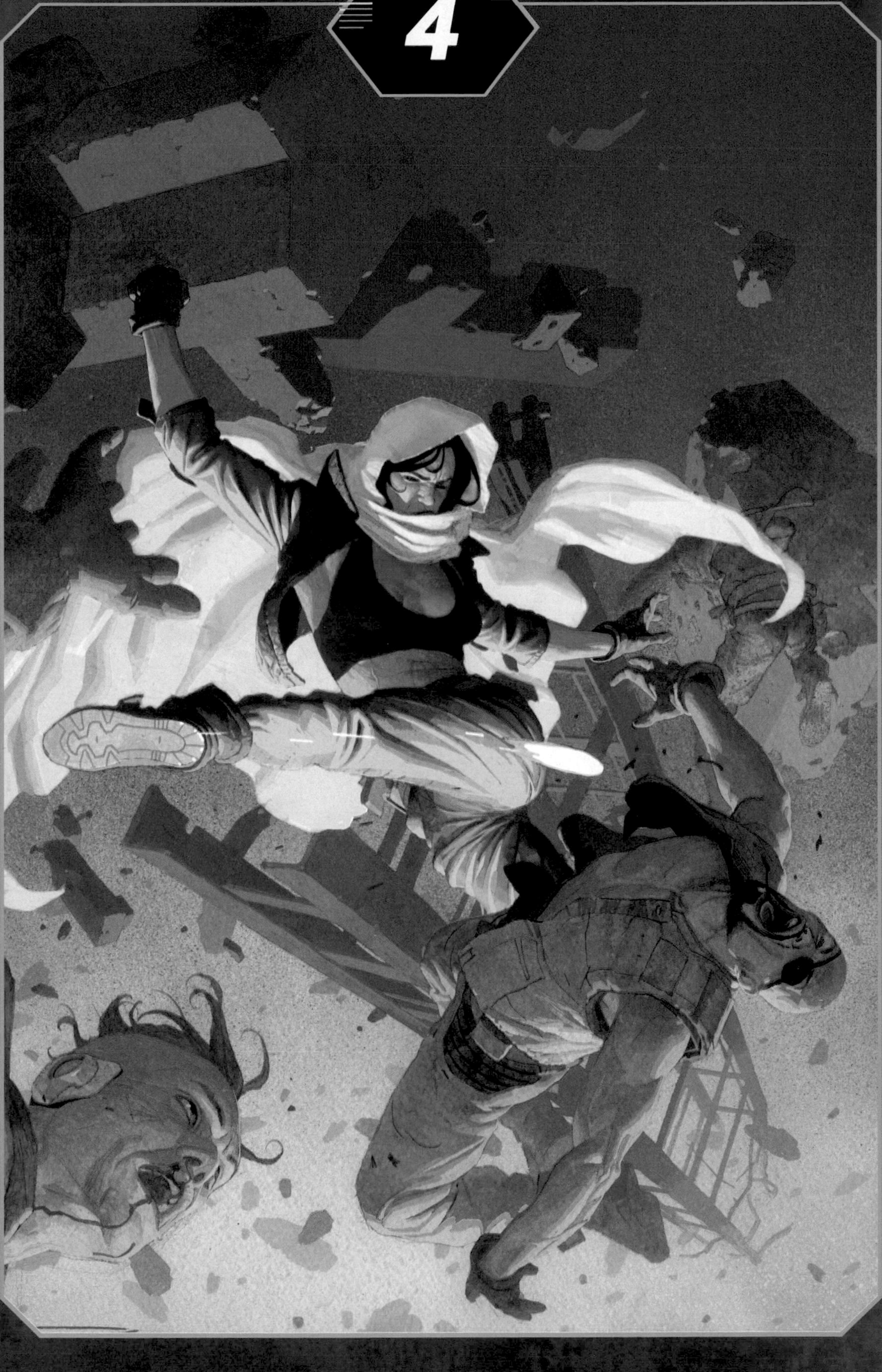

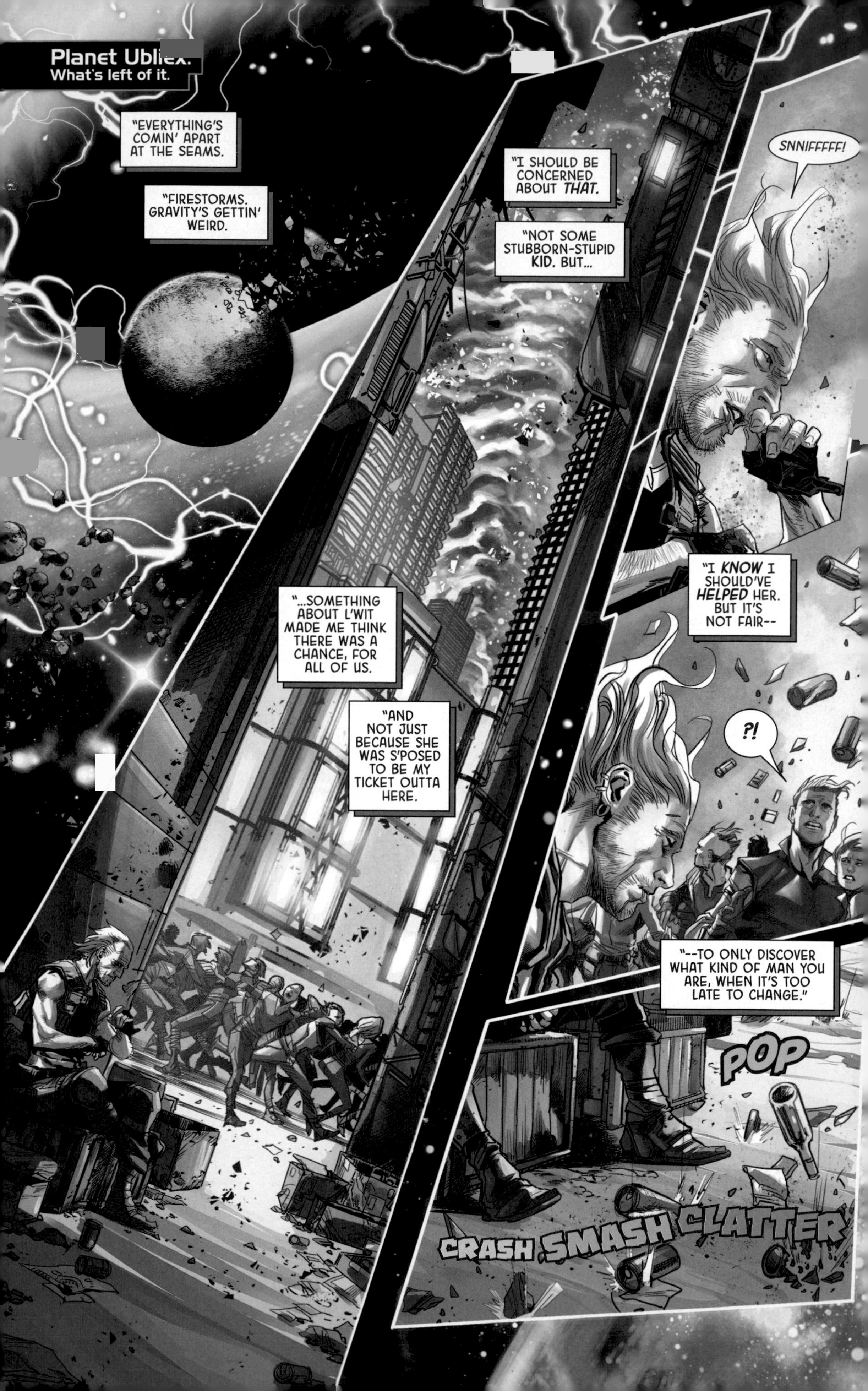
Planet Ubliex.
What's left of it.
"EVERYTHING'S COMIN' APART AT THE SEAMS.
"FIRESTORMS. GRAVITY'S GETTIN' WEIRD.
"I SHOULD BE CONCERNED ABOUT THAT.
"NOT SOME STUBBORN-STUPID KID. BUT...
"...SOMETHING ABOUT L'WIT MADE ME THINK THERE WAS A CHANCE, FOR ALL OF US.
"AND NOT JUST BECAUSE SHE WAS S'POSED TO BE MY TICKET OUTTA HERE.
SNNIFFFFF!
"I KNOW I SHOULD'VE HELPED HER. BUT IT'S NOT FAIR--
?!
"--TO ONLY DISCOVER WHAT KIND OF MAN YOU ARE, WHEN IT'S TOO LATE TO CHANGE."
POP
CRASH SMASH CLATTER

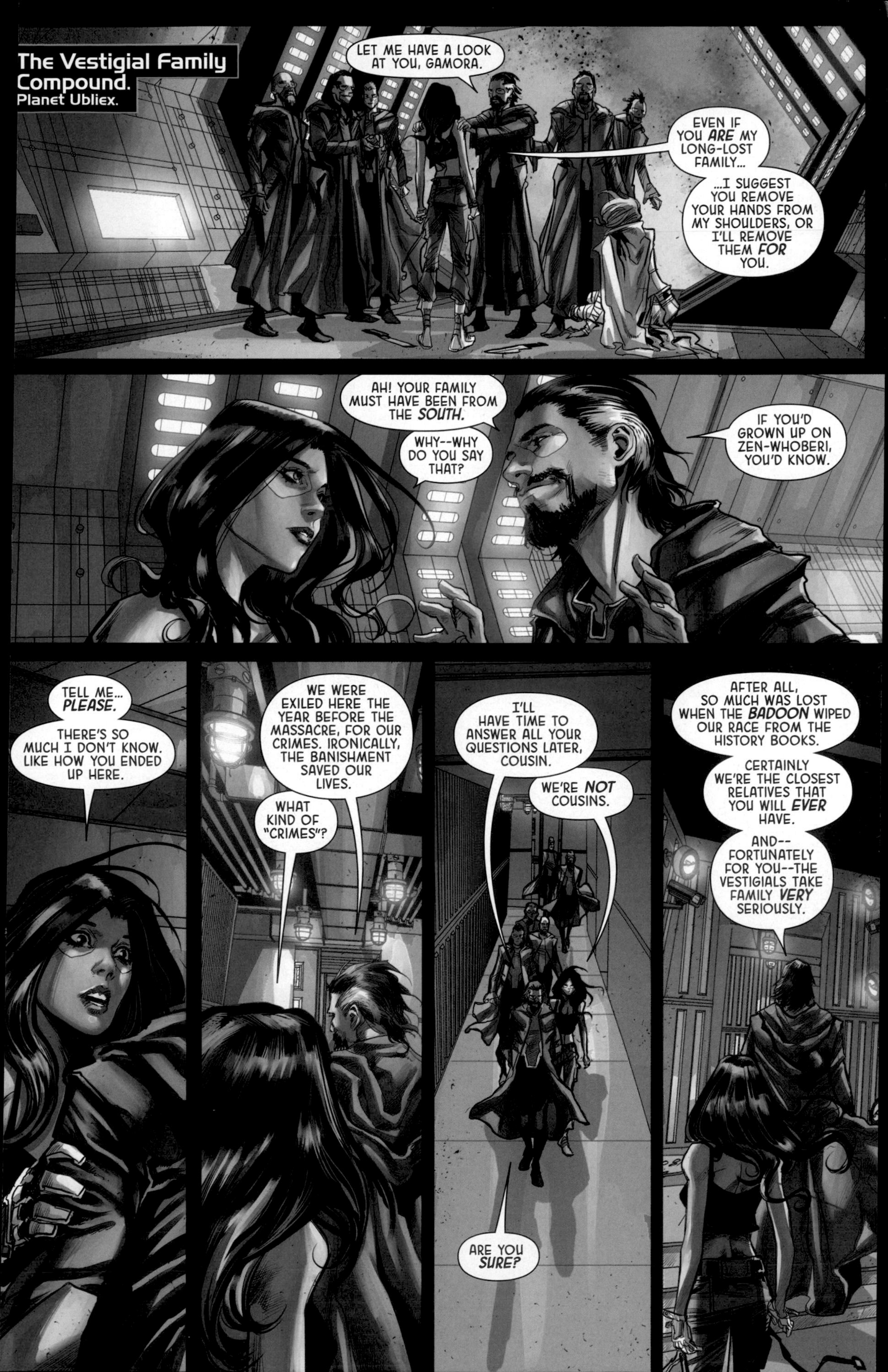

The Vestigial Family Compound.
Planet Ubliex.
LET ME HAVE A LOOK AT YOU, GAMORA.
EVEN IF YOU ARE MY LONG-LOST FAMILY...
...I SUGGEST YOU REMOVE YOUR HANDS FROM MY SHOULDERS, OR I'LL REMOVE THEM FOR YOU.
AH! YOUR FAMILY MUST HAVE BEEN FROM THE SOUTH.
WHY--WHY DO YOU SAY THAT?
IF YOU'D GROWN UP ON ZEN-WHOBERI, YOU'D KNOW.
TELL ME... PLEASE.
THERE'S SO MUCH I DON'T KNOW. LIKE HOW YOU ENDED UP HERE.
WE WERE EXILED HERE THE YEAR BEFORE THE MASSACRE, FOR OUR CRIMES. IRONICALLY, THE BANISHMENT SAVED OUR LIVES.
WHAT KIND OF "CRIMES"?
I'LL HAVE TIME TO ANSWER ALL YOUR QUESTIONS LATER, COUSIN.
WE'RE NOT COUSINS.
ARE YOU SURE?
AFTER ALL, SO MUCH WAS LOST WHEN THE BADOON WIPED OUR RACE FROM THE HISTORY BOOKS.
CERTAINLY WE'RE THE CLOSEST RELATIVES THAT YOU WILL EVER HAVE.
AND--FORTUNATELY FOR YOU--THE VESTIGIALS TAKE FAMILY VERY SERIOUSLY.

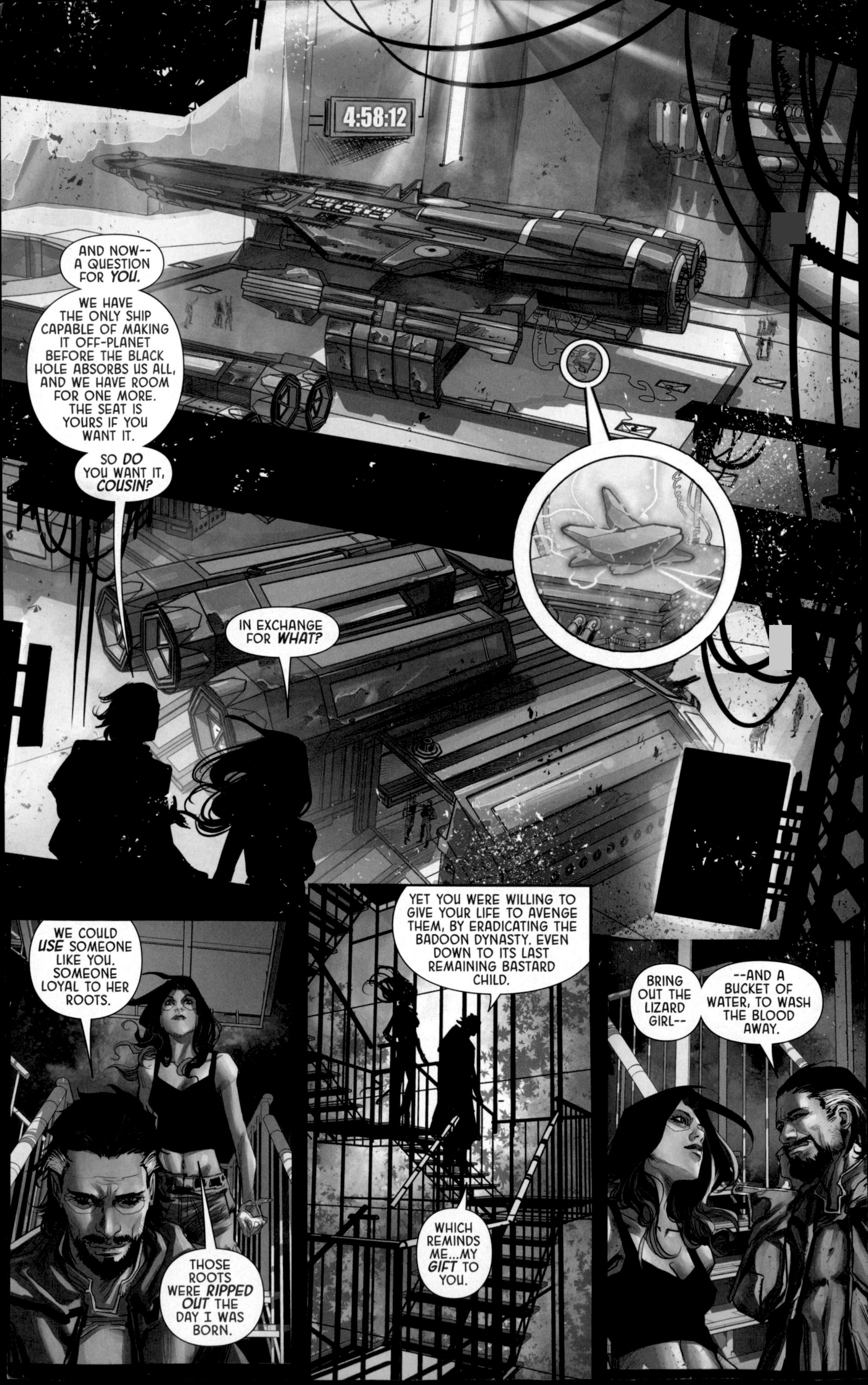
4:58:12
AND NOW-- A QUESTION FOR YOU.
WE HAVE THE ONLY SHIP CAPABLE OF MAKING IT OFF-PLANET BEFORE THE BLACK HOLE ABSORBS US ALL, AND WE HAVE ROOM FOR ONE MORE. THE SEAT IS YOURS IF YOU WANT IT.
SO DO YOU WANT IT, COUSIN?
IN EXCHANGE FOR WHAT?
WE COULD USE SOMEONE LIKE YOU. SOMEONE LOYAL TO HER ROOTS.
THOSE ROOTS WERE RIPPED OUT THE DAY I WAS BORN.
YET YOU WERE WILLING TO GIVE YOUR LIFE TO AVENGE THEM, BY ERADICATING THE BADOON DYNASTY. EVEN DOWN TO ITS LAST REMAINING BASTARD CHILD.
WHICH REMINDS ME...MY GIFT TO YOU.
BRING OUT THE LIZARD GIRL--
--AND A BUCKET OF WATER, TO WASH THE BLOOD AWAY.

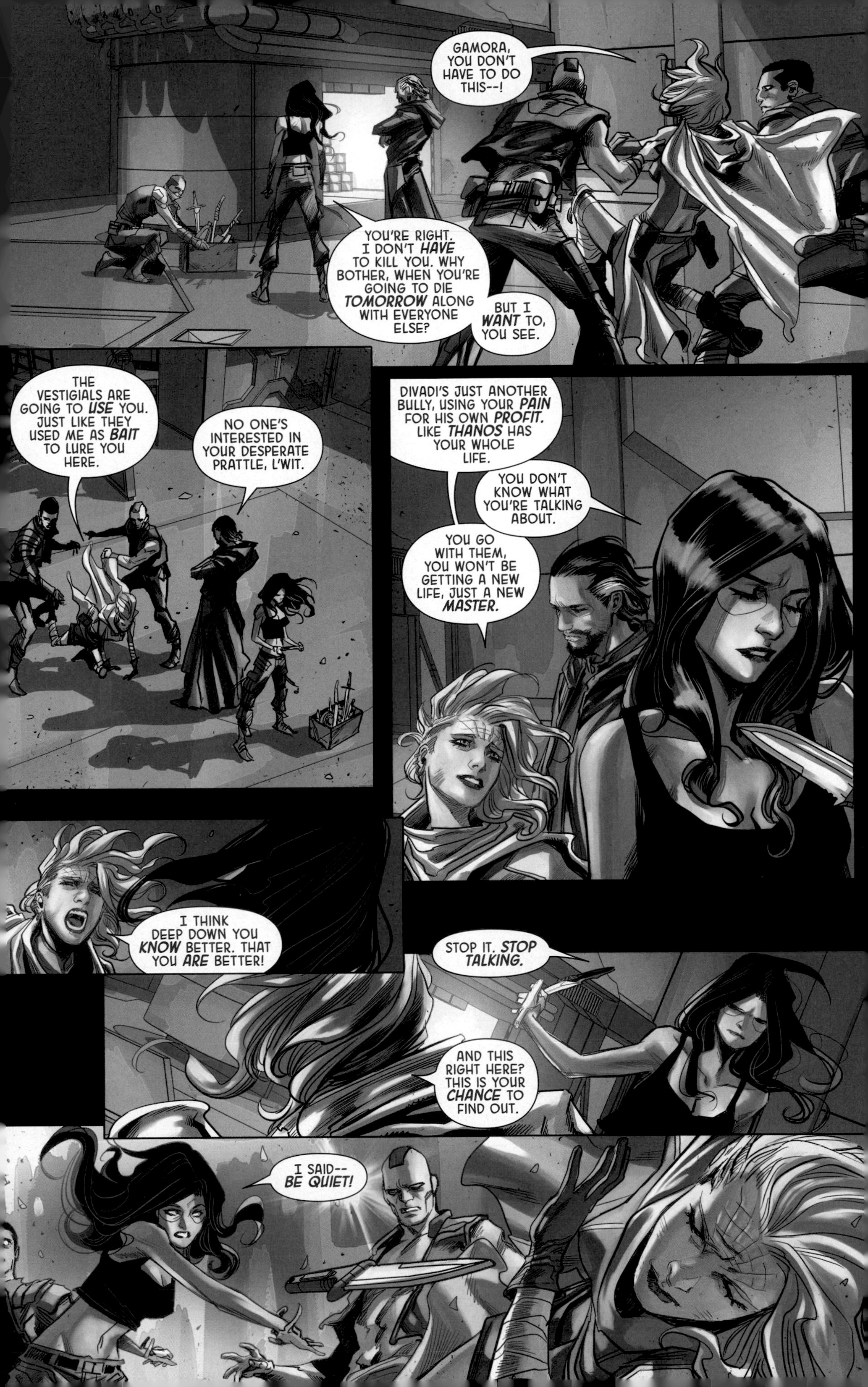
GAMORA, YOU DON'T HAVE TO DO THIS--!
YOU'RE RIGHT. I DON'T HAVE TO KILL YOU. WHY BOTHER, WHEN YOU'RE GOING TO DIE TOMORROW ALONG WITH EVERYONE ELSE?
BUT I WANT TO, YOU SEE.
THE VESTIGIALS ARE GOING TO USE YOU. JUST LIKE THEY USED ME AS BAIT TO LURE YOU HERE.
NO ONE'S INTERESTED IN YOUR DESPERATE PRATTLE, L'WIT.
DIVADI'S JUST ANOTHER BULLY, USING YOUR PAIN FOR HIS OWN PROFIT. LIKE THANOS HAS YOUR WHOLE LIFE.
YOU DON'T KNOW WHAT YOU'RE TALKING ABOUT.
YOU GO WITH THEM, YOU WON'T BE GETTING A NEW LIFE, JUST A NEW MASTER.
I THINK DEEP DOWN YOU KNOW BETTER. THAT YOU ARE BETTER!
STOP IT. STOP TALKING.
AND THIS RIGHT HERE? THIS IS YOUR CHANCE TO FIND OUT.
I SAID-- BE QUIET!

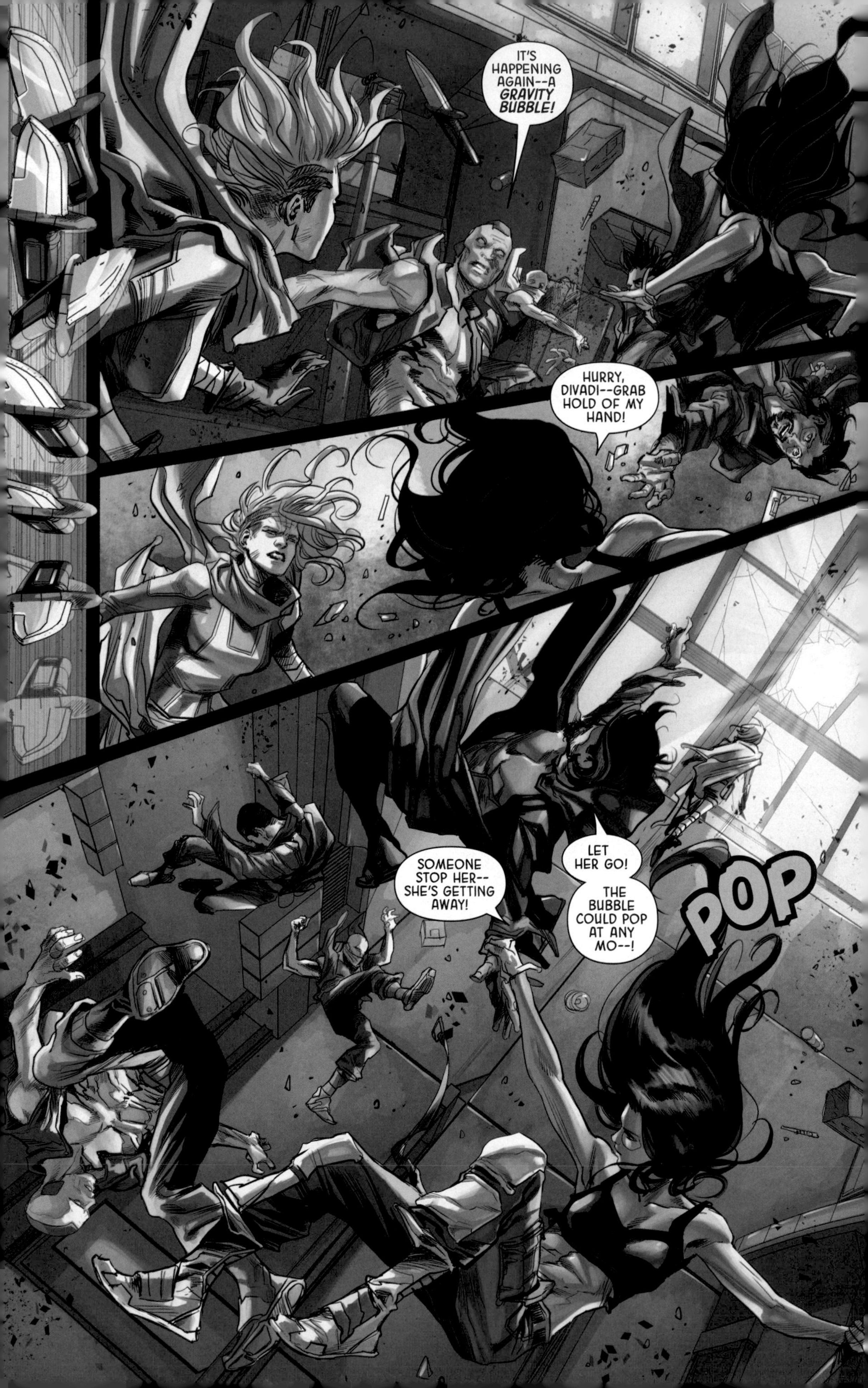

IT'S HAPPENING AGAIN--A GRAVITY BUBBLE!
HURRY, DIVADI--GRAB HOLD OF MY HAND!
SOMEONE STOP HER-- SHE'S GETTING AWAY!
LET HER GO!
THE BUBBLE COULD POP AT ANY MO--!
POP

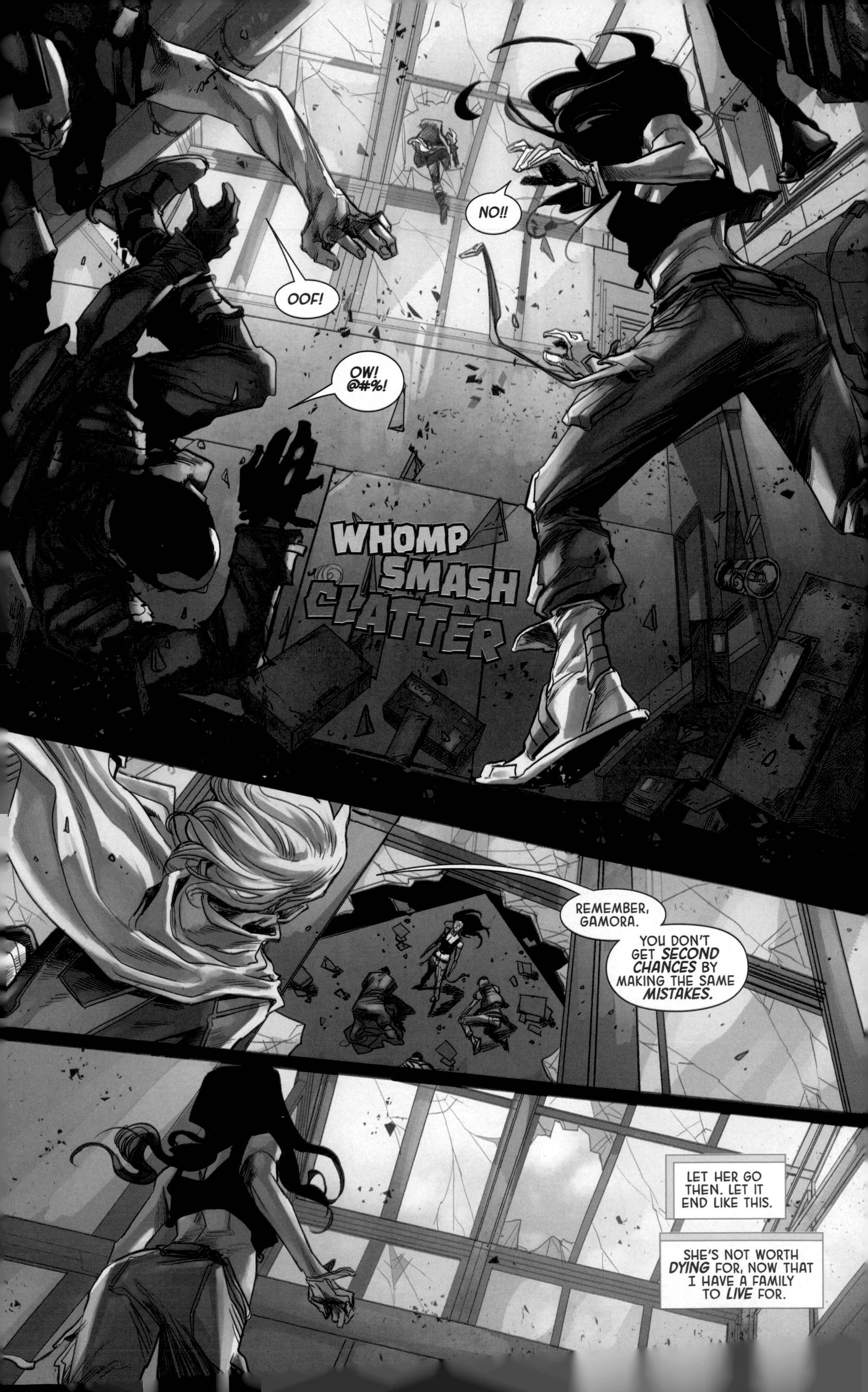
NO!!
OOF!
OW! @#%!
WHOMP
SMASH
CLATTER
REMEMBER, GAMORA.
YOU DON'T GET *SECOND CHANCES* BY MAKING THE SAME *MISTAKES.*
LET HER GO THEN. LET IT END LIKE THIS.
SHE'S NOT WORTH *DYING* FOR, NOW THAT I HAVE A FAMILY TO *LIVE* FOR.

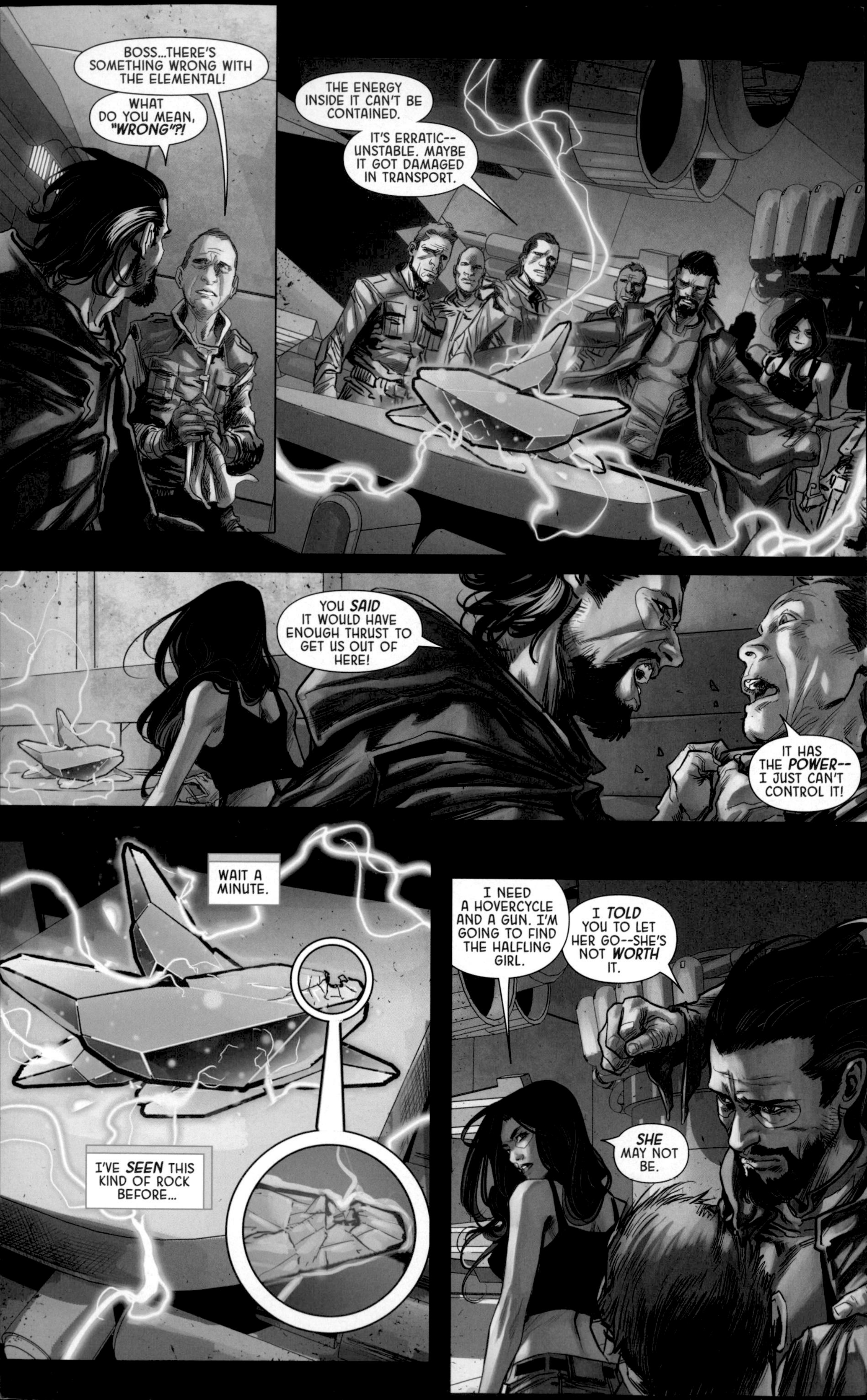
BOSS...THERE'S SOMETHING WRONG WITH THE ELEMENTAL!
WHAT DO YOU MEAN, "WRONG"?!
THE ENERGY INSIDE IT CAN'T BE CONTAINED.
IT'S ERRATIC-- UNSTABLE. MAYBE IT GOT DAMAGED IN TRANSPORT.
YOU SAID IT WOULD HAVE ENOUGH THRUST TO GET US OUT OF HERE!
IT HAS THE POWER-- I JUST CAN'T CONTROL IT!
WAIT A MINUTE.
I'VE SEEN THIS KIND OF ROCK BEFORE...
I NEED A HOVERCYCLE AND A GUN. I'M GOING TO FIND THE HALFLING GIRL.
I TOLD YOU TO LET HER GO--SHE'S NOT WORTH IT.
SHE MAY NOT BE.

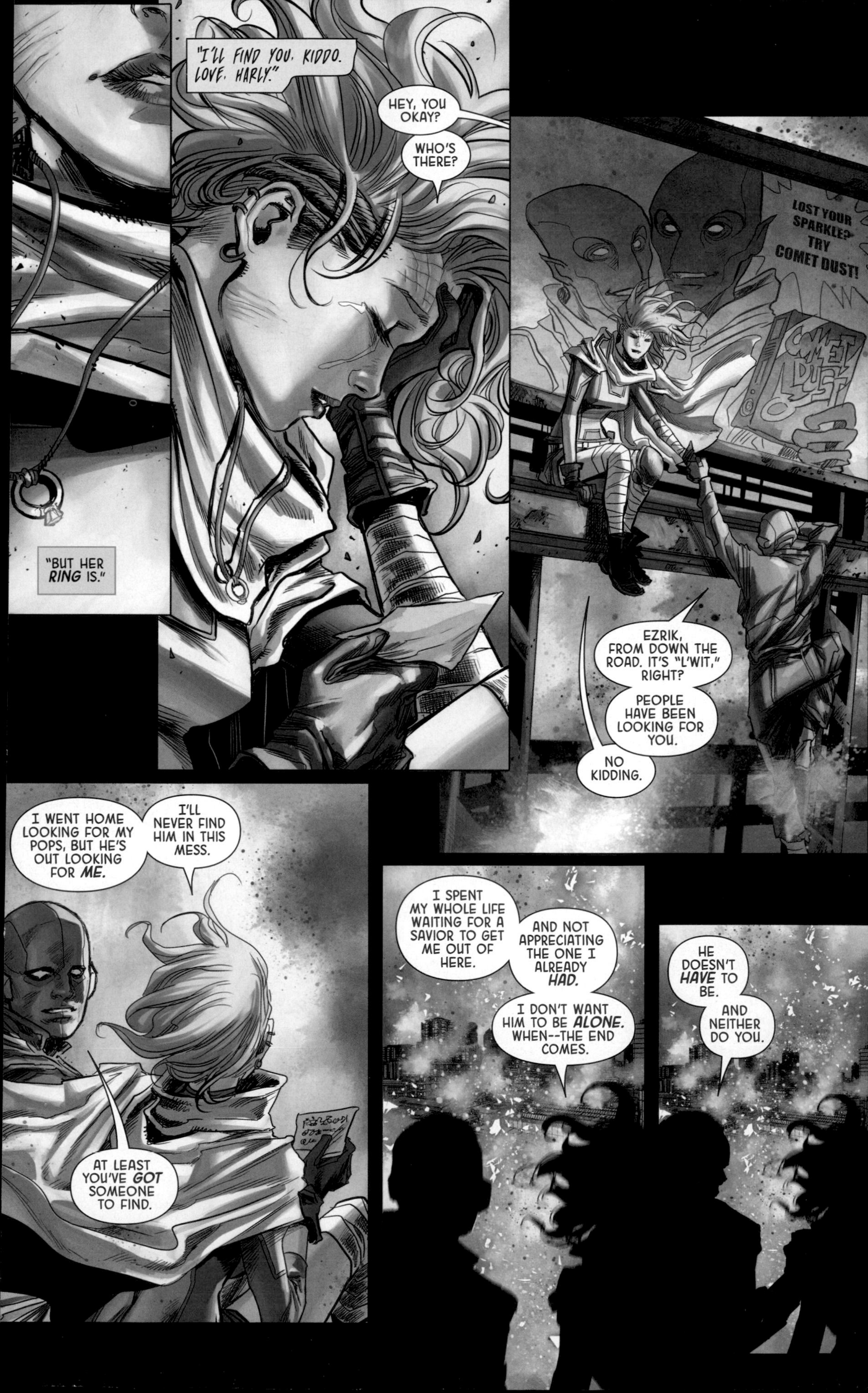
"BUT HER RING IS."
"I'LL FIND YOU, KIDDO. LOVE, HARLY."
HEY, YOU OKAY?
WHO'S THERE?
LOST YOUR SPARKLE? TRY COMET DUST!
COMET DUST
EZRIK, FROM DOWN THE ROAD. IT'S "L'WIT," RIGHT?
PEOPLE HAVE BEEN LOOKING FOR YOU.
NO KIDDING.
I WENT HOME LOOKING FOR MY POPS, BUT HE'S OUT LOOKING FOR ME.
I'LL NEVER FIND HIM IN THIS MESS.
AT LEAST YOU'VE GOT SOMEONE TO FIND.
I SPENT MY WHOLE LIFE WAITING FOR A SAVIOR TO GET ME OUT OF HERE.
AND NOT APPRECIATING THE ONE I ALREADY HAD.
I DON'T WANT HIM TO BE ALONE. WHEN--THE END COMES.
HE DOESN'T HAVE TO BE.
AND NEITHER DO YOU.

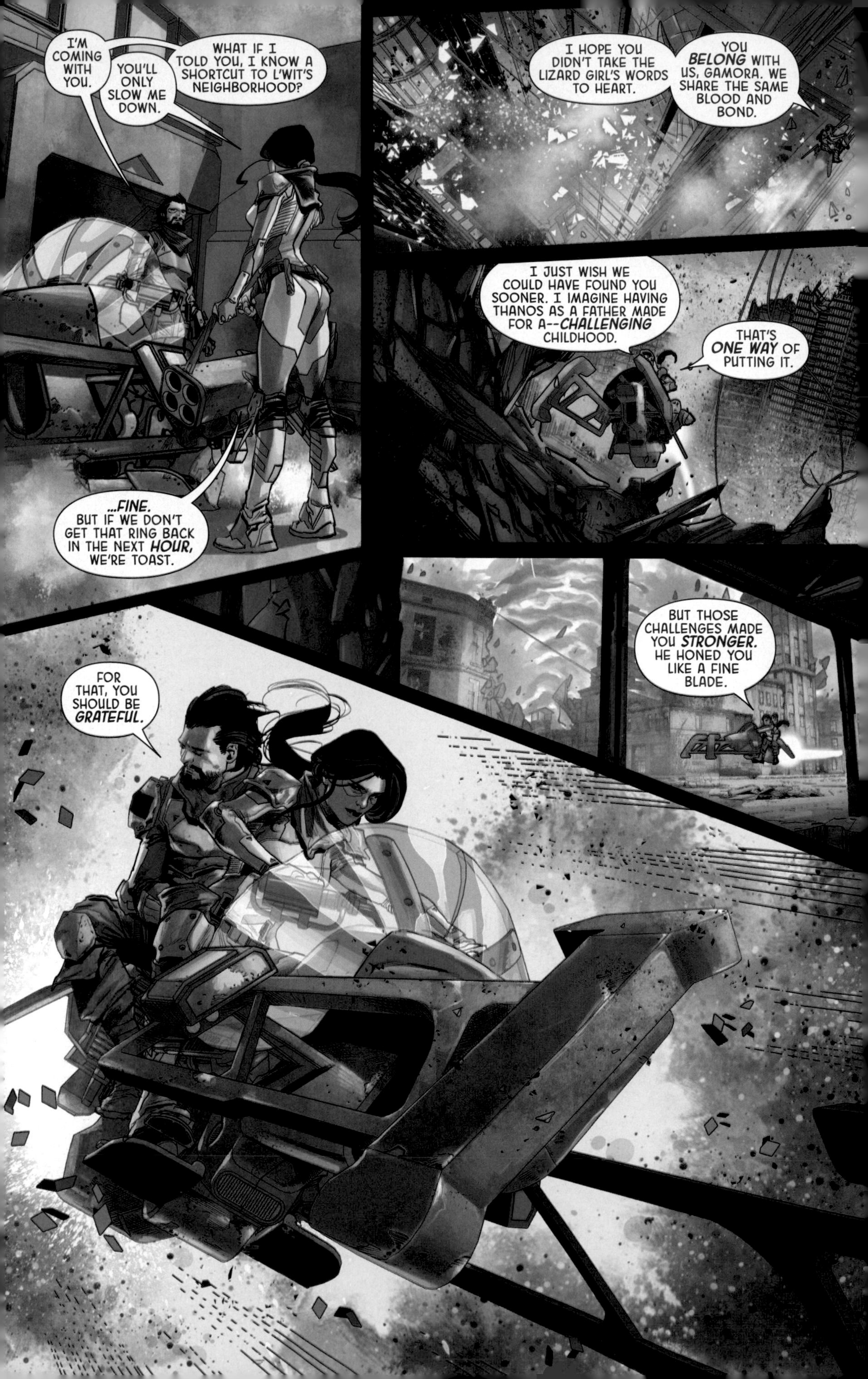
I'M COMING WITH YOU.
YOU'LL ONLY SLOW ME DOWN.
WHAT IF I TOLD YOU, I KNOW A SHORTCUT TO L'WIT'S NEIGHBORHOOD?
...FINE. BUT IF WE DON'T GET THAT RING BACK IN THE NEXT HOUR, WE'RE TOAST.
I HOPE YOU DIDN'T TAKE THE LIZARD GIRL'S WORDS TO HEART.
YOU BELONG WITH US, GAMORA. WE SHARE THE SAME BLOOD AND BOND.
I JUST WISH WE COULD HAVE FOUND YOU SOONER. I IMAGINE HAVING THANOS AS A FATHER MADE FOR A--CHALLENGING CHILDHOOD.
THAT'S ONE WAY OF PUTTING IT.
BUT THOSE CHALLENGES MADE YOU STRONGER. HE HONED YOU LIKE A FINE BLADE.
FOR THAT, YOU SHOULD BE GRATEFUL.

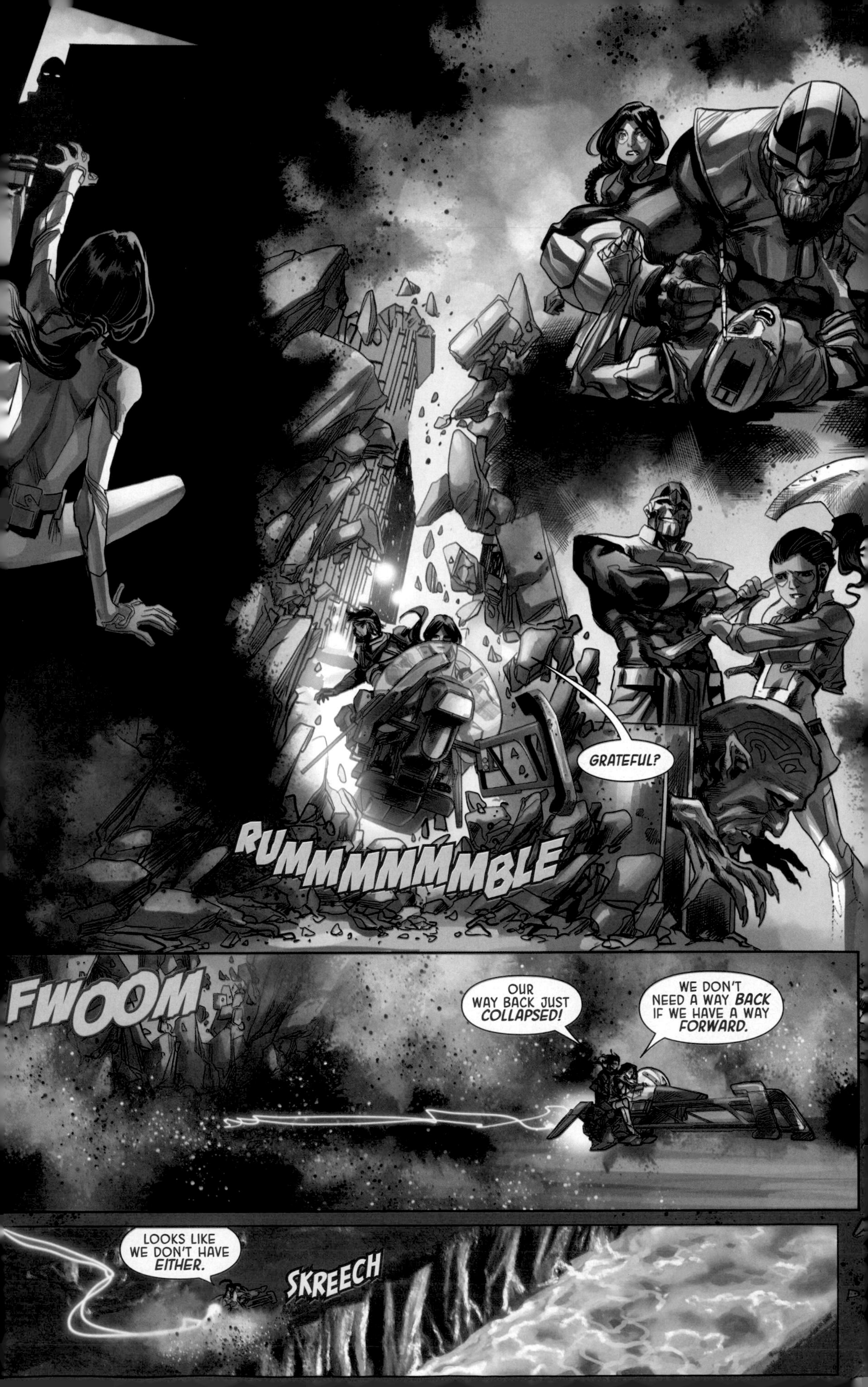
GRATEFUL?
RUMMMMMMMBLE
FWOOM
OUR WAY BACK JUST COLLAPSED!
WE DON'T NEED A WAY BACK IF WE HAVE A WAY FORWARD.
LOOKS LIKE WE DON'T HAVE EITHER.
SKREECH

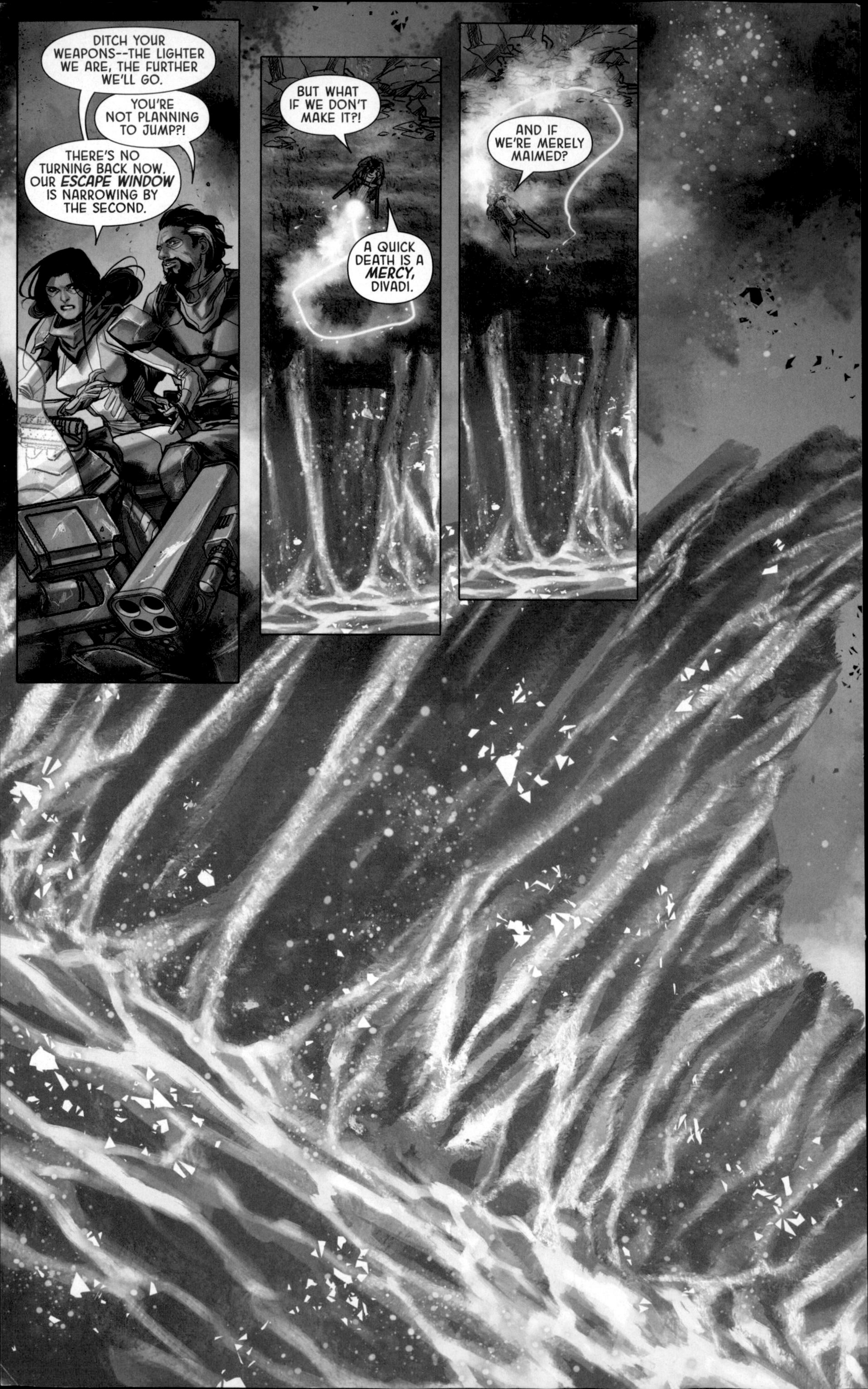
DITCH YOUR WEAPONS--THE LIGHTER WE ARE, THE FURTHER WE'LL GO.
YOU'RE NOT PLANNING TO JUMP?!
THERE'S NO TURNING BACK NOW. OUR *ESCAPE WINDOW* IS NARROWING BY THE SECOND.
BUT WHAT IF WE DON'T MAKE IT?!
A QUICK DEATH IS A *MERCY,* DIVADI.
AND IF WE'RE MERELY MAIMED?

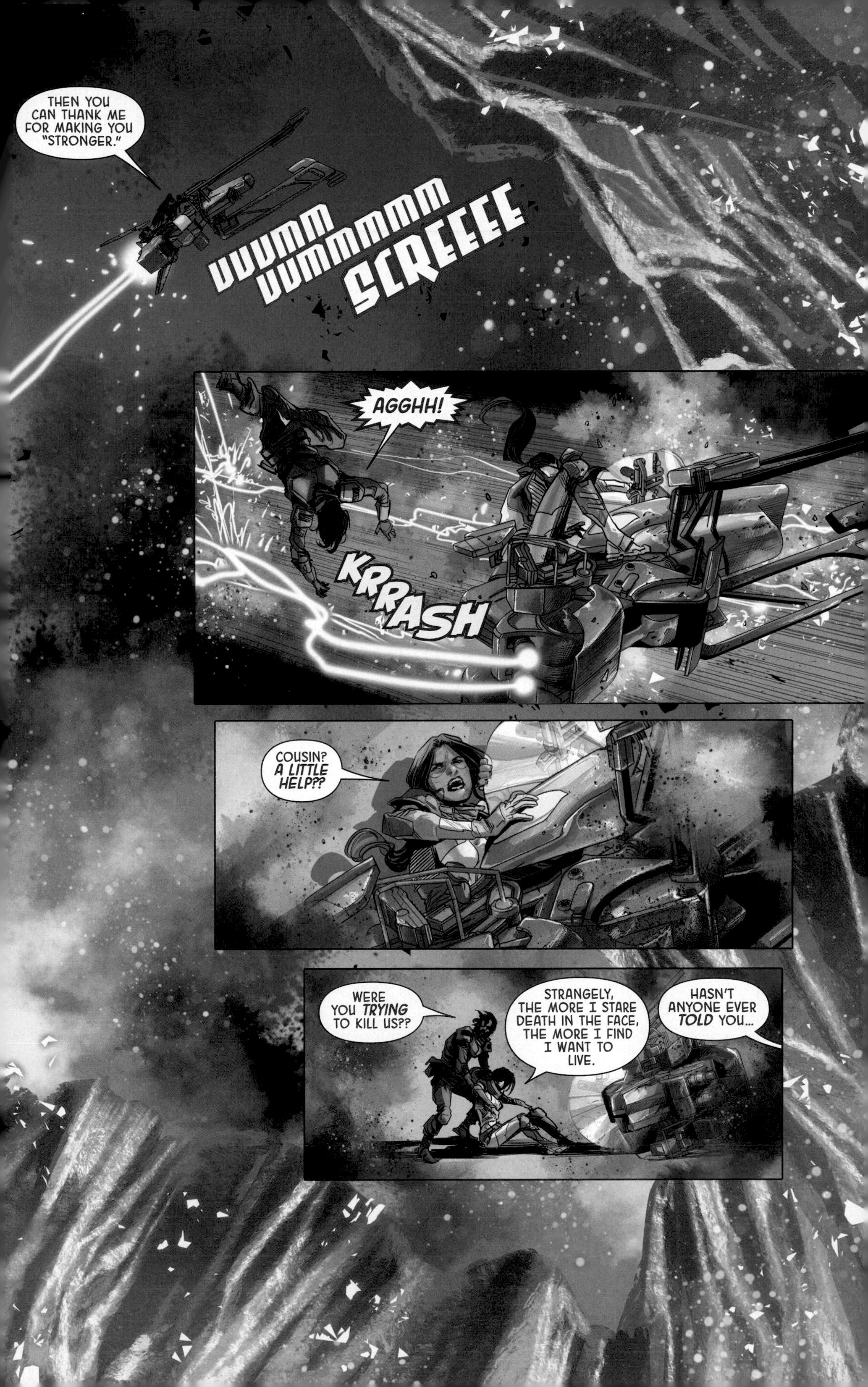
THEN YOU CAN THANK ME FOR MAKING YOU "STRONGER."
VVVMM VVMMMMM SCREEEE
AGGHH!
KRRASH
COUSIN? A LITTLE HELP??
WERE YOU TRYING TO KILL US??
STRANGELY, THE MORE I STARE DEATH IN THE FACE, THE MORE I FIND I WANT TO LIVE.
HASN'T ANYONE EVER TOLD YOU...

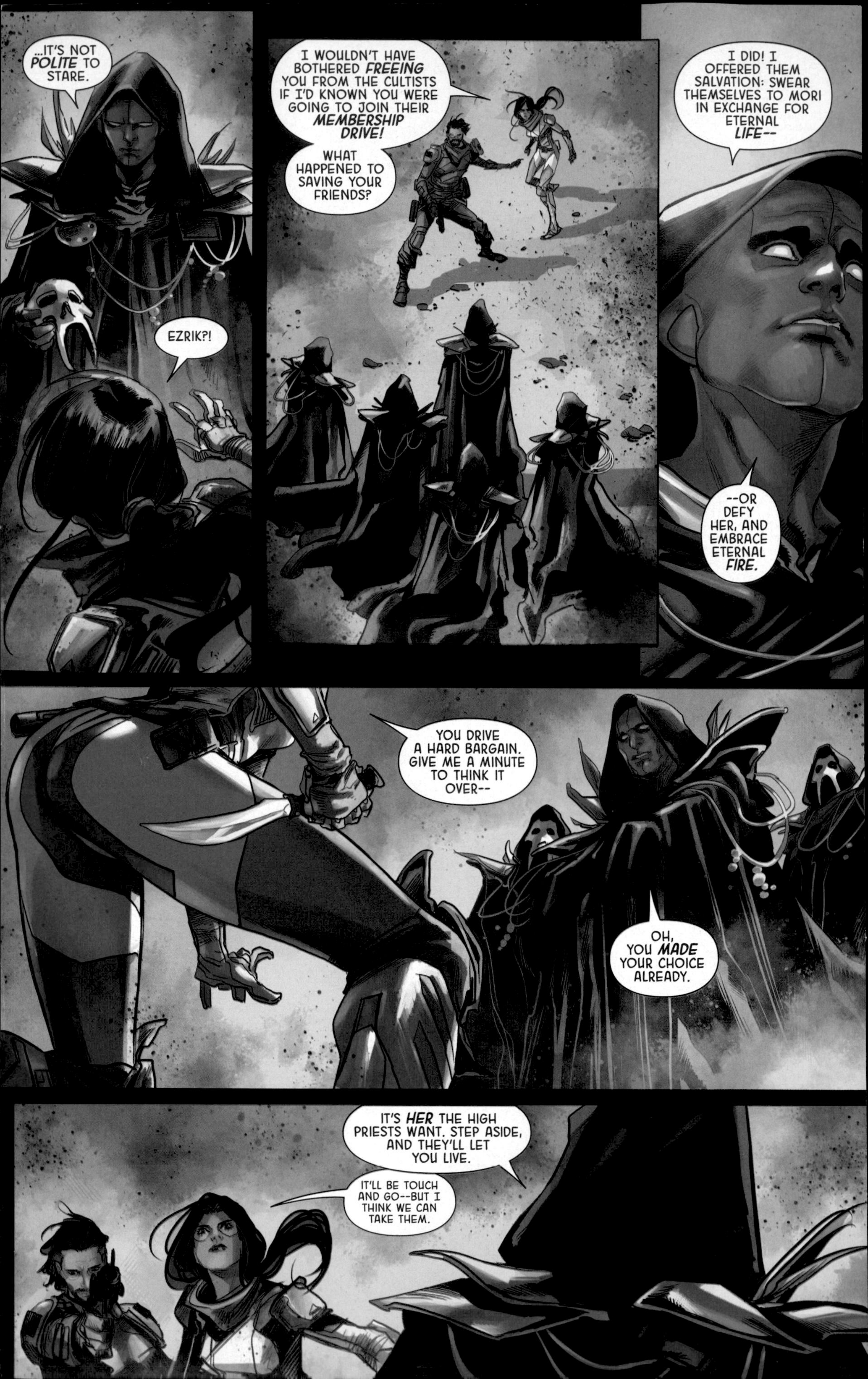
...IT'S NOT POLITE TO STARE.
EZRIK?!
I WOULDN'T HAVE BOTHERED FREEING YOU FROM THE CULTISTS IF I'D KNOWN YOU WERE GOING TO JOIN THEIR MEMBERSHIP DRIVE!
WHAT HAPPENED TO SAVING YOUR FRIENDS?
I DID! I OFFERED THEM SALVATION: SWEAR THEMSELVES TO MORI IN EXCHANGE FOR ETERNAL LIFE--
--OR DEFY HER, AND EMBRACE ETERNAL FIRE.
YOU DRIVE A HARD BARGAIN. GIVE ME A MINUTE TO THINK IT OVER--
OH, YOU MADE YOUR CHOICE ALREADY.
IT'S HER THE HIGH PRIESTS WANT. STEP ASIDE, AND THEY'LL LET YOU LIVE.
IT'LL BE TOUCH AND GO--BUT I THINK WE CAN TAKE THEM.

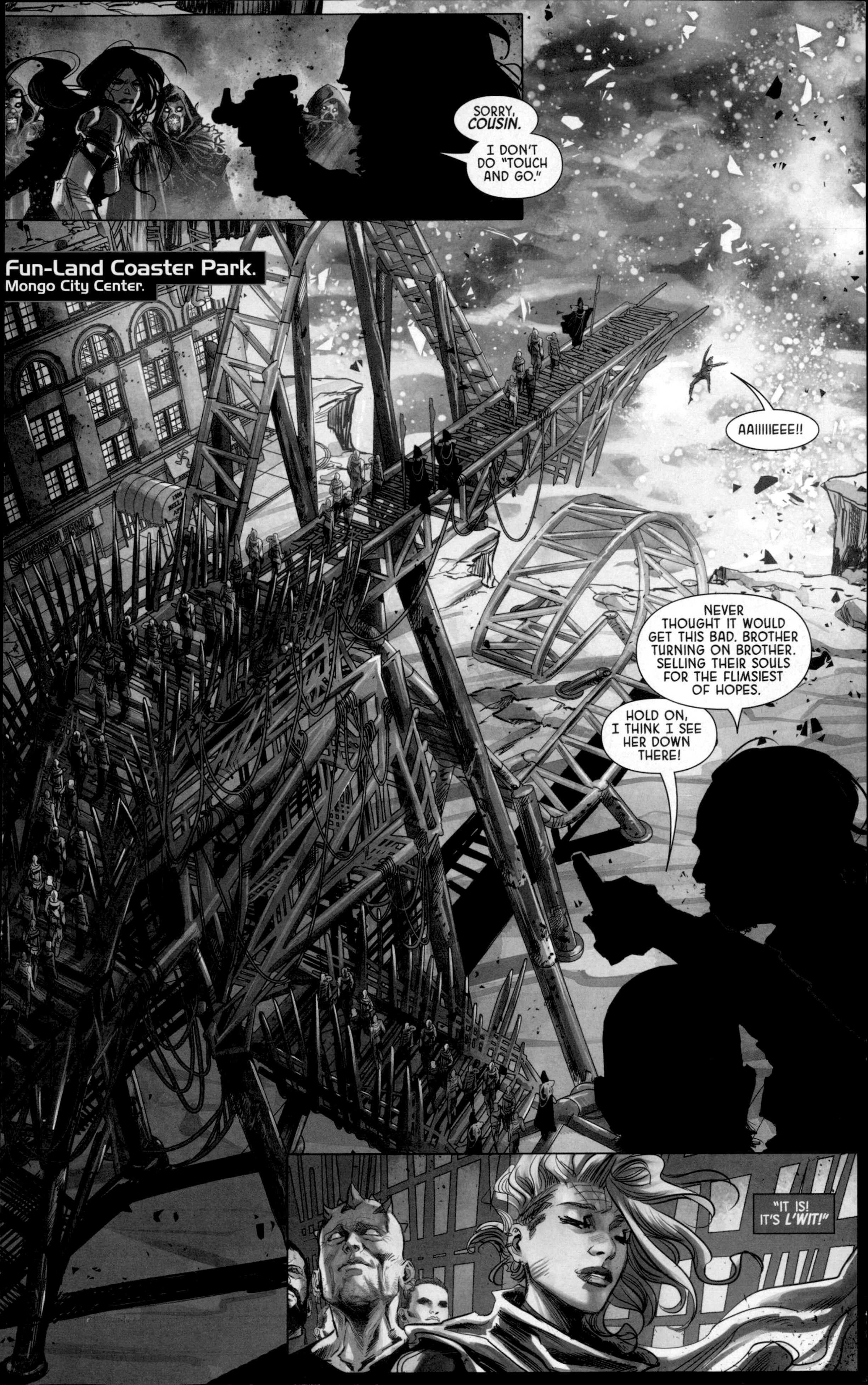
SORRY, COUSIN.
I DON'T DO "TOUCH AND GO."
Fun-Land Coaster Park.
Mongo City Center.
AAIIIIIEEE!!
NEVER THOUGHT IT WOULD GET THIS BAD. BROTHER TURNING ON BROTHER. SELLING THEIR SOULS FOR THE FLIMSIEST OF HOPES.
HOLD ON, I THINK I SEE HER DOWN THERE!
"IT IS! IT'S L'WIT!"

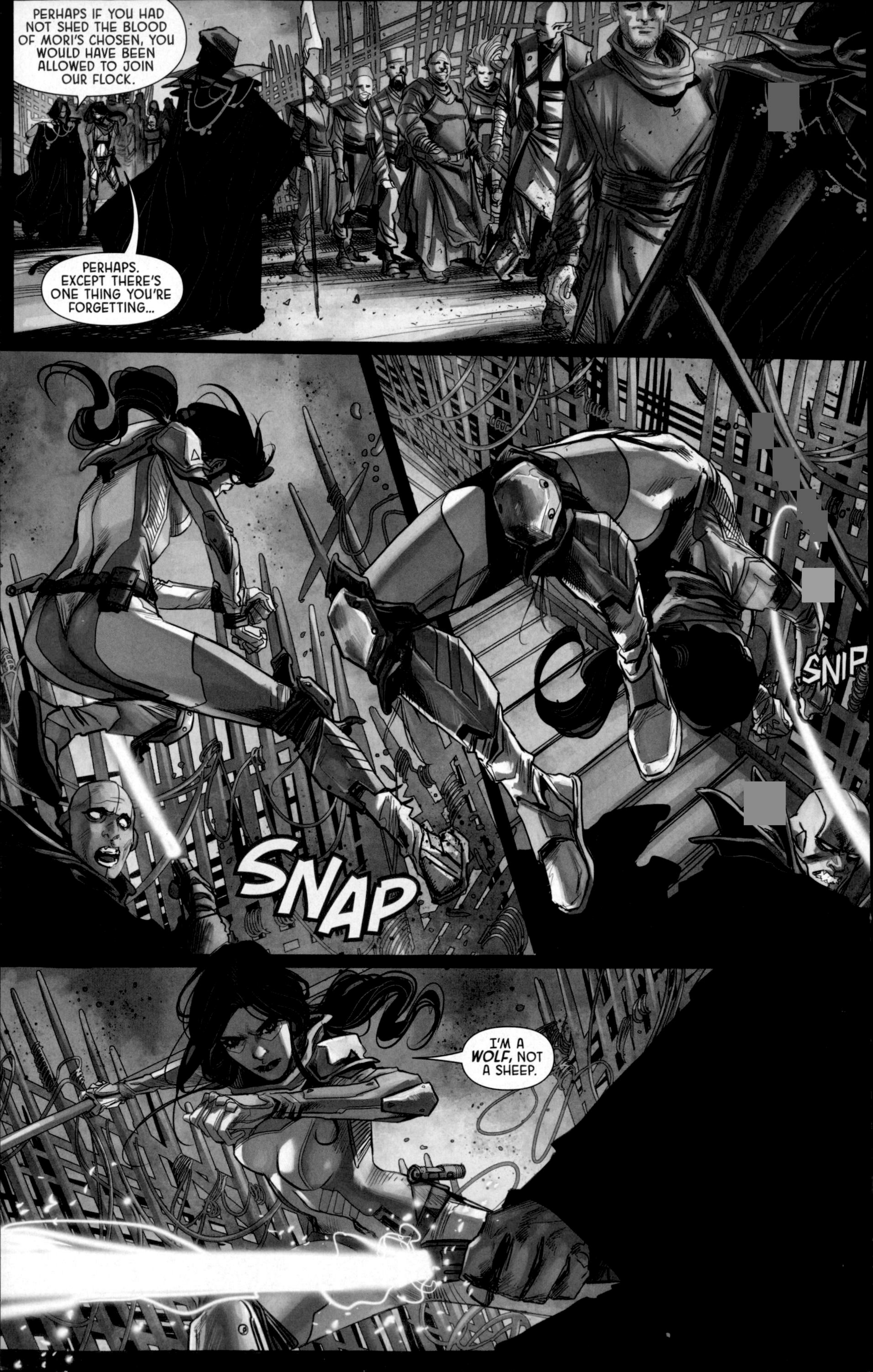
PERHAPS IF YOU HAD NOT SHED THE BLOOD OF MORI'S CHOSEN, YOU WOULD HAVE BEEN ALLOWED TO JOIN OUR FLOCK.
PERHAPS. EXCEPT THERE'S ONE THING YOU'RE FORGETTING...
SNAP
SNIP
I'M A *WOLF*, NOT A SHEEP.

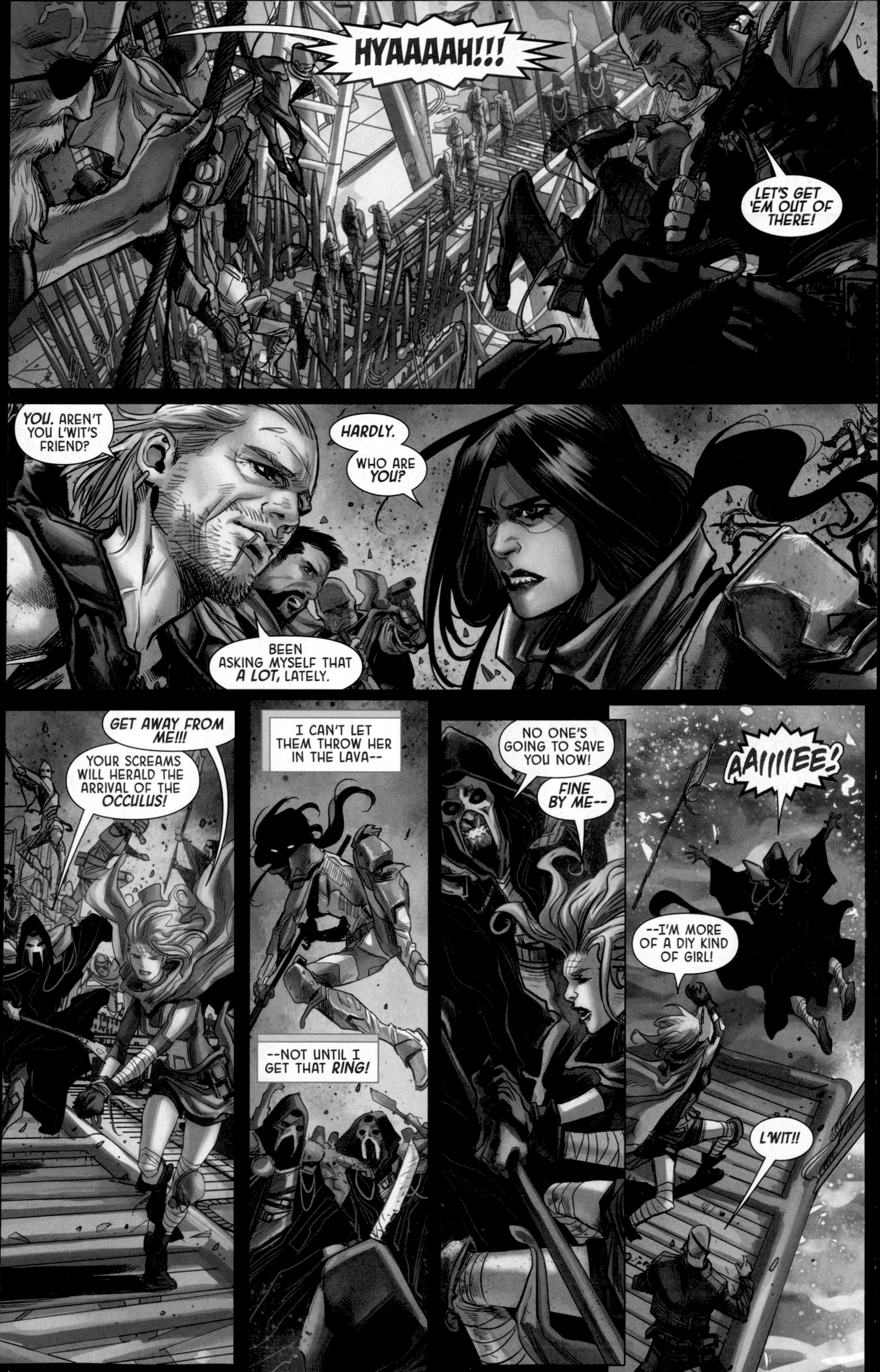
HYAAAAH!!!
LET'S GET 'EM OUT OF THERE!
YOU. AREN'T YOU L'WIT'S FRIEND?
HARDLY.
WHO ARE YOU?
BEEN ASKING MYSELF THAT A LOT, LATELY.
GET AWAY FROM ME!!!
YOUR SCREAMS WILL HERALD THE ARRIVAL OF THE OCCULUS!
I CAN'T LET THEM THROW HER IN THE LAVA--
--NOT UNTIL I GET THAT RING!
NO ONE'S GOING TO SAVE YOU NOW!
FINE BY ME--
AAIIIIEE!
--I'M MORE OF A DIY KIND OF GIRL!
L'WIT!!

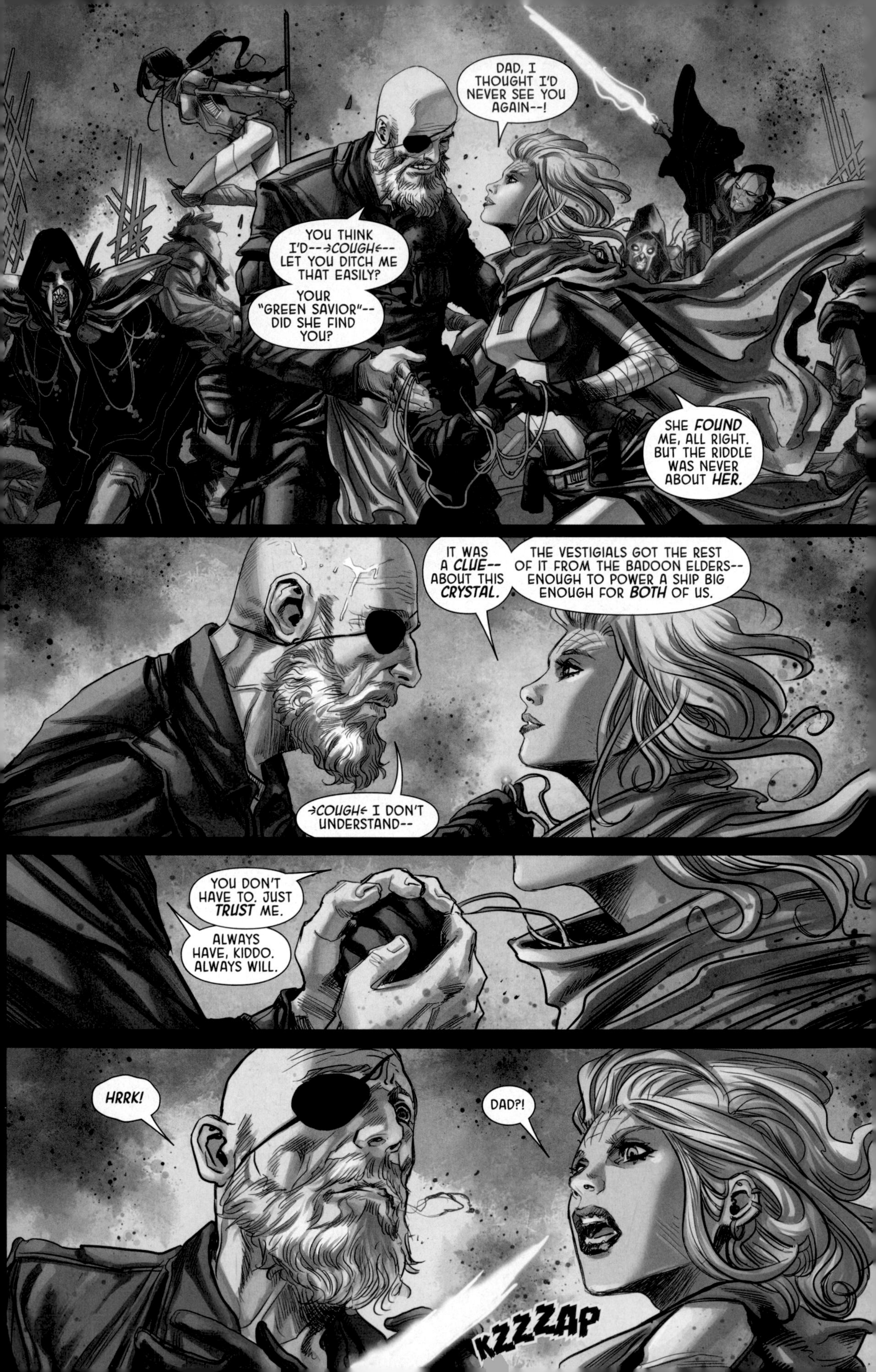
DAD, I THOUGHT I'D NEVER SEE YOU AGAIN--!
YOU THINK I'D-- ≯COUGH≮-- LET YOU DITCH ME THAT EASILY?
YOUR "GREEN SAVIOR"-- DID SHE FIND YOU?
SHE *FOUND* ME, ALL RIGHT. BUT THE RIDDLE WAS NEVER ABOUT *HER.*
IT WAS A *CLUE*-- ABOUT THIS *CRYSTAL.*
THE VESTIGIALS GOT THE REST OF IT FROM THE BADOON ELDERS-- ENOUGH TO POWER A SHIP BIG ENOUGH FOR *BOTH* OF US.
≯COUGH≮ I DON'T UNDERSTAND--
YOU DON'T HAVE TO. JUST *TRUST* ME.
ALWAYS HAVE, KIDDO. ALWAYS WILL.
HRRK!
DAD?!
KZZZAP

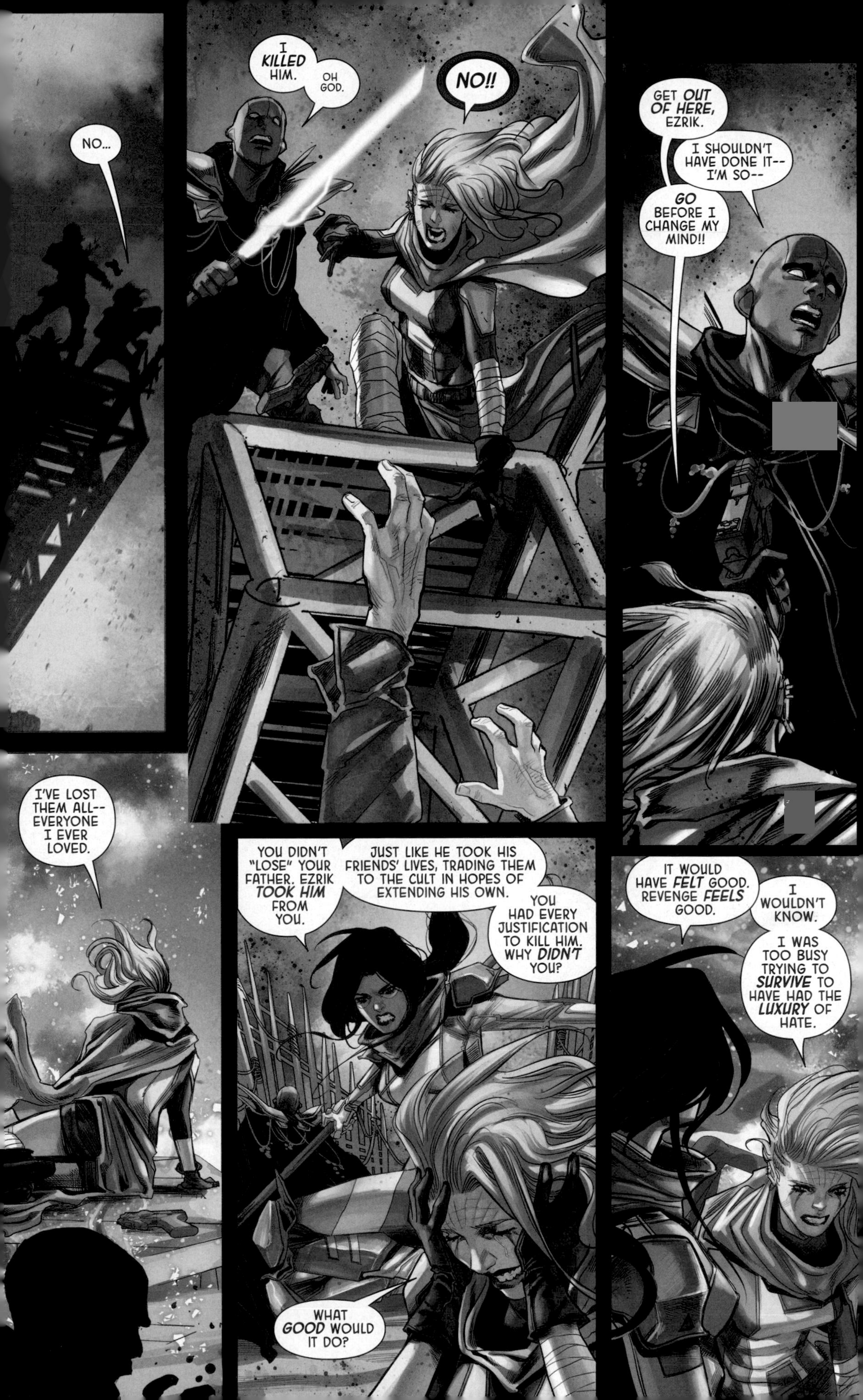
NO...
I KILLED HIM.
OH GOD.
NO!!
GET OUT OF HERE, EZRIK.
I SHOULDN'T HAVE DONE IT-- I'M SO--
GO BEFORE I CHANGE MY MIND!!
I'VE LOST THEM ALL-- EVERYONE I EVER LOVED.
YOU DIDN'T "LOSE" YOUR FATHER. EZRIK TOOK HIM FROM YOU.
JUST LIKE HE TOOK HIS FRIENDS' LIVES, TRADING THEM TO THE CULT IN HOPES OF EXTENDING HIS OWN.
YOU HAD EVERY JUSTIFICATION TO KILL HIM. WHY DIDN'T YOU?
WHAT GOOD WOULD IT DO?
IT WOULD HAVE FELT GOOD. REVENGE FEELS GOOD.
I WOULDN'T KNOW.
I WAS TOO BUSY TRYING TO SURVIVE TO HAVE HAD THE LUXURY OF HATE.

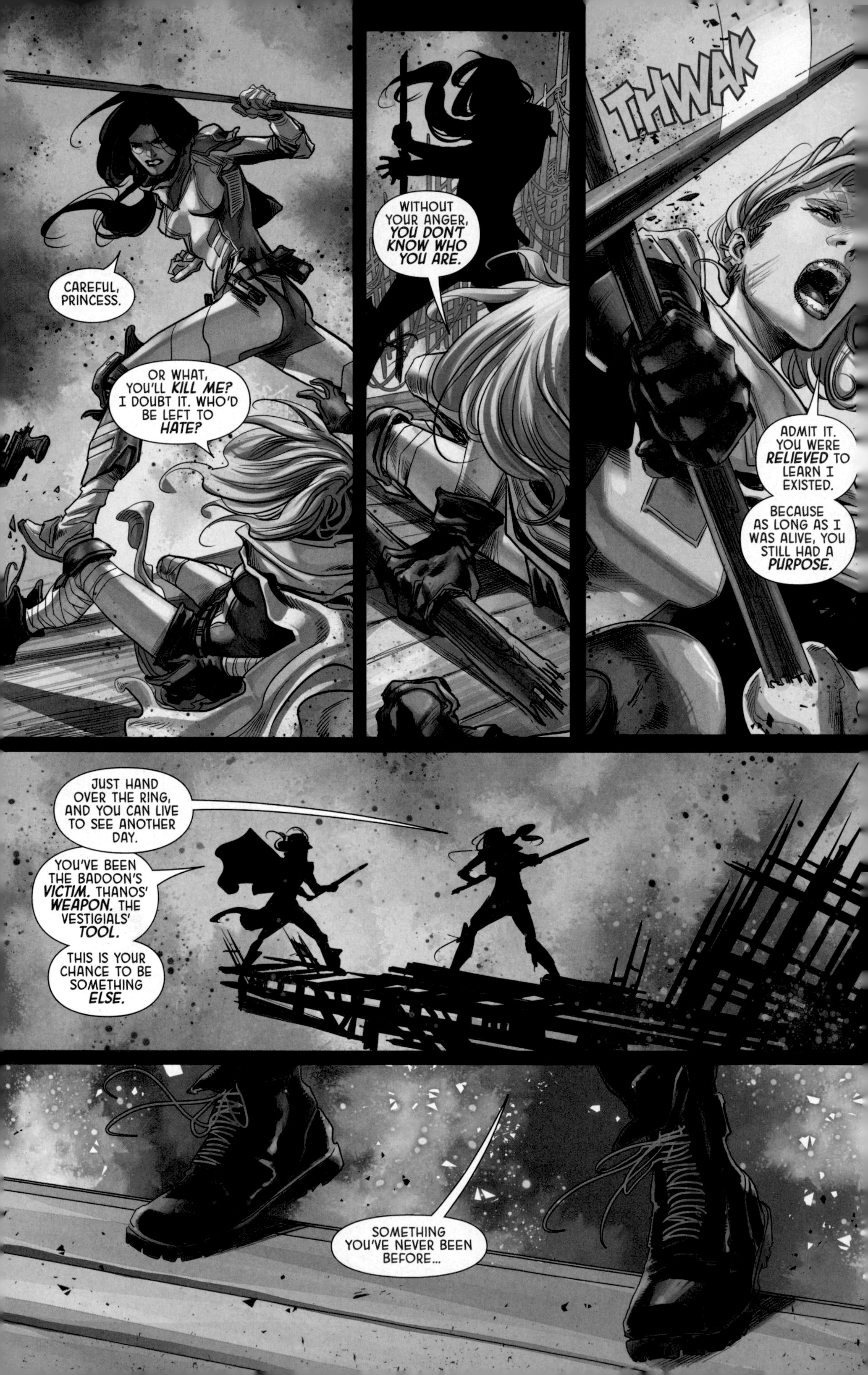
CAREFUL, PRINCESS.
OR WHAT, YOU'LL KILL ME? I DOUBT IT. WHO'D BE LEFT TO HATE?
WITHOUT YOUR ANGER, YOU DON'T KNOW WHO YOU ARE.
THWAK
ADMIT IT. YOU WERE RELIEVED TO LEARN I EXISTED.
BECAUSE AS LONG AS I WAS ALIVE, YOU STILL HAD A PURPOSE.
JUST HAND OVER THE RING, AND YOU CAN LIVE TO SEE ANOTHER DAY.
YOU'VE BEEN THE BADOON'S VICTIM. THANOS' WEAPON. THE VESTIGIALS' TOOL.
THIS IS YOUR CHANCE TO BE SOMETHING ELSE.
SOMETHING YOU'VE NEVER BEEN BEFORE...

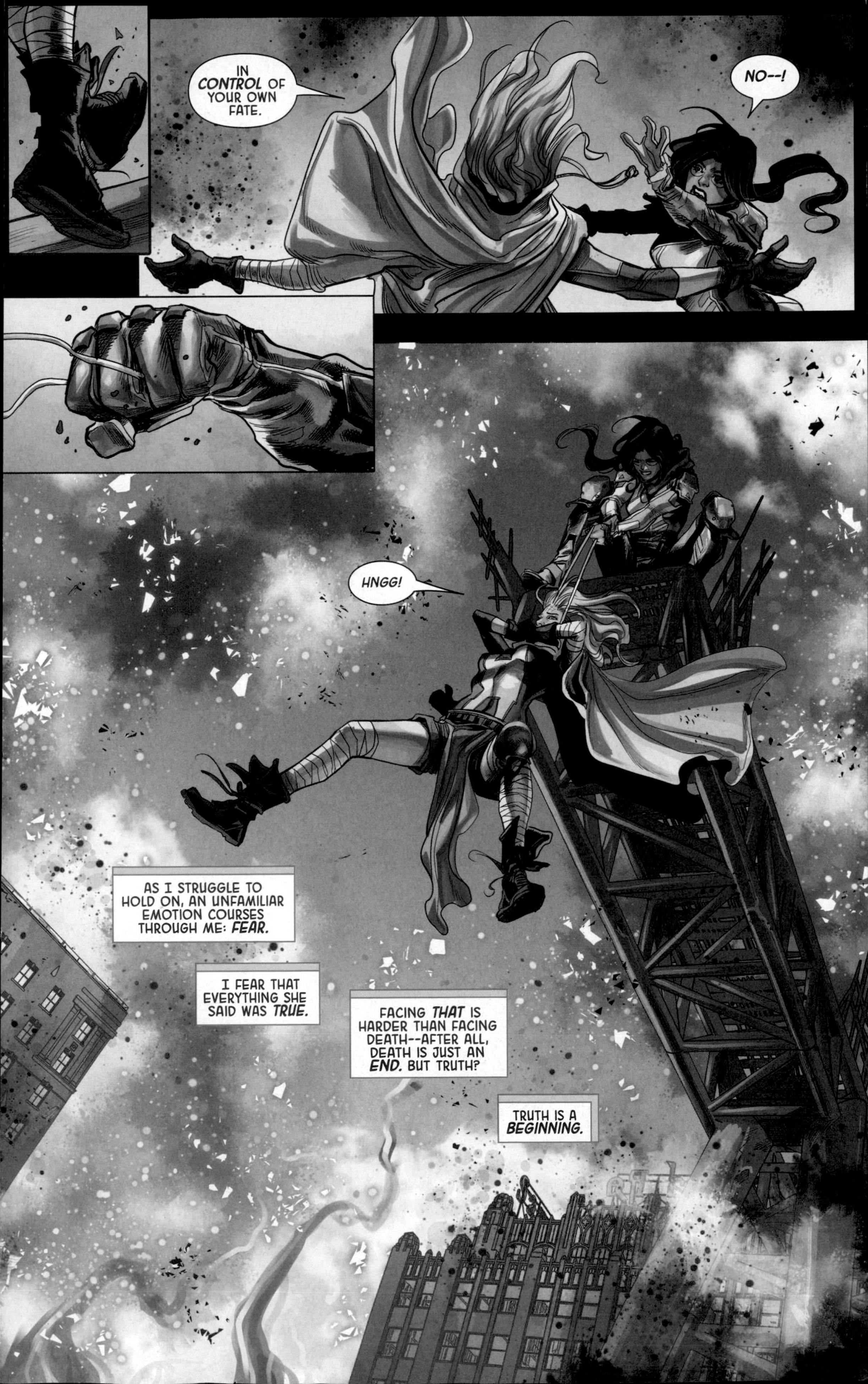
IN CONTROL OF YOUR OWN FATE.
NO--!
HNGG!
AS I STRUGGLE TO HOLD ON, AN UNFAMILIAR EMOTION COURSES THROUGH ME: FEAR.
I FEAR THAT EVERYTHING SHE SAID WAS TRUE.
FACING THAT IS HARDER THAN FACING DEATH--AFTER ALL, DEATH IS JUST AN END. BUT TRUTH?
TRUTH IS A BEGINNING.

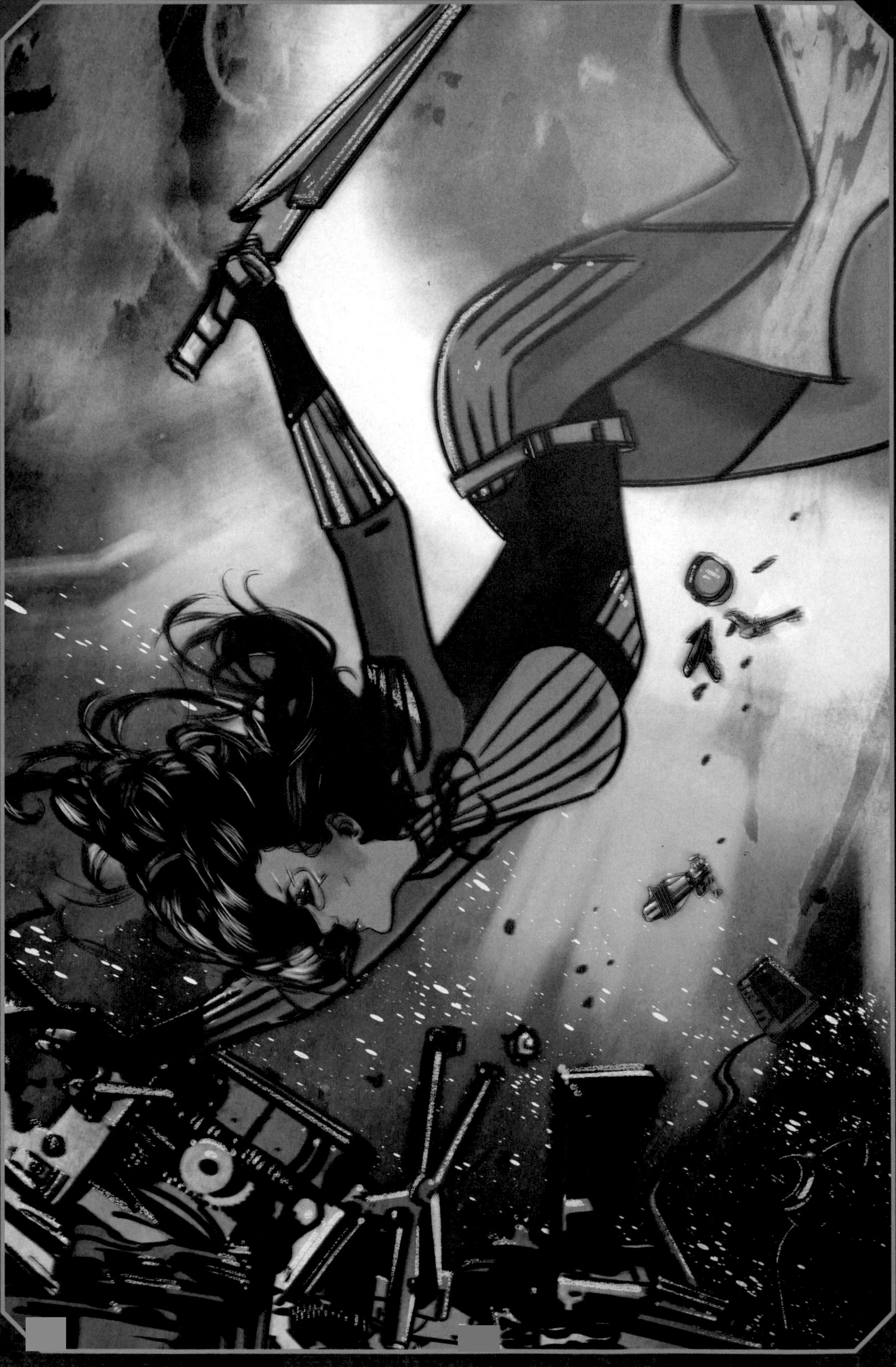

#1 VARIANT BY **TULA LOTAY**

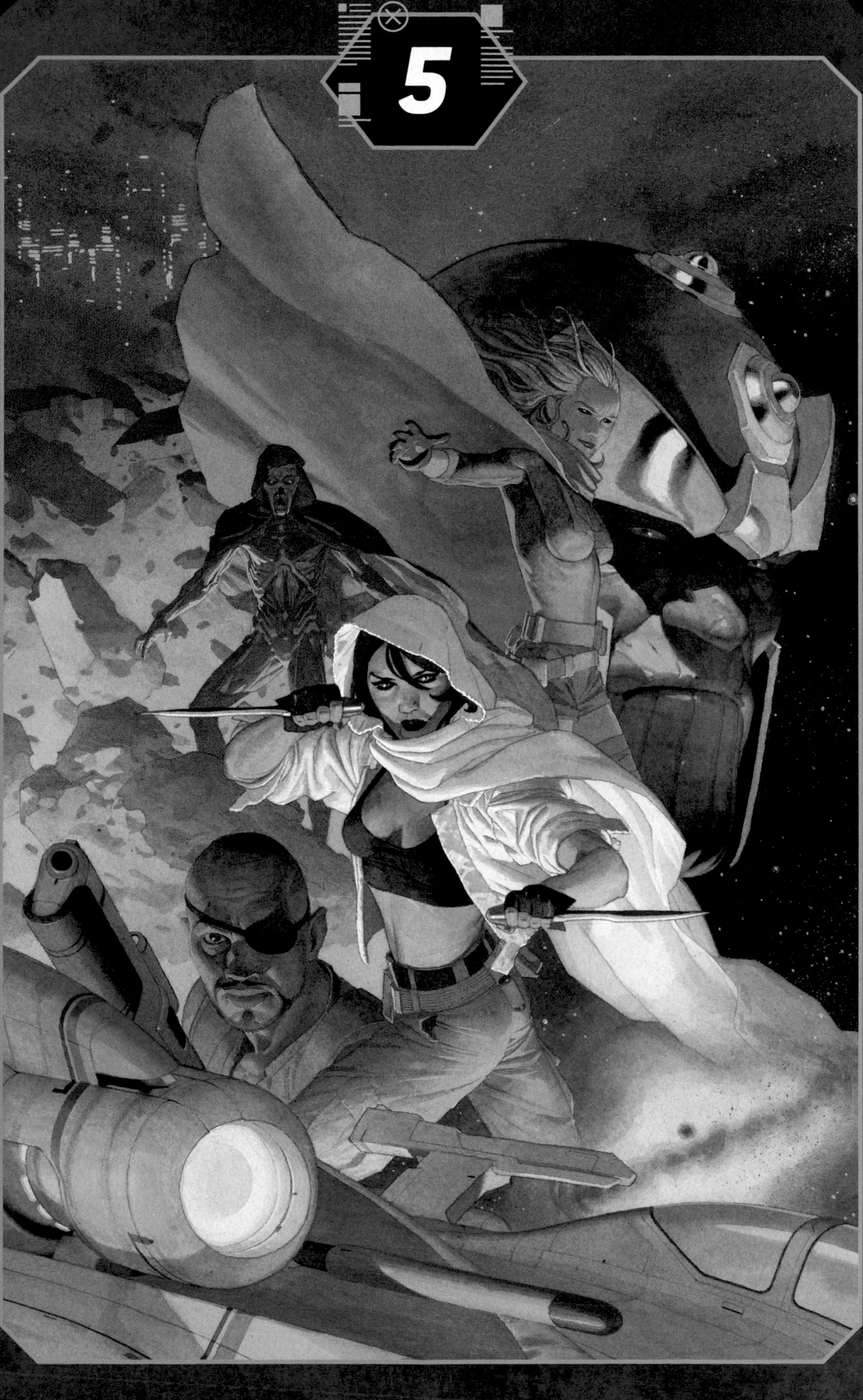
5

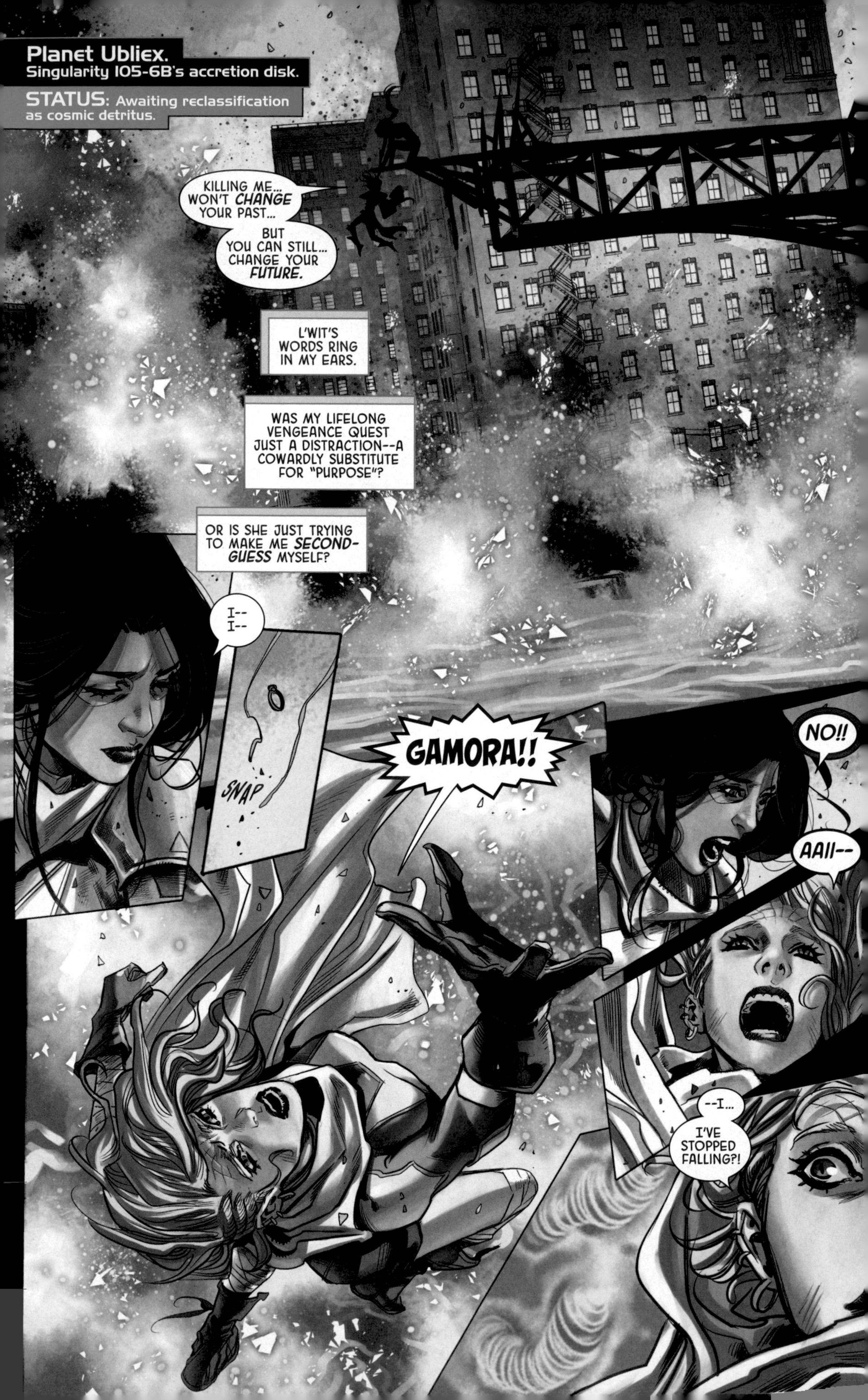
Planet Ubliex.
Singularity 105-6B's accretion disk.
STATUS: Awaiting reclassification as cosmic detritus.
KILLING ME... WON'T CHANGE YOUR PAST...
BUT YOU CAN STILL... CHANGE YOUR FUTURE.
L'WIT'S WORDS RING IN MY EARS.
WAS MY LIFELONG VENGEANCE QUEST JUST A DISTRACTION--A COWARDLY SUBSTITUTE FOR "PURPOSE"?
OR IS SHE JUST TRYING TO MAKE ME SECOND-GUESS MYSELF?
I-- I--
SNAP
GAMORA!!
NO!!
AAII--
--I... I'VE STOPPED FALLING?!

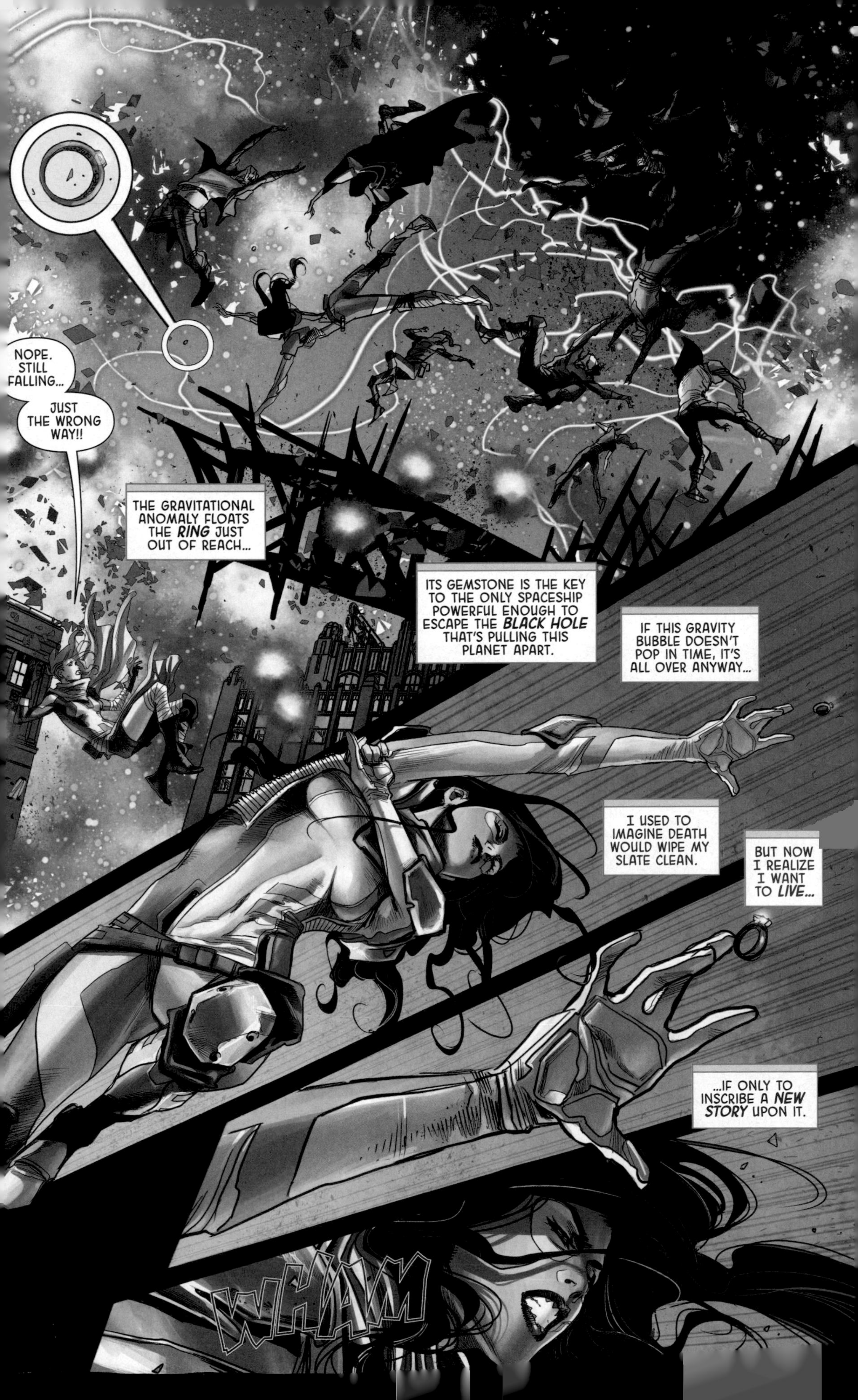
NOPE. STILL FALLING...
JUST THE WRONG WAY!!
THE GRAVITATIONAL ANOMALY FLOATS THE RING JUST OUT OF REACH...
ITS GEMSTONE IS THE KEY TO THE ONLY SPACESHIP POWERFUL ENOUGH TO ESCAPE THE BLACK HOLE THAT'S PULLING THIS PLANET APART.
IF THIS GRAVITY BUBBLE DOESN'T POP IN TIME, IT'S ALL OVER ANYWAY...
I USED TO IMAGINE DEATH WOULD WIPE MY SLATE CLEAN.
BUT NOW I REALIZE I WANT TO LIVE...
...IF ONLY TO INSCRIBE A NEW STORY UPON IT.
WHAM

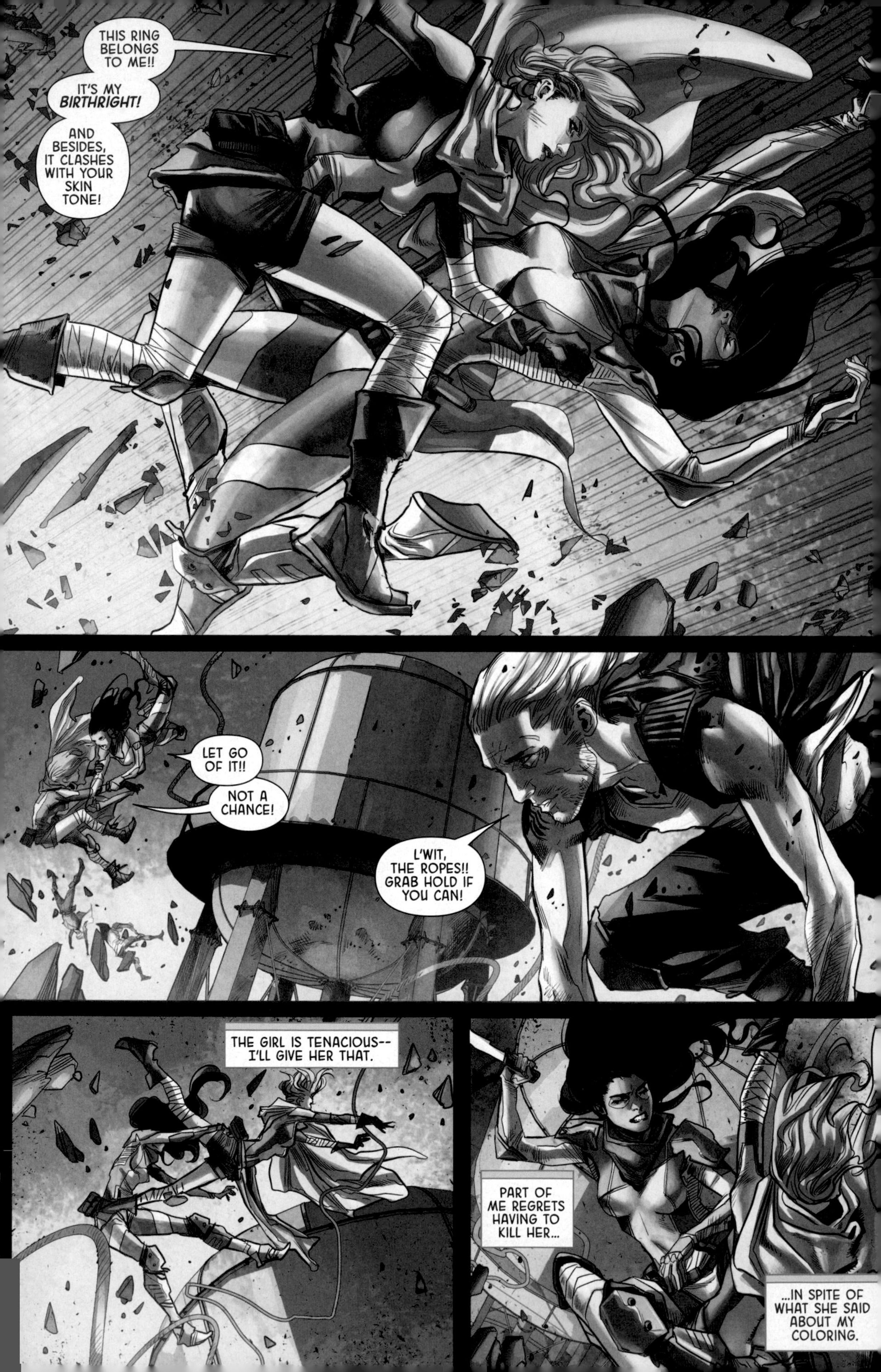
THIS RING BELONGS TO ME!!
IT'S MY *BIRTHRIGHT!*
AND BESIDES, IT CLASHES WITH YOUR SKIN TONE!
LET GO OF IT!!
NOT A CHANCE!
L'WIT, THE ROPES!! GRAB HOLD IF YOU CAN!
THE GIRL IS TENACIOUS-- I'LL GIVE HER THAT.
PART OF ME REGRETS HAVING TO KILL HER...
...IN SPITE OF WHAT SHE SAID ABOUT MY COLORING.

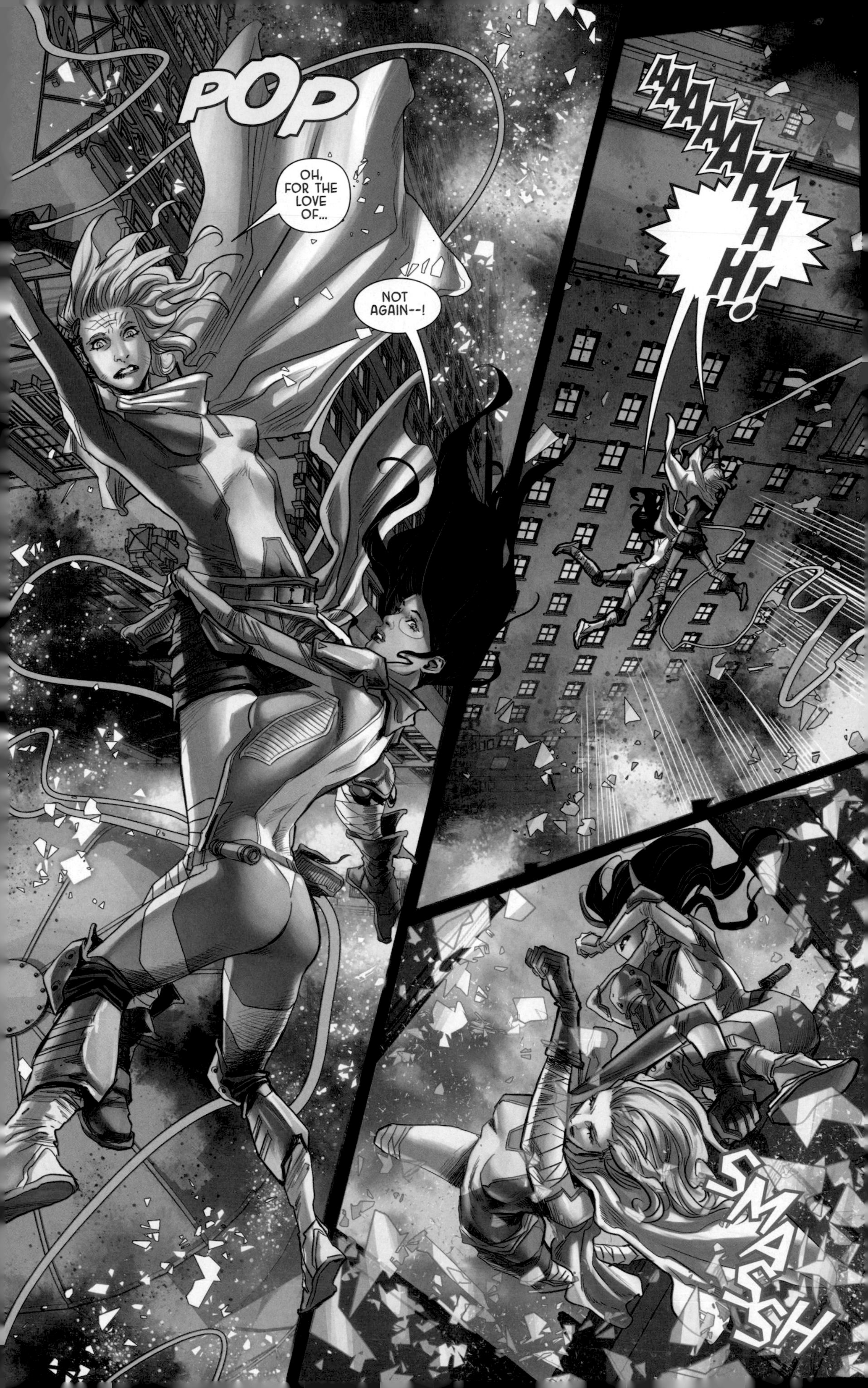
POP
OH, FOR THE LOVE OF...
NOT AGAIN--!
AAAAAAHHHHH!
SMASH

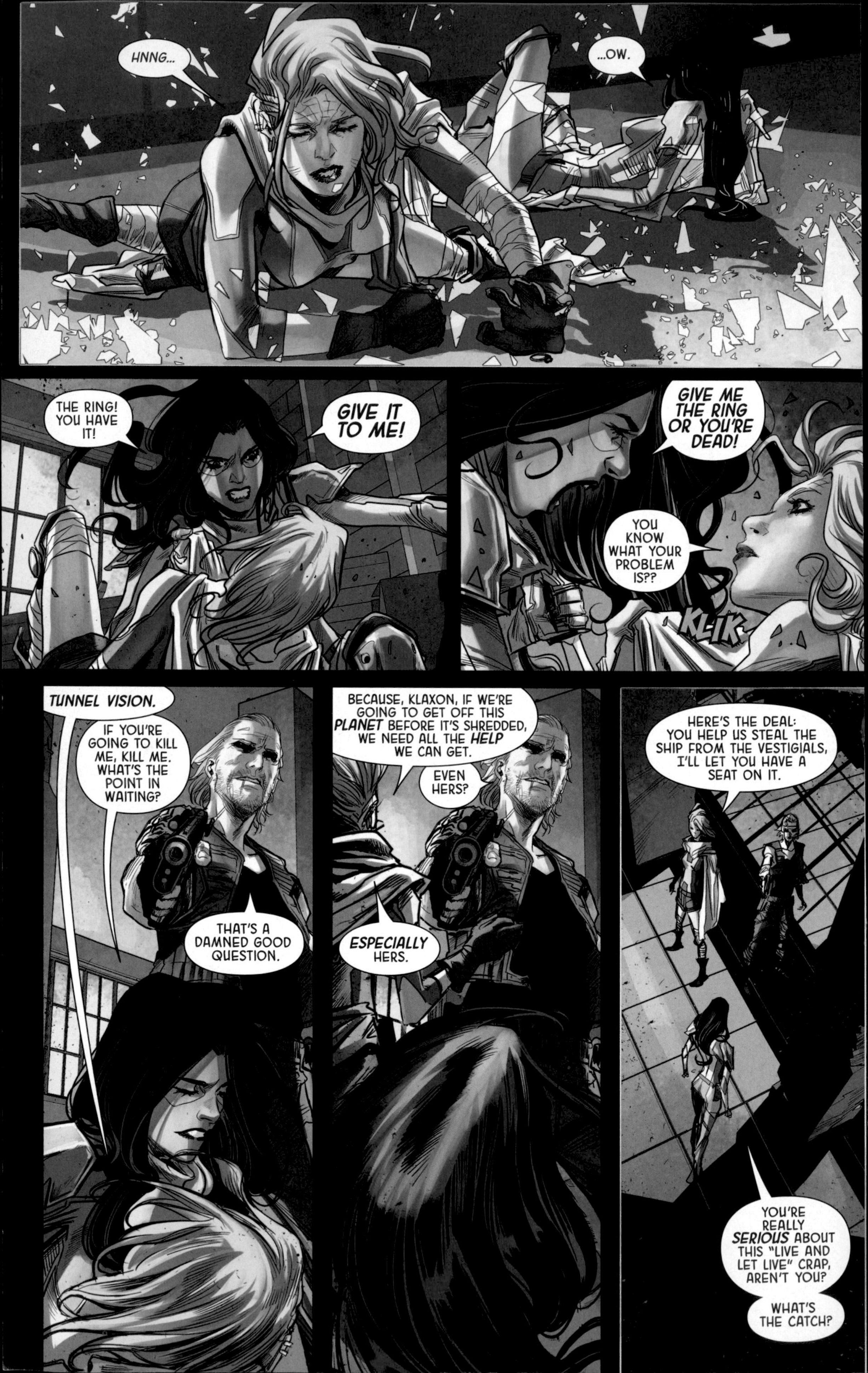
HNNG...
...OW.
THE RING! YOU HAVE IT!
GIVE IT TO ME!
GIVE ME THE RING OR YOU'RE DEAD!
YOU KNOW WHAT YOUR PROBLEM IS??
KLIK
TUNNEL VISION.
IF YOU'RE GOING TO KILL ME, KILL ME. WHAT'S THE POINT IN WAITING?
THAT'S A DAMNED GOOD QUESTION.
BECAUSE, KLAXON, IF WE'RE GOING TO GET OFF THIS PLANET BEFORE IT'S SHREDDED, WE NEED ALL THE HELP WE CAN GET.
EVEN HERS?
ESPECIALLY HERS.
HERE'S THE DEAL: YOU HELP US STEAL THE SHIP FROM THE VESTIGIALS, I'LL LET YOU HAVE A SEAT ON IT.
YOU'RE REALLY SERIOUS ABOUT THIS "LIVE AND LET LIVE" CRAP, AREN'T YOU?
WHAT'S THE CATCH?

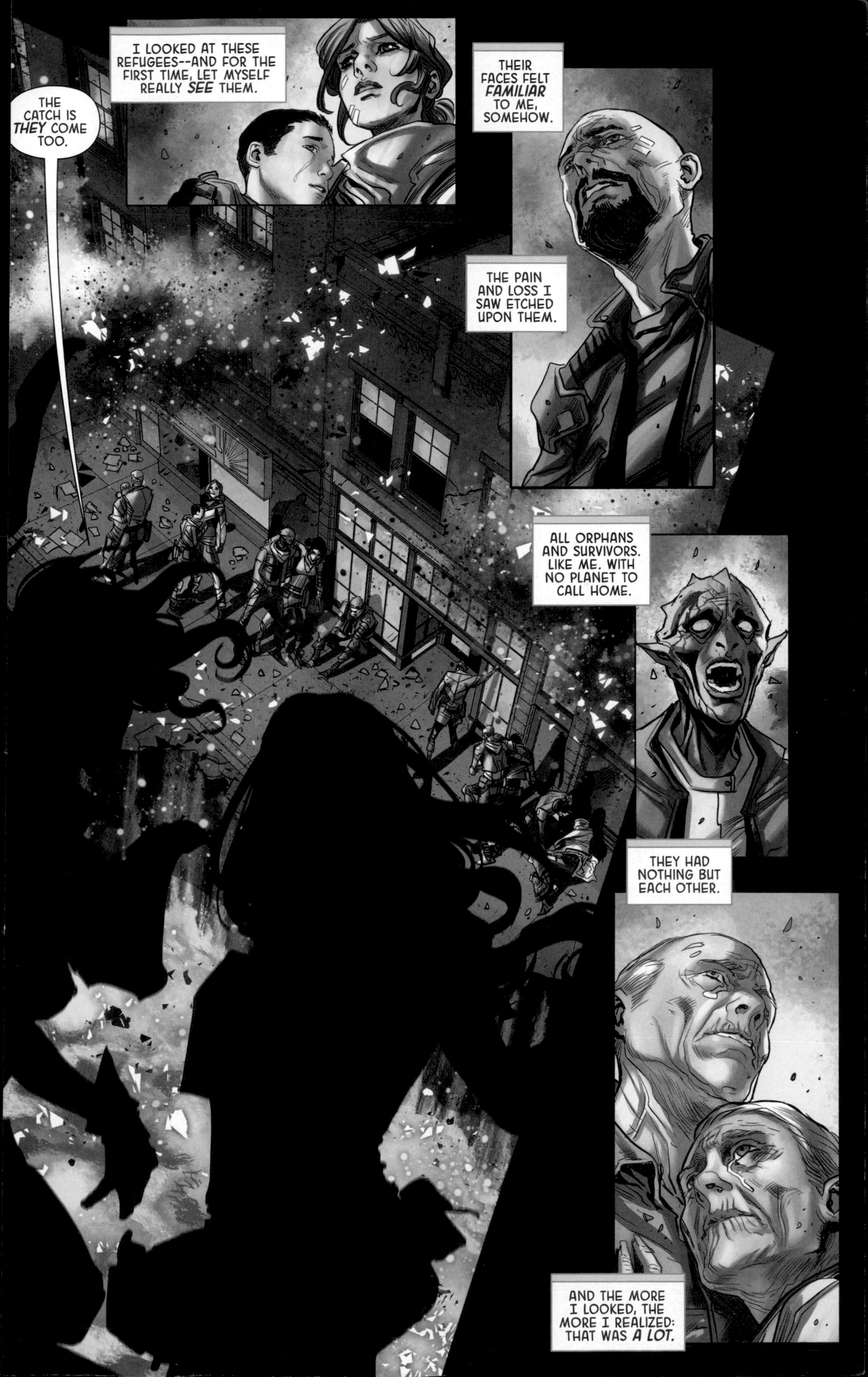

I LOOKED AT THESE REFUGEES--AND FOR THE FIRST TIME, LET MYSELF REALLY SEE THEM.
THE CATCH IS THEY COME TOO.
THEIR FACES FELT FAMILIAR TO ME, SOMEHOW.
THE PAIN AND LOSS I SAW ETCHED UPON THEM.
ALL ORPHANS AND SURVIVORS. LIKE ME. WITH NO PLANET TO CALL HOME.
THEY HAD NOTHING BUT EACH OTHER.
AND THE MORE I LOOKED, THE MORE I REALIZED: THAT WAS A LOT.

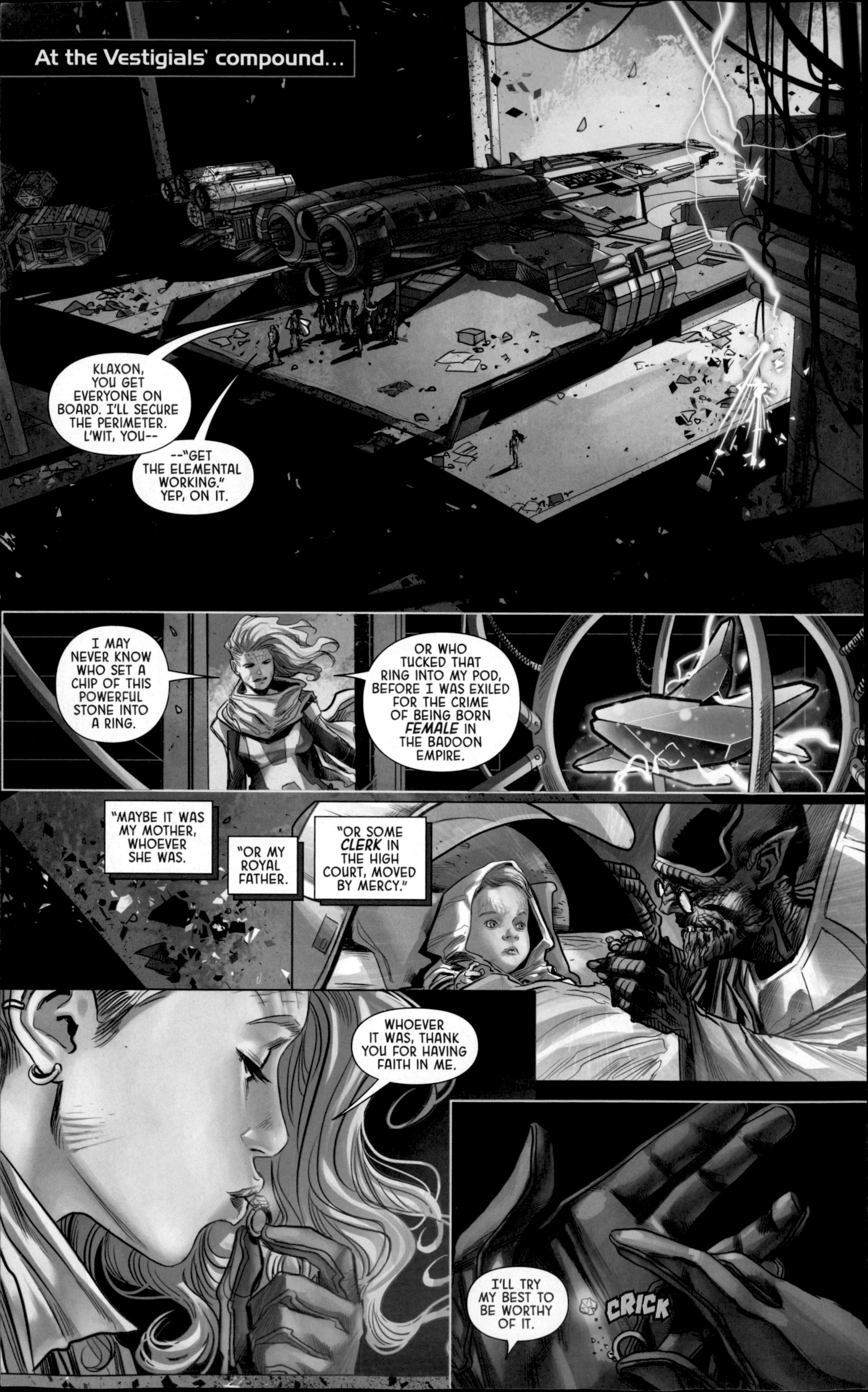
At the Vestigials' compound...
KLAXON, YOU GET EVERYONE ON BOARD. I'LL SECURE THE PERIMETER. L'WIT, YOU--
--"GET THE ELEMENTAL WORKING." YEP, ON IT.
I MAY NEVER KNOW WHO SET A CHIP OF THIS POWERFUL STONE INTO A RING.
OR WHO TUCKED THAT RING INTO MY POD, BEFORE I WAS EXILED FOR THE CRIME OF BEING BORN FEMALE IN THE BADOON EMPIRE.
"MAYBE IT WAS MY MOTHER, WHOEVER SHE WAS.
"OR MY ROYAL FATHER.
"OR SOME CLERK IN THE HIGH COURT, MOVED BY MERCY."
WHOEVER IT WAS, THANK YOU FOR HAVING FAITH IN ME.
I'LL TRY MY BEST TO BE WORTHY OF IT.
CRICK

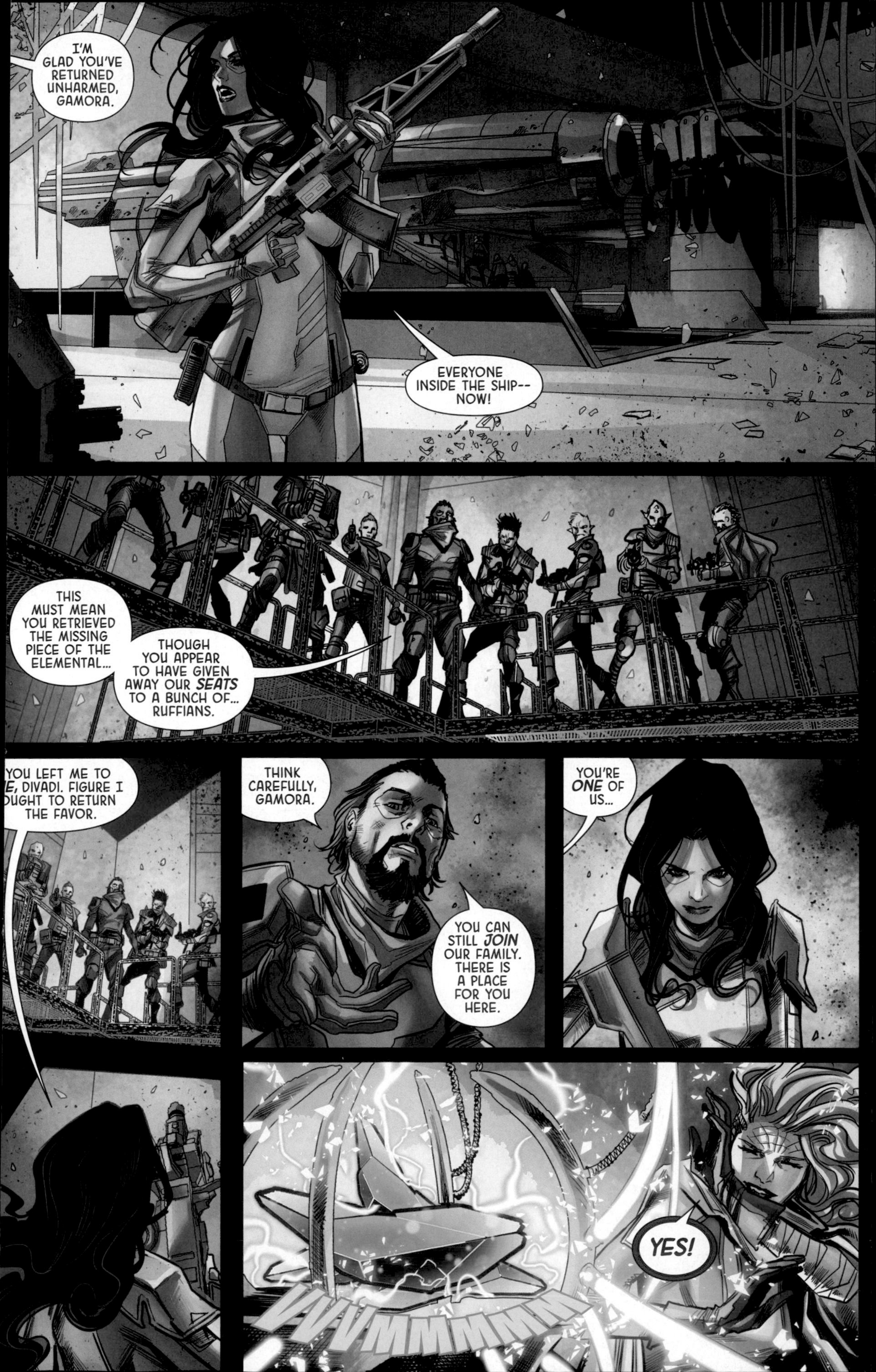
I'M GLAD YOU'VE RETURNED UNHARMED, GAMORA.
EVERYONE INSIDE THE SHIP-- NOW!
THIS MUST MEAN YOU RETRIEVED THE MISSING PIECE OF THE ELEMENTAL...
THOUGH YOU APPEAR TO HAVE GIVEN AWAY OUR SEATS TO A BUNCH OF... RUFFIANS.
YOU LEFT ME TO E, DIVADI. FIGURE I OUGHT TO RETURN THE FAVOR.
THINK CAREFULLY, GAMORA.
YOU CAN STILL JOIN OUR FAMILY. THERE IS A PLACE FOR YOU HERE.
YOU'RE ONE OF US...
YES!
VVVMMMMMM

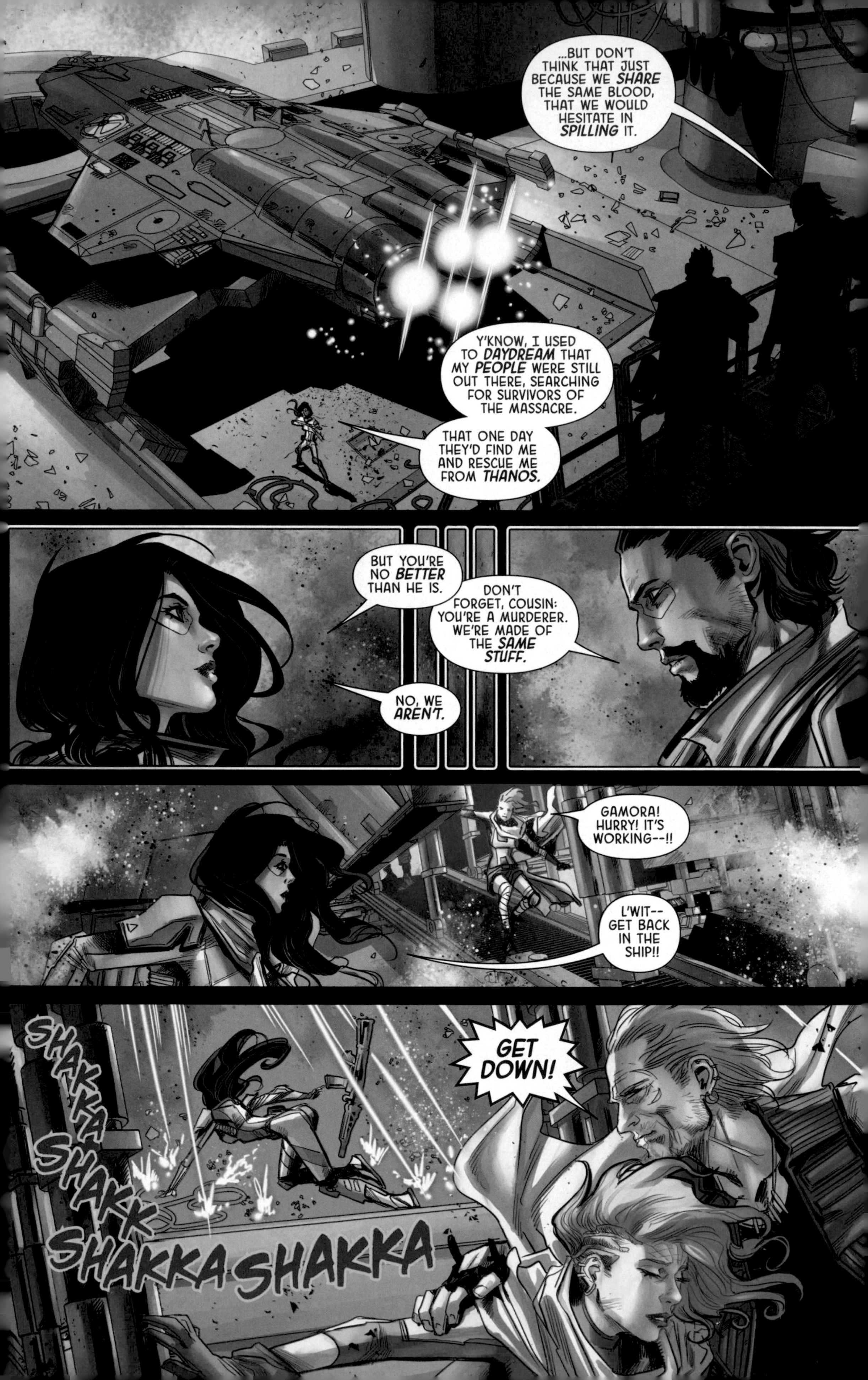
...BUT DON'T THINK THAT JUST BECAUSE WE SHARE THE SAME BLOOD, THAT WE WOULD HESITATE IN SPILLING IT.
Y'KNOW, I USED TO DAYDREAM THAT MY PEOPLE WERE STILL OUT THERE, SEARCHING FOR SURVIVORS OF THE MASSACRE.
THAT ONE DAY THEY'D FIND ME AND RESCUE ME FROM THANOS.
BUT YOU'RE NO BETTER THAN HE IS.
DON'T FORGET, COUSIN: YOU'RE A MURDERER. WE'RE MADE OF THE SAME STUFF.
NO, WE AREN'T.
GAMORA! HURRY! IT'S WORKING--!!
L'WIT-- GET BACK IN THE SHIP!!
GET DOWN!
SHAKKA
SHAKK
SHAKKA SHAKKA

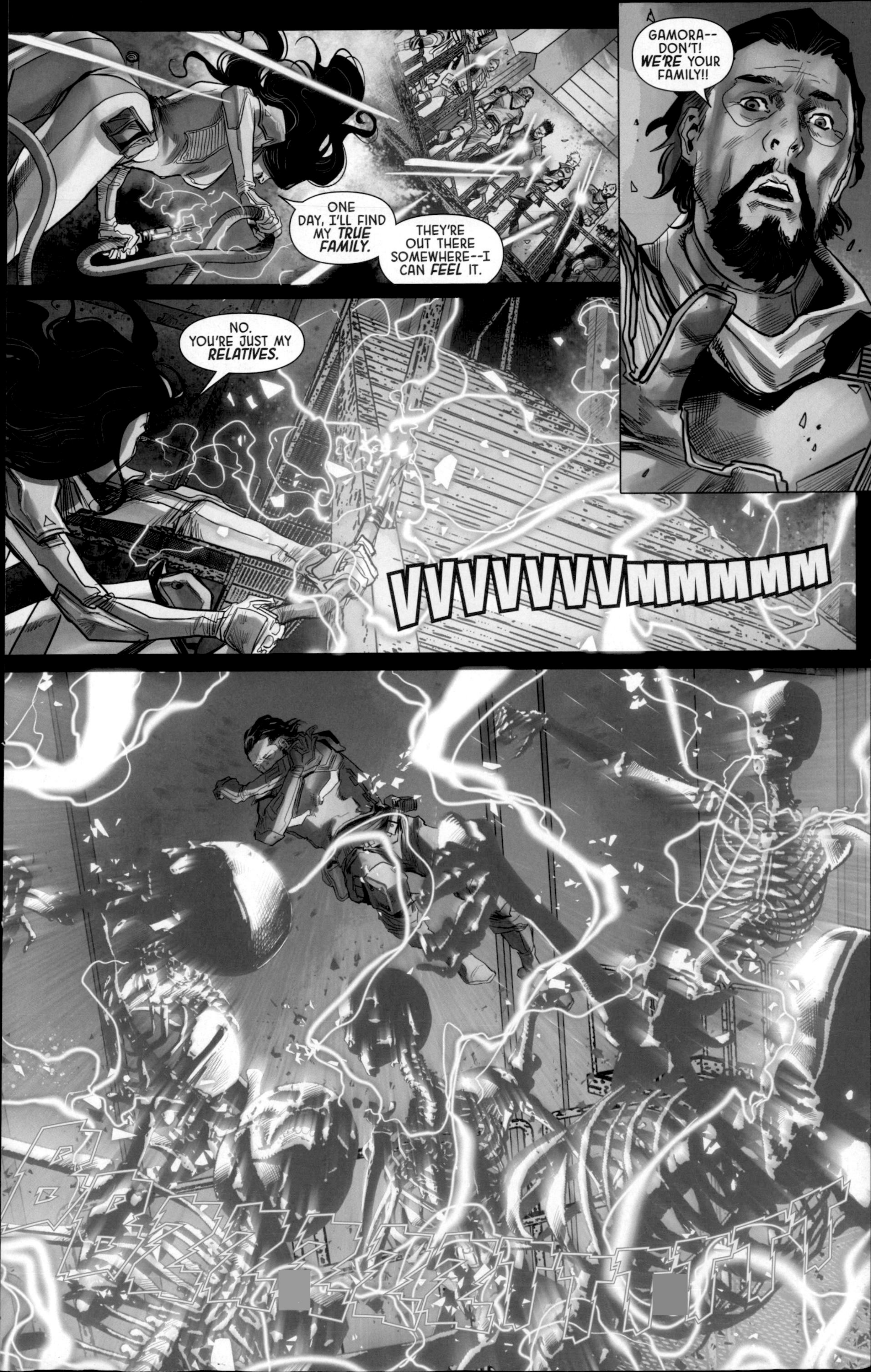
ONE DAY, I'LL FIND MY TRUE FAMILY.
THEY'RE OUT THERE SOMEWHERE--I CAN FEEL IT.
GAMORA-- DON'T! WE'RE YOUR FAMILY!!
NO. YOU'RE JUST MY RELATIVES.
VVVVVVVMMMMMM

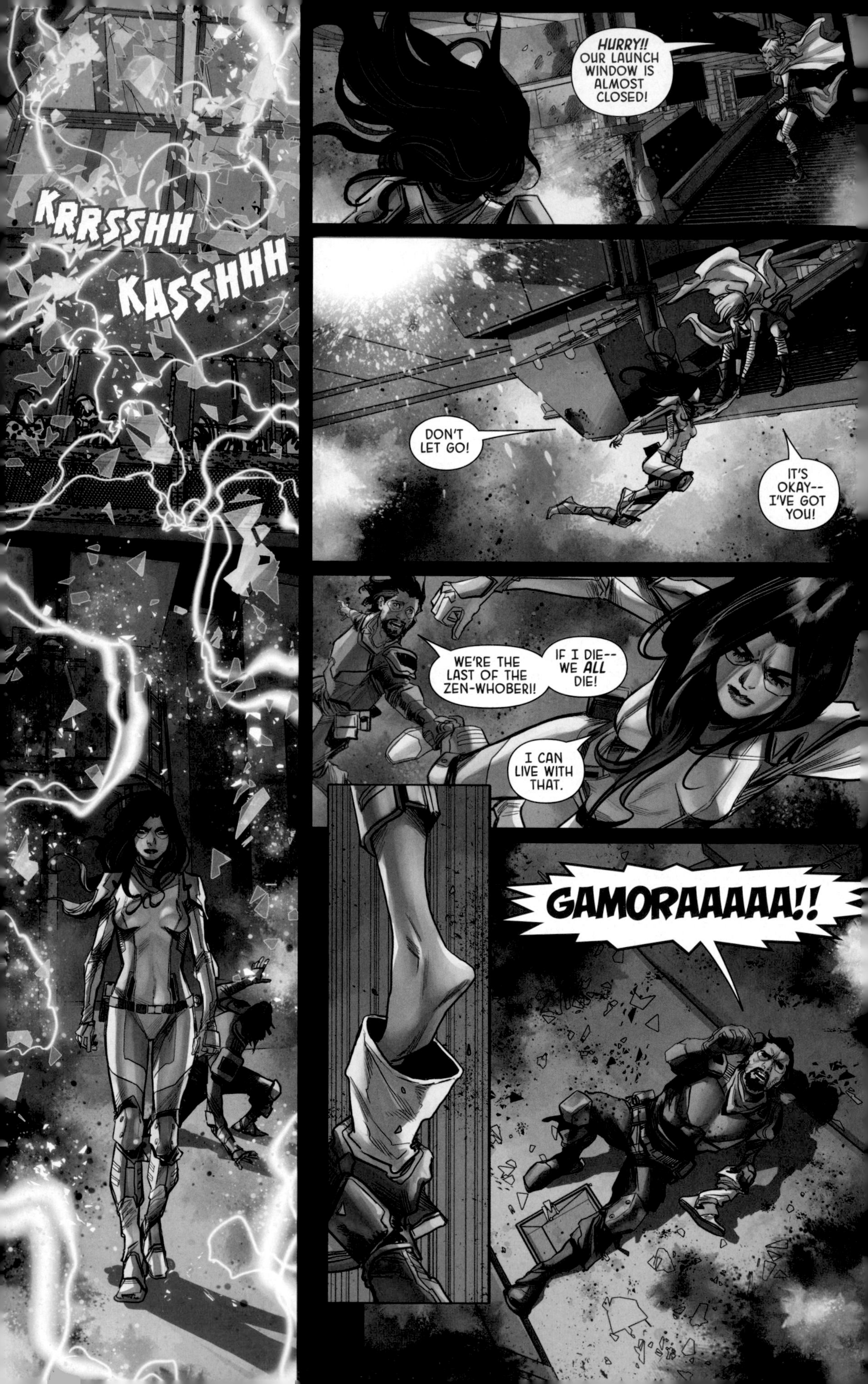
KRRSSHH
KASSHHH
HURRY!! OUR LAUNCH WINDOW IS ALMOST CLOSED!
DON'T LET GO!
IT'S OKAY-- I'VE GOT YOU!
WE'RE THE LAST OF THE ZEN-WHOBERI!
IF I DIE-- WE ALL DIE!
I CAN LIVE WITH THAT.
GAMORAAAAA!!

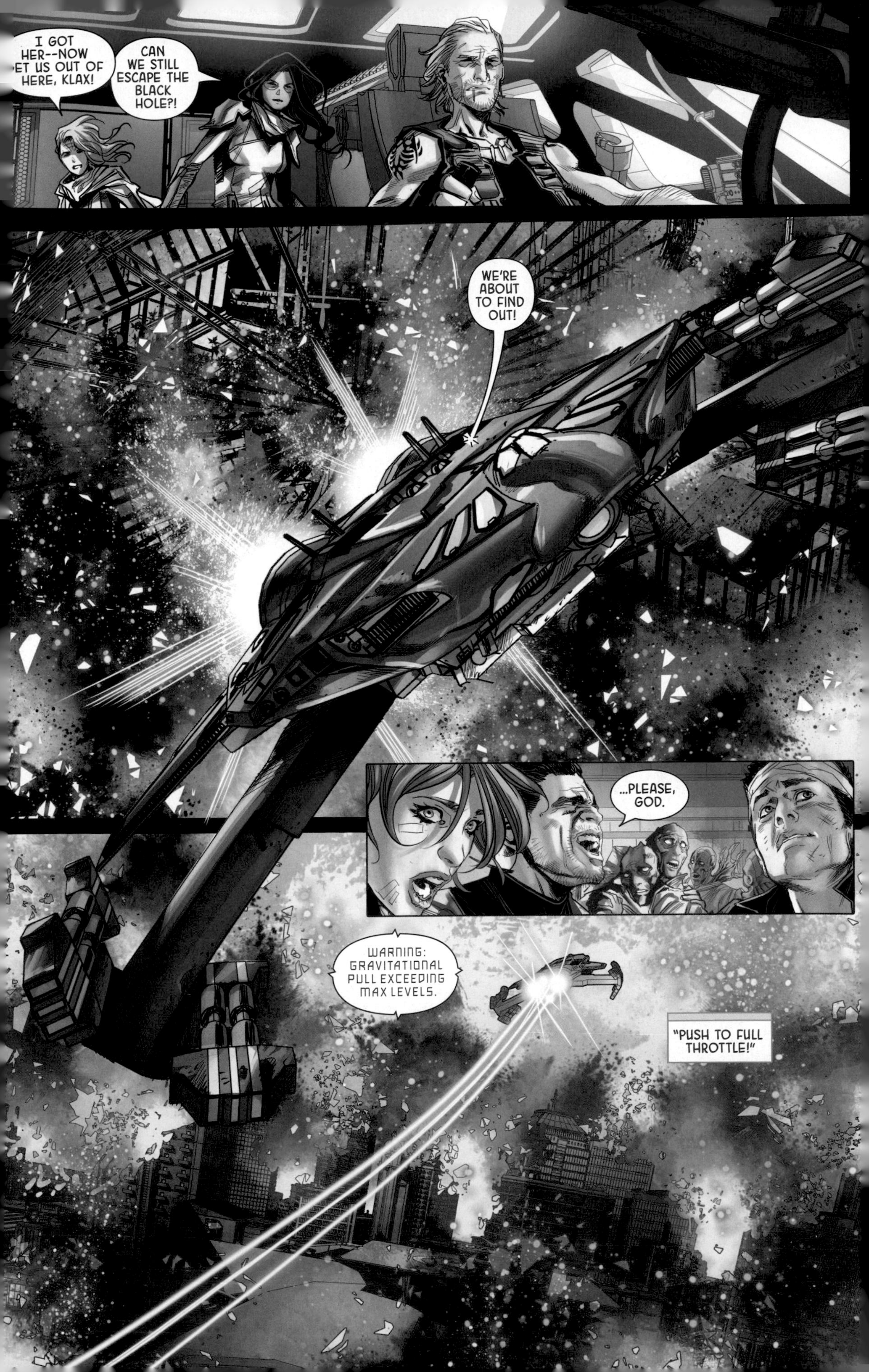
I GOT HER--NOW LET US OUT OF HERE, KLAX!
CAN WE STILL ESCAPE THE BLACK HOLE?!
WE'RE ABOUT TO FIND OUT!
...PLEASE, GOD.
WARNING: GRAVITATIONAL PULL EXCEEDING MAX LEVELS.
"PUSH TO FULL THROTTLE!"

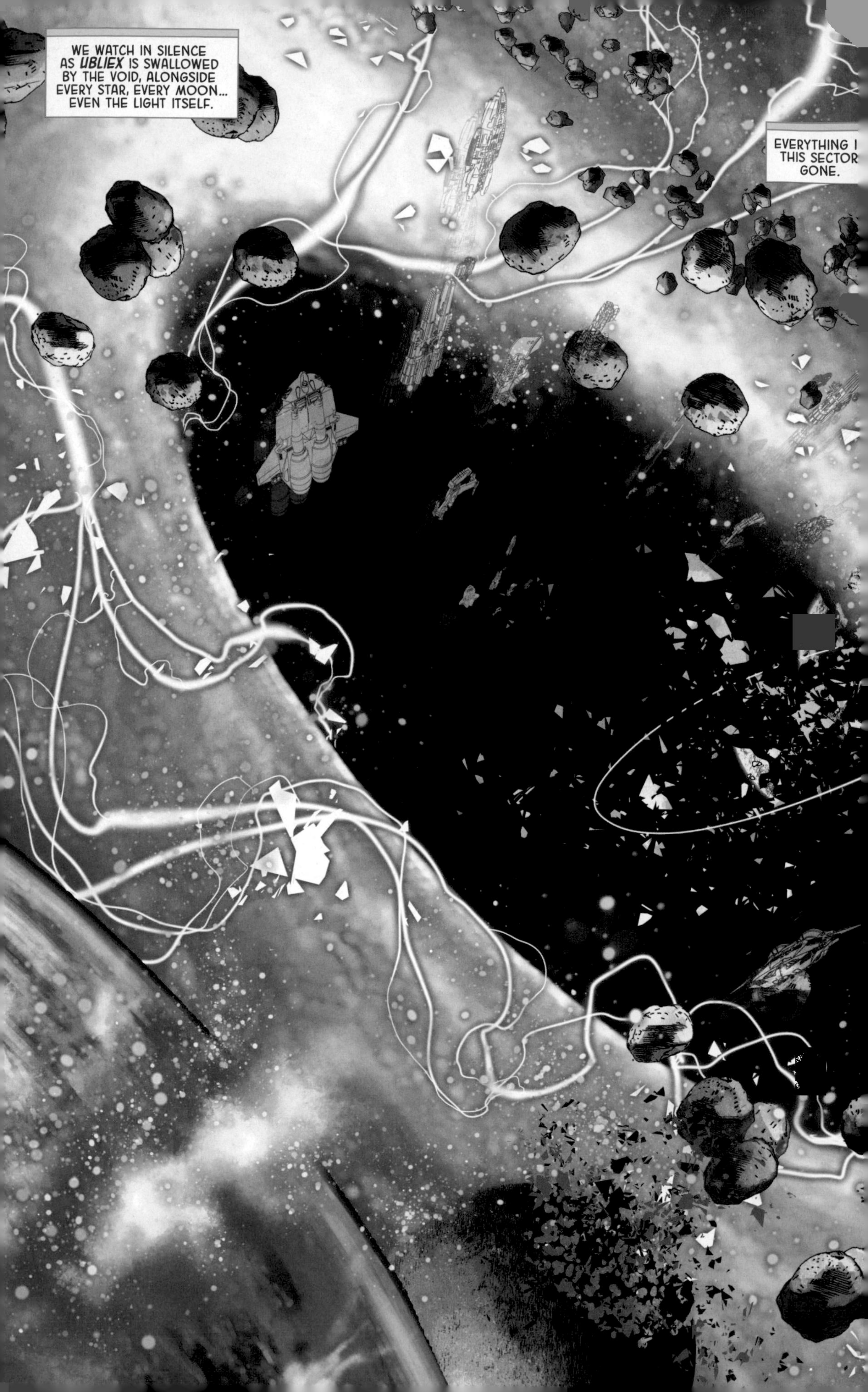
WE WATCH IN SILENCE AS UBLIEX IS SWALLOWED BY THE VOID, ALONGSIDE EVERY STAR, EVERY MOON... EVEN THE LIGHT ITSELF.
EVERYTHING I THIS SECTOR GONE.

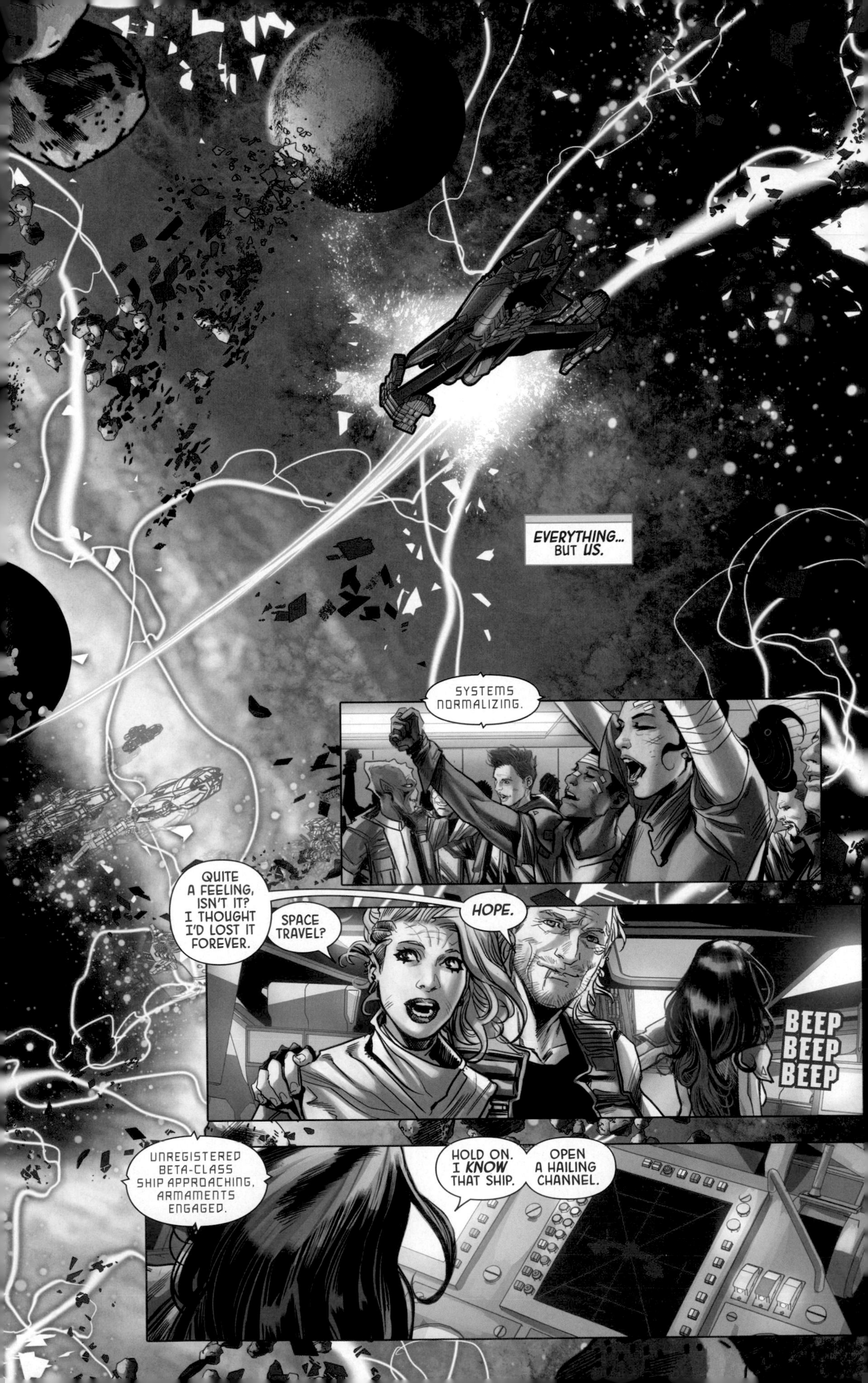
EVERYTHING... BUT US.
SYSTEMS NORMALIZING.
QUITE A FEELING, ISN'T IT?
SPACE TRAVEL?
HOPE.
I THOUGHT I'D LOST IT FOREVER.
BEEP BEEP BEEP
UNREGISTERED BETA-CLASS SHIP APPROACHING. ARMAMENTS ENGAGED.
HOLD ON. I KNOW THAT SHIP.
OPEN A HAILING CHANNEL.

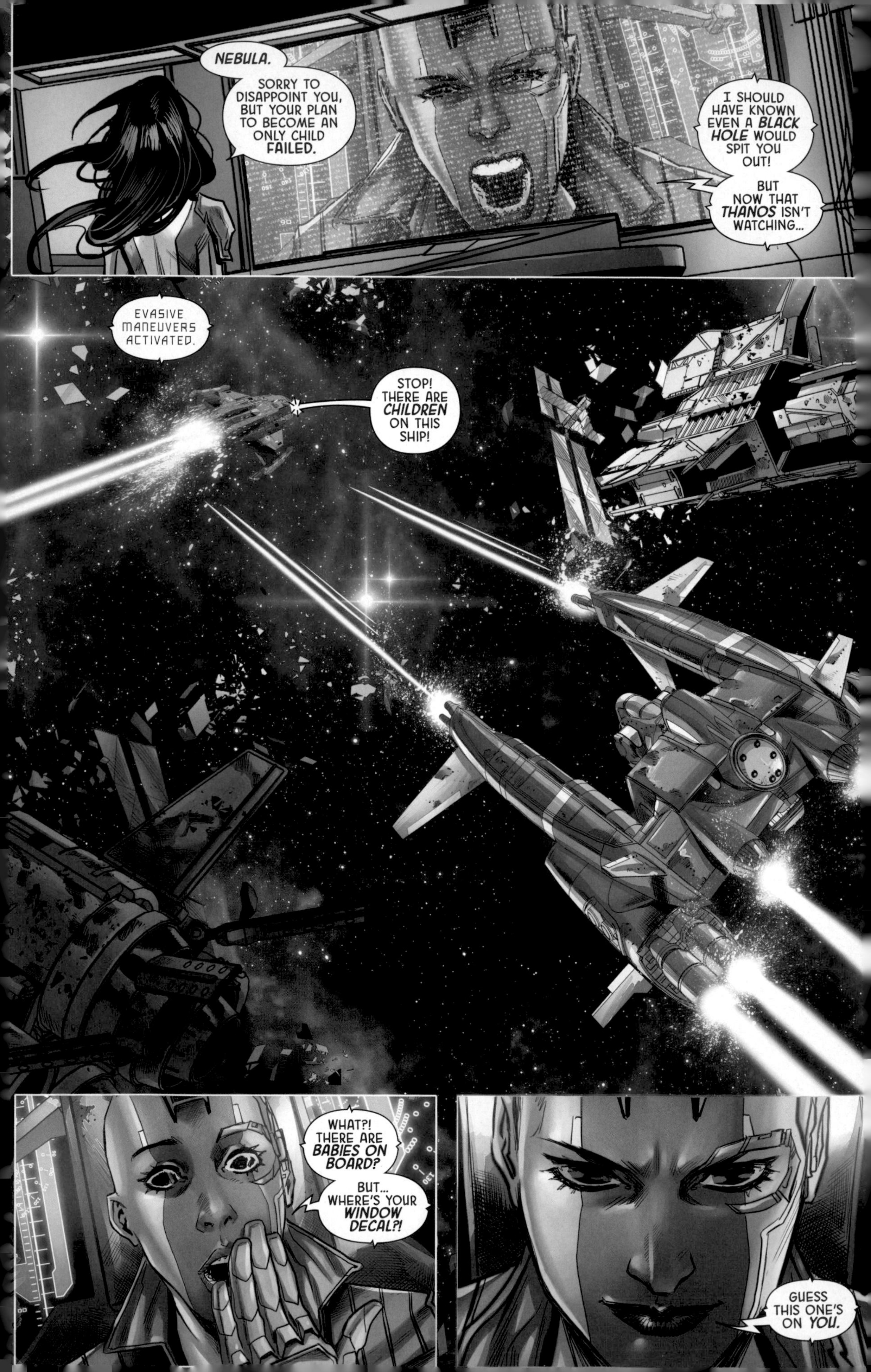

NEBULA.
SORRY TO DISAPPOINT YOU, BUT YOUR PLAN TO BECOME AN ONLY CHILD FAILED.
I SHOULD HAVE KNOWN EVEN A BLACK HOLE WOULD SPIT YOU OUT!
BUT NOW THAT THANOS ISN'T WATCHING...
EVASIVE MANEUVERS ACTIVATED.
STOP! THERE ARE CHILDREN ON THIS SHIP!
WHAT?! THERE ARE BABIES ON BOARD?
BUT... WHERE'S YOUR WINDOW DECAL?!
GUESS THIS ONE'S ON YOU.

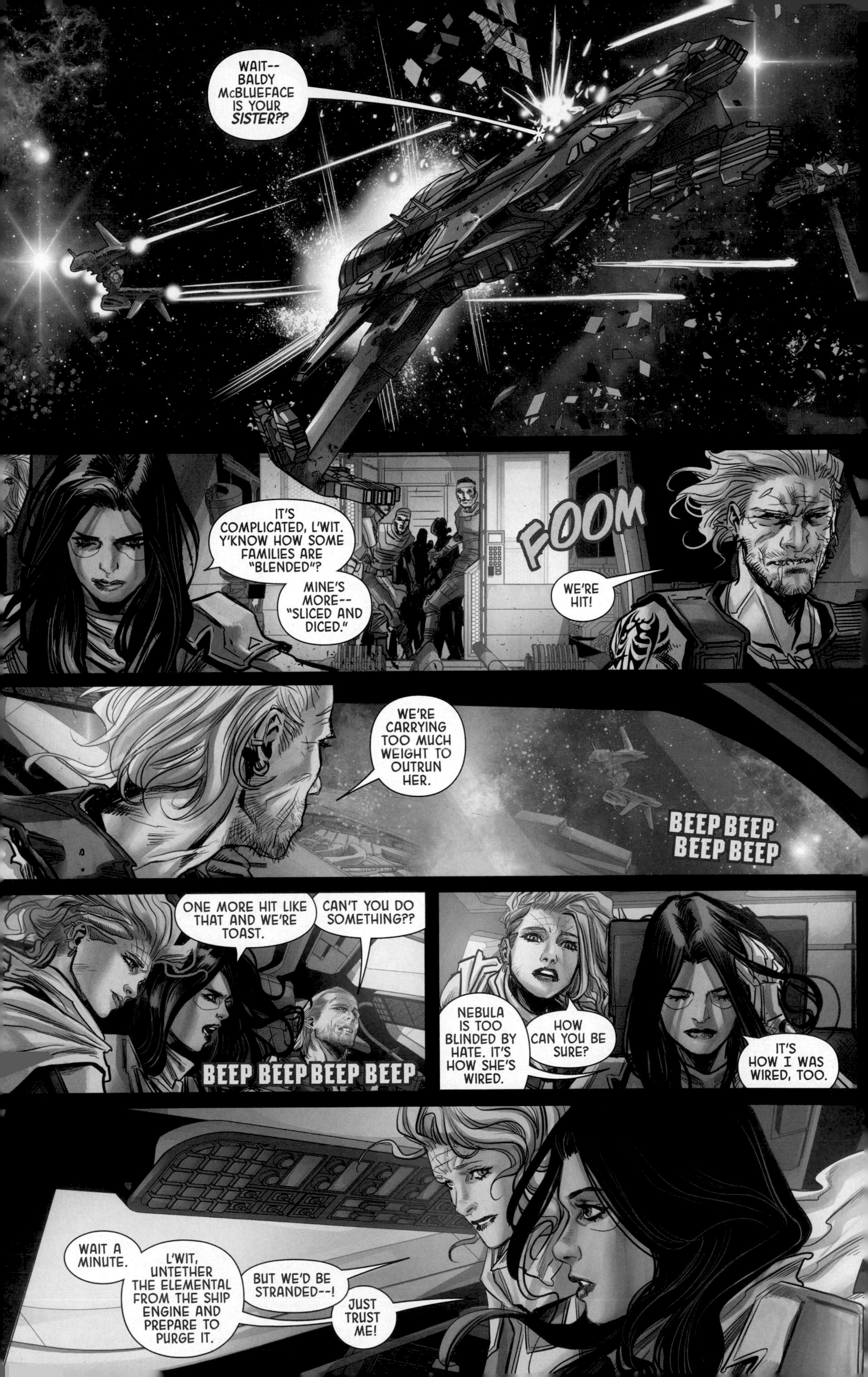
WAIT--
BALDY McBLUEFACE IS YOUR SISTER??
IT'S COMPLICATED, L'WIT. Y'KNOW HOW SOME FAMILIES ARE "BLENDED"?
MINE'S MORE-- "SLICED AND DICED."
FOOM
WE'RE HIT!
WE'RE CARRYING TOO MUCH WEIGHT TO OUTRUN HER.
BEEP BEEP BEEP BEEP
ONE MORE HIT LIKE THAT AND WE'RE TOAST.
CAN'T YOU DO SOMETHING??
BEEP BEEP BEEP BEEP
NEBULA IS TOO BLINDED BY HATE. IT'S HOW SHE'S WIRED.
HOW CAN YOU BE SURE?
IT'S HOW I WAS WIRED, TOO.
WAIT A MINUTE.
L'WIT, UNTETHER THE ELEMENTAL FROM THE SHIP ENGINE AND PREPARE TO PURGE IT.
BUT WE'D BE STRANDED--!
JUST TRUST ME!

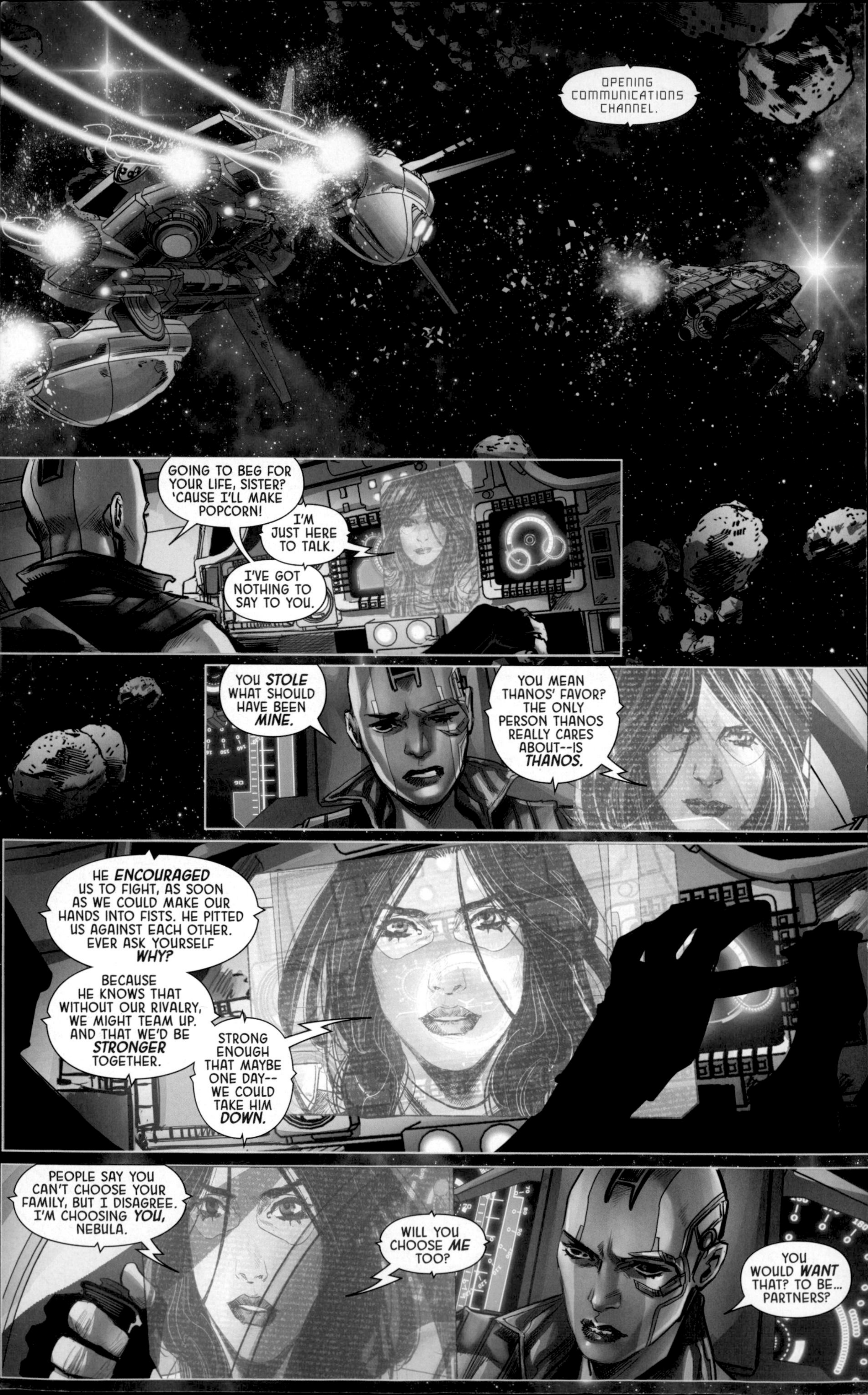
OPENING COMMUNICATIONS CHANNEL.
GOING TO BEG FOR YOUR LIFE, SISTER? 'CAUSE I'LL MAKE POPCORN!
I'M JUST HERE TO TALK.
I'VE GOT NOTHING TO SAY TO YOU.
YOU STOLE WHAT SHOULD HAVE BEEN MINE.
YOU MEAN THANOS' FAVOR? THE ONLY PERSON THANOS REALLY CARES ABOUT--IS THANOS.
HE ENCOURAGED US TO FIGHT, AS SOON AS WE COULD MAKE OUR HANDS INTO FISTS. HE PITTED US AGAINST EACH OTHER. EVER ASK YOURSELF WHY?
BECAUSE HE KNOWS THAT WITHOUT OUR RIVALRY, WE MIGHT TEAM UP. AND THAT WE'D BE STRONGER TOGETHER.
STRONG ENOUGH THAT MAYBE ONE DAY-- WE COULD TAKE HIM DOWN.
PEOPLE SAY YOU CAN'T CHOOSE YOUR FAMILY, BUT I DISAGREE. I'M CHOOSING YOU, NEBULA.
WILL YOU CHOOSE ME TOO?
YOU WOULD WANT THAT? TO BE... PARTNERS?

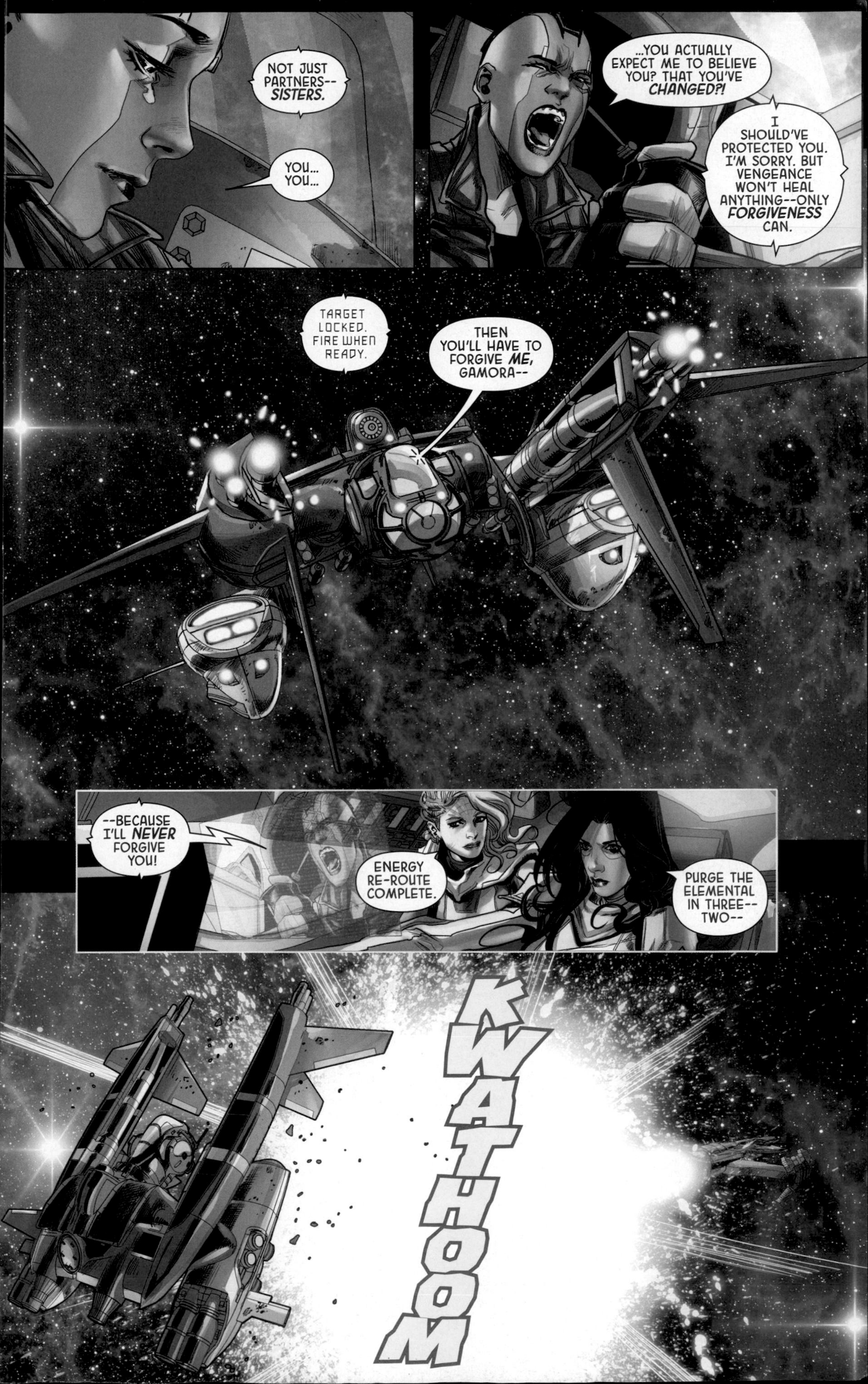
NOT JUST PARTNERS-- SISTERS.
YOU... YOU...
...YOU ACTUALLY EXPECT ME TO BELIEVE YOU? THAT YOU'VE CHANGED?!
I SHOULD'VE PROTECTED YOU. I'M SORRY. BUT VENGEANCE WON'T HEAL ANYTHING--ONLY FORGIVENESS CAN.
TARGET LOCKED. FIRE WHEN READY.
THEN YOU'LL HAVE TO FORGIVE ME, GAMORA--
--BECAUSE I'LL NEVER FORGIVE YOU!
ENERGY RE-ROUTE COMPLETE.
PURGE THE ELEMENTAL IN THREE-- TWO--
KWATHOOM

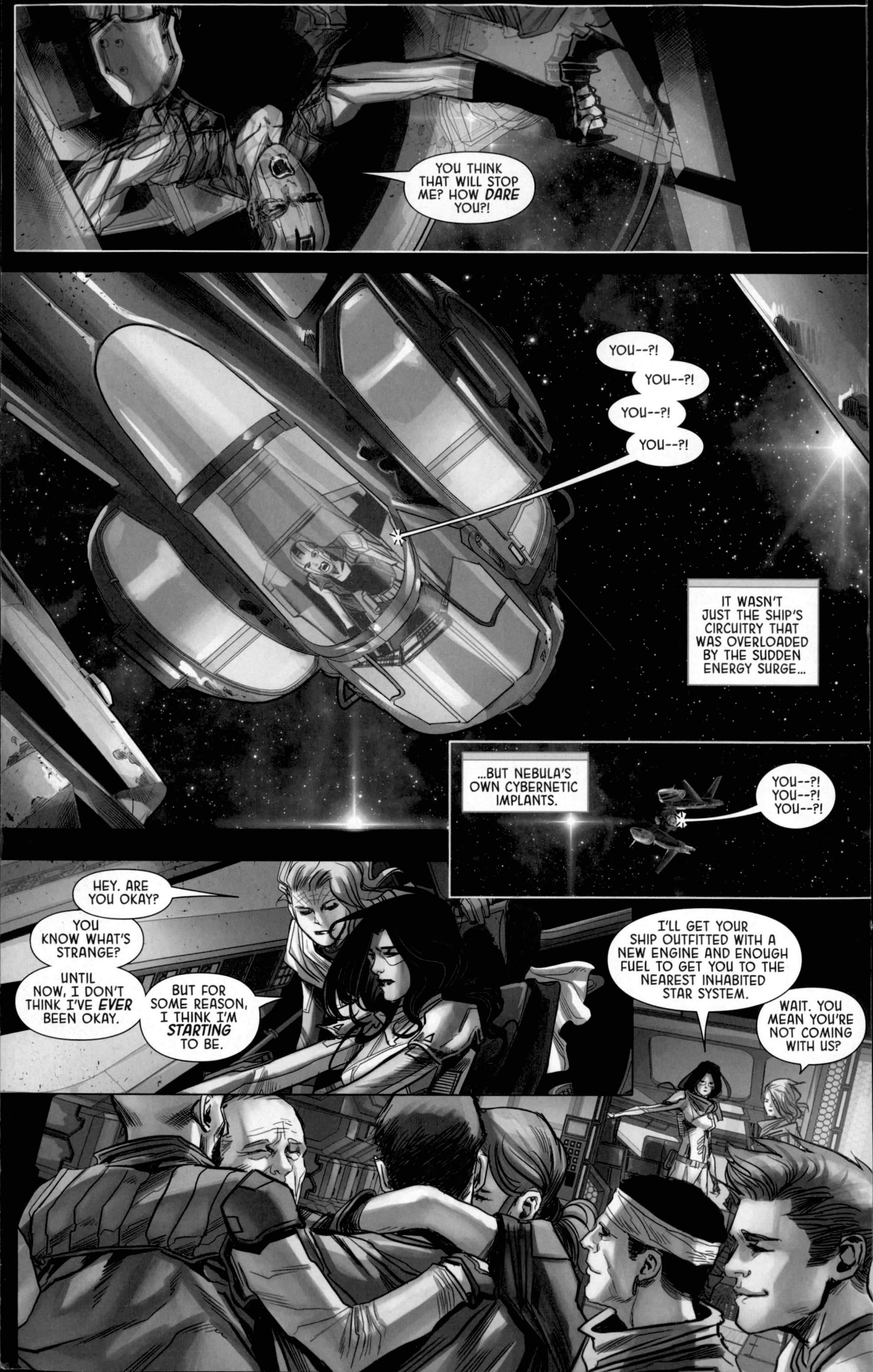

YOU THINK THAT WILL STOP ME? HOW DARE YOU?!
YOU--?!
YOU--?!
YOU--?!
YOU--?!
IT WASN'T JUST THE SHIP'S CIRCUITRY THAT WAS OVERLOADED BY THE SUDDEN ENERGY SURGE...
...BUT NEBULA'S OWN CYBERNETIC IMPLANTS.
YOU--?! YOU--?! YOU--?!
HEY. ARE YOU OKAY?
YOU KNOW WHAT'S STRANGE?
UNTIL NOW, I DON'T THINK I'VE EVER BEEN OKAY.
BUT FOR SOME REASON, I THINK I'M STARTING TO BE.
I'LL GET YOUR SHIP OUTFITTED WITH A NEW ENGINE AND ENOUGH FUEL TO GET YOU TO THE NEAREST INHABITED STAR SYSTEM.
WAIT. YOU MEAN YOU'RE NOT COMING WITH US?

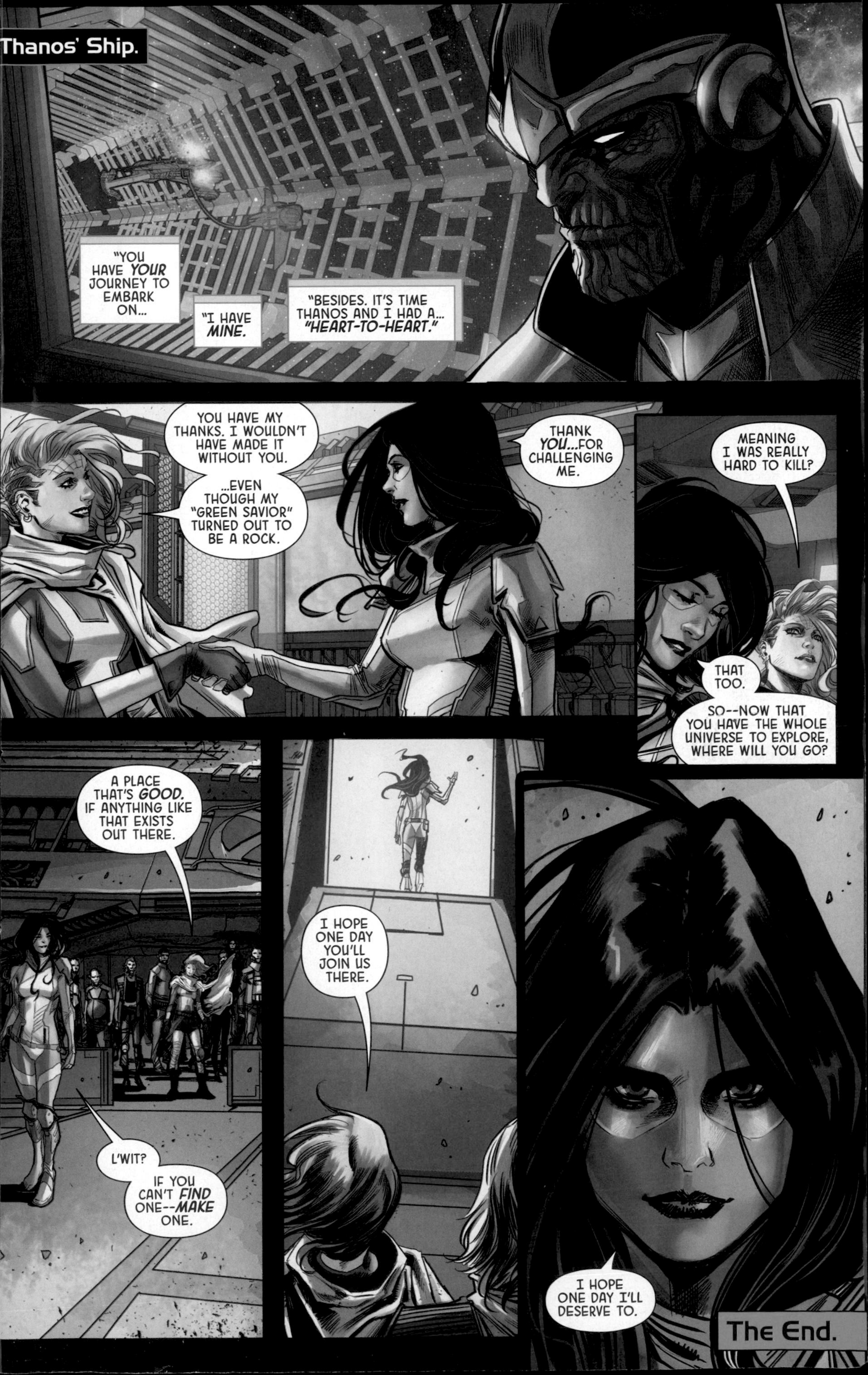

Thanos' Ship.
"YOU HAVE YOUR JOURNEY TO EMBARK ON...
"I HAVE MINE.
"BESIDES. IT'S TIME THANOS AND I HAD A... "HEART-TO-HEART."
YOU HAVE MY THANKS. I WOULDN'T HAVE MADE IT WITHOUT YOU.
...EVEN THOUGH MY "GREEN SAVIOR" TURNED OUT TO BE A ROCK.
THANK YOU...FOR CHALLENGING ME.
MEANING I WAS REALLY HARD TO KILL?
THAT TOO.
SO--NOW THAT YOU HAVE THE WHOLE UNIVERSE TO EXPLORE, WHERE WILL YOU GO?
A PLACE THAT'S GOOD. IF ANYTHING LIKE THAT EXISTS OUT THERE.
L'WIT?
IF YOU CAN'T FIND ONE--MAKE ONE.
I HOPE ONE DAY YOU'LL JOIN US THERE.
I HOPE ONE DAY I'LL DESERVE TO.
The End.

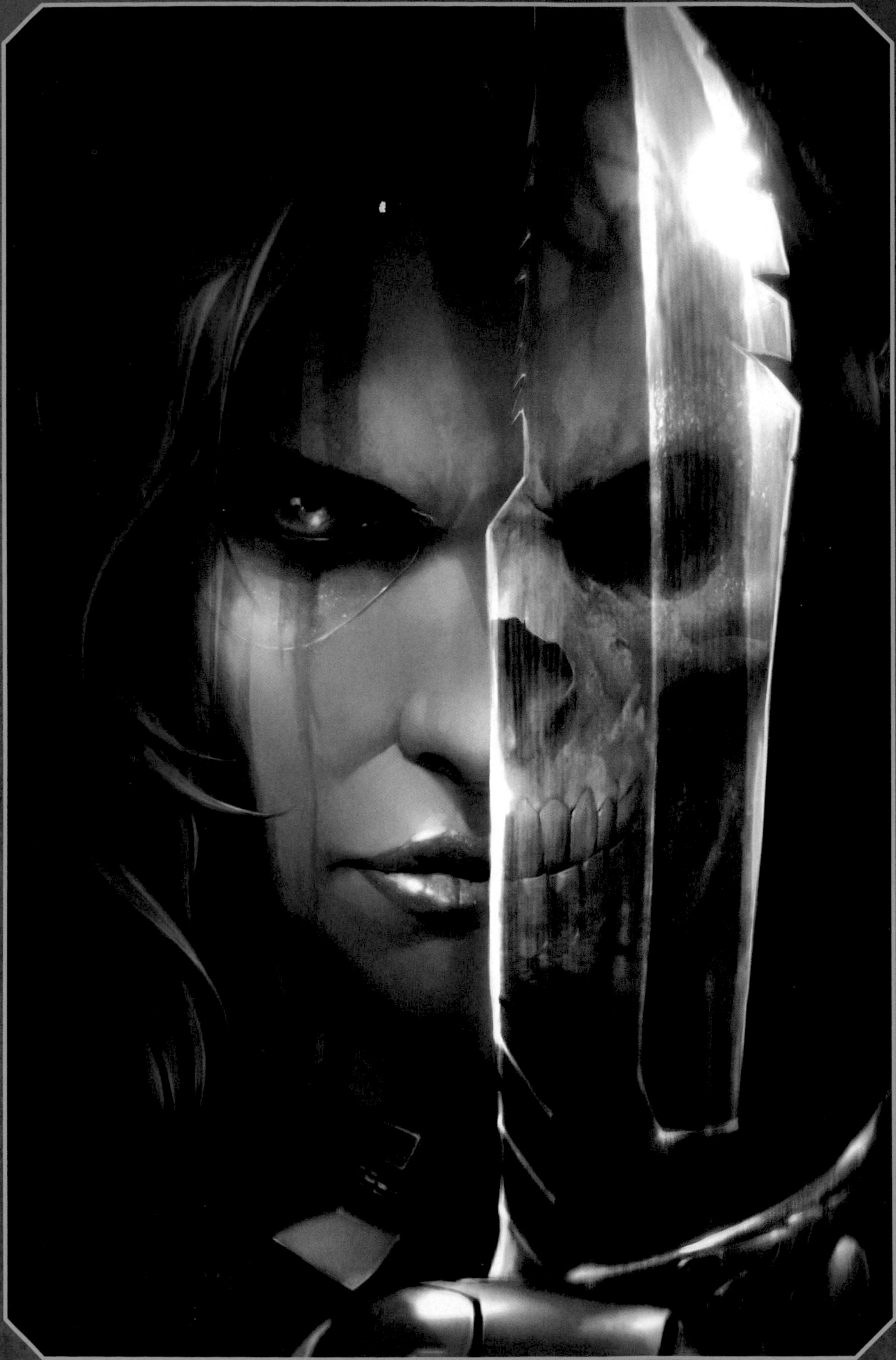

#2 VARIANT BY **FRANCESCO MATTINA**

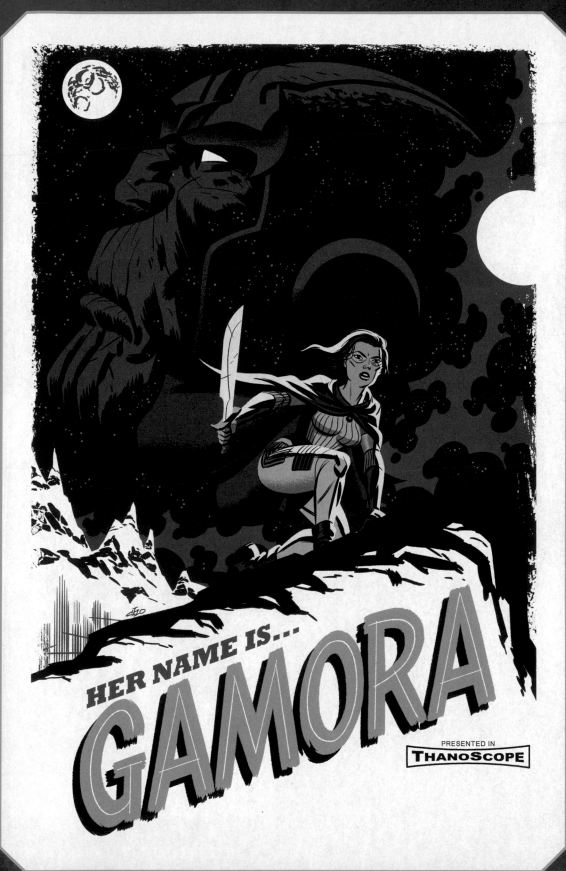

HER NAME IS...
GAMORA

PRESENTED IN
THANOSCOPE

#4 VENOMIZED VARIANT
BY **STEPHANIE HANS**

#1 TEASER VARIANT
BY **MIKE DEODATO JR.** & **FRANK MARTIN**